Vincent *of* Lérins

Foundations of Theological Exegesis and Christian Spirituality

Hans Boersma and Matthew Levering, series editors

Available in the Series
Athanasius, by Peter J. Leithart

Vincent *of* Lérins
AND THE
Development OF Christian Doctrine

Thomas G. Guarino

Baker Academic
a division of Baker Publishing Group
www.BakerAcademic.com

© 2013 by Thomas G. Guarino

Published by Baker Academic
a division of Baker Publishing Group
P.O. Box 6287, Grand Rapids, MI 49516-6287
www.bakeracademic.com

Printed in the United States of America

ISBN 978-0-8010-4909-5

Library of Congress Cataloging-in-Publication Data is on file at the Library of Congress, Washington, DC.

Scripture is the author's translation from Vincent's text or the Latin Vulgate.

The internet addresses, email addresses, and phone numbers in this book are accurate at the time of publication. They are provided as a resource. Baker Publishing Group does not endorse them or vouch for their content or permanence.

13   14   15   16   17   18   19   7   6   5   4   3   2   1

Contents

Series Preface

Recent decades have witnessed a growing desire among Orthodox, Catholics, and Protestants to engage and retrieve the exegetical, theological, and doctrinal resources of the early church. If the affirmations of the first four councils constitute a common inheritance for ecumenical Christian witness, then in the Nicene Creed Christians find a particularly rich vein for contemporary exploration of the realities of faith. These fruits of the patristic period were, as the fathers themselves repeatedly attest, the embodiment of a personally and ecclesially engaged exegetical, theological, and metaphysical approach to articulating the Christian faith. In the Foundations of Theological Exegesis and Christian Spirituality series, we will explore this patristic witness to our common Nicene faith.

Each volume of the present series explores how biblical exegesis, dogmatic theology, and participatory metaphysics relate in the thought of a particular church father. In addition to serving as introductions to the theological world of the fathers, the volumes of the series break new ecumenical and theological ground by taking as their starting point three related convictions. First, at the core of the Foundations series lies the conviction that *ressourcement*, or retrieval, of the shared inheritance of the Nicene faith is an important entry point to all ecumenical endeavor. Nicene Christianity, which received its authoritative shape at the councils of Constantinople (381) and Chalcedon (451), was the result of more than three centuries of ecclesial engagement with the implications of the incarnation and of the adoration of Father, Son, and Holy Spirit in the liturgy of the church. Particularly since the 1940s, when Catholic scholars such as Henri de Lubac, Jean Daniélou, and others reached back to the church fathers for inspiration and contemporary cultural and ecclesial renewal, *ressourcement* has made significant contributions to theological development and ecumenical discussion. The last few decades have also witnessed growing evangelical interest in an approach to the church fathers that reads them not only for academic reasons but also with a view to giving them a voice in today's discussions. Accordingly, this series is based on the conviction that a contemporary retrieval of the church fathers is essential also to the flourishing and further development of Christian theology.

Second, since the Nicene consensus was based on a thorough engagement with the Scriptures, renewed attention to the exegetical approaches of the church fathers is an important aspect of *ressourcement*. In particular, the series works on the assumption that Nicene theology was the result of the early church's conviction that historical and spiritual interpretation of the Scriptures were intimately connected and that both the Old and the New Testaments speak of the realities of Christ, of the church, and of eternal life in fellowship with the Triune God. Although today we may share the dogmatic inheritance of the Nicene faith regardless of our exegetical approach, it is much less clear that the Nicene convictions—such as the doctrines of the Trinity and of the person of Christ—can be sustained without the spiritual approaches to interpretation that were common among the fathers. Doctrine, after all, is the outcome of biblical interpretation. Thus, theological renewal requires attention to the way in which the church fathers approached Scripture. Each of the volumes of this series will therefore explore a church father's theological approach(es) to the biblical text.

Finally, it is our conviction that such a *ressourcement* of spiritual interpretation may contribute significantly toward offsetting the fragmentation—ecclesial, moral, economical, and social—of contemporary society. This fragmentation is closely connected to the loss of the Platonic-Christian synthesis of Nicene Christianity. Whereas this earlier synthesis recognized a web of relationships as a result of God's creative act in and through Christ, many today find it much more difficult to recognize, or even to pursue, common life together. A participatory metaphysic, which many of the church fathers took as axiomatic, implies that all of created reality finds its point of mutual connection in the eternal Word of God, in which it lies anchored. It is this christological anchor that allows for the recognition of a common origin and a common end, and thus for shared commitments. While the modern mindset tends to separate nature and the supernatural (often explicitly excluding the latter), Nicene Christianity recognized that the created order exists by virtue of God's graciously allowing it to participate, in a creaturely fashion, in his goodness, truth, and beauty as revealed in Christ through the Spirit. A participatory metaphysic, therefore, is one of the major presuppositions of the creed's articulation of the realities of faith.

In short, rooted in the wisdom of the Christian past, the volumes of the series speak from the conviction that the above-mentioned convictions informed the life and work of the church fathers and that these convictions are in need of *ressourcement* for the sake of today's theological, philosophical, and exegetical debates. In light of a growing appreciation of the early Christians, the series aims to publish erudite introductions that will be of interest in seminary and university courses on doctrine and biblical exegesis and that will be accessible to educated lay readers with interest in how early Christians appropriated and passed on divine revelation.

Hans Boersma and Matthew Levering, series editors

Acknowledgments

I would like to acknowledge, even if briefly and incompletely, the many people who have aided my research on this book over the past two years.

Pride of place belongs to the Rev. Dr. Robert Coleman, dean of the school of theology at Seton Hall University, for his continual support.

I also thank my colleagues who read various parts of the manuscript. These include Anthony Ziccardi, Ellen Scully, Gerard McCarren, Jack Radano, Robert Wister, Lawrence Porter, Douglas Milewski, and Eduardo Echeverria. I likewise acknowledge with gratitude the insightful comments received from Paul Rorem of Princeton Theological Seminary and Joseph Lienhard, SJ, of Fordham University.

I owe a special debt of gratitude to the libraries of my home institution. The dean of Seton Hall libraries, Chrysanthy Grieco, graciously provided me with space for undisturbed writing, while the staffs of both the Walsh and Turro libraries were most helpful in obtaining the necessary research materials. Cathy Xavier, for her part, never failed to accommodate my many book-related requests.

I also thank the Center of Theological Inquiry and its director, William Storrar, for always providing a warm welcome when I was working in the Princeton area.

Finally, I am grateful to the editors of this series, Hans Boersma and Matthew Levering, for their helpful suggestions.

Needless to add, any deficiencies in the book are my responsibility alone.

Preface

When the editors of this series asked me to participate in a new set of theological commentaries on the fathers of the church, I was eager to take part, immediately suggesting Vincent of Lérins as a possible candidate. Although Vincent was not on the original list compiled by the editors, they graciously acceded to my request. I thought the Lérinian a perfect subject for prolonged study for several reasons. In the first place, Vincent is an attractive figure because he is a man who, even in the early fifth century, was well aware that we live in a world deeply affected by change, historicity, and shifting circumstances. In this sense, Vincent is a theologian marked by historical consciousness, grappling with the questions of continuity and change as they affect Christian faith and doctrine.

A second reason that a contemporary study on Vincent's thought is important is its potential for advancing ecumenical discussions. All theological investigation must contend, ultimately, with the issue of proper development over time. How are we to understand the developments that took place in Christianity from the apostolic age to the great trinitarian and christological councils of the early centuries? Is there a notion of progression to be found that may be applied to later developments in the church as well? And is there a way of understanding precisely *how* later developments—according to determinate criteria—occurred? In other words, how does Vincent understand theological "knowing" to proceed accurately and appropriately? What kind of theological epistemology does he offer for today's Christians?

Third, there has been little recently written on Vincent, in English or in other languages, despite the fact that his main work (the *Commonitorium*) was considered extraordinary in the sixteenth century (going through thirty-five editions) and then again in the nineteenth century as, under historical and philosophical pressures of evolutionary thinking, the idea of development was accorded greater theological attention. The contemporary lapse in serious studies on the monk of Lérins indicates that it is a good time, once again, to bring his incisive theology to the fore.

Why has Vincent been ignored of late, especially in an age that has prided itself on patristic recovery and *ressourcement*? One reason is that the Lérinian's complex thought on Christian doctrine is often reduced to a memorable slogan (called the Vincentian canon, or first rule): *id teneamus quod ubique, quod semper, quod ab omnibus creditum est* (we hold that faith which has been believed everywhere, always, and by everyone). Even noteworthy patristic and theological dictionaries are wont to place the accent solely on this celebrated axiom. And it has become de rigueur for authors to add that Vincent's catchy maxim—a doctrinal teaching is warranted only if attested everywhere, always, and by everyone—though constituting an interesting attempt to distinguish truth from heresy, is ultimately a failed and even hopelessly mistaken criterion.

The current lack of interest in Vincent's thought may also be traced to the fact that the theologian of Lérins is sometimes dismissed as a mere antiquarian, exceedingly concerned with preserving the faith in its original purity, but without any significant interest in its development over time. Even as astute a theologian as the young Joseph Ratzinger somewhat breezily dismissed Vincent as holding a notion of historical change and development that is untenable in the contemporary age.[1] A similarly insightful commentator, who has written an oft-cited monument to the Lérinian's work, comes close to accusing him of mummifying doctrine, so great is his concern zealously to protect "the faith once delivered to the saints" (Jude 3).[2] The prosecutorial charge is that Vincent is so profoundly concerned to protect old-time religion that he fails to allow the Christian faith to meet new challenges and develop new insights. The theologian of Lérins was indeed interested in preserving the faith in its pristine purity. But if we cast Vincent as a mere antiquarian, then we read him in a highly restrictive manner and therefore miss significant dimensions of his theological incisiveness. It is for this reason, too, that a new study of Vincent's work seems essential.

It is my argument that Vincent's small book may be of significant theological and ecumenical interest in addressing the complex question of the authentic development of doctrine, thereby bringing Protestant, Eastern Orthodox, and Roman Catholic churches into deeper communion. This study, then, while interested in the historical reception of Vincent's thought, is also concerned with the contemporary role that the Lérinian's theology, with its twin accent on faithfulness to the apostolic heritage *and* the need for proper development, can play in the performative life of contemporary Christianity. One of the intentions of this series is to employ the theological riches of the undivided church for the sake of affirming a common Christian patrimony and discovering new resources for unity. It is my hope that this book engages theological reflection in service to ecumenism and to the renewal of the church.[3]

An essential part of present-day theology, and indeed of all contemporary Christian life, has to do with the proper balance between continuity and change. It may even be argued that many serious theological discussions are about achieving an appropriate symmetry on just this issue. How does the church assimilate new ideas, even while remaining entirely faithful to "the faith once delivered to the saints"? How does the church maintain unity, identity, and continuity amid inescapable diversity, plurality, and historicity? These are the crucial questions for Christians as the faith makes its way through history, societies, and cultures. And responding to them is precisely Vincent's métier. In fact, Vincent is the only early Christian writer to treat the issue of proper development *ex professo*. He is asking in his time, as we are asking in ours, "How does the Spirit faithfully guide the church in continually facing new challenges?"

It is my intention, then, that this book serve two purposes:

1. It provides a historical introduction to the rich theology of Vincent of Lérins.
2. It offers a creative appropriation of the Lérinian's thought in service to theological and ecumenical renewal.

This volume attempts to show that Vincent's chief work, the *Commonitorium*, can still yield an abundant harvest for contemporary Christian theology.

In pursuit of these purposes, the book will offer, first, an introduction to Vincent's life and works; second, a theological analysis of Vincent's *Commonitorium*, especially the crucially important terms and phrases that he employs and their theological significance (chap. 1); third, a review of how Vincent's work has been "received" by one important thinker, John Henry Newman, during both his Anglican and Roman Catholic periods (chap. 2); and finally, a speculative and constructive discussion on how Vincent's insights may bear theological and ecumenical fruit for the church today (chap. 3).

I hope that one outcome of this book will be the end of naive citations of the theologian of Lérins, wherein authors claim that his threefold criteria for Christian doctrine—ubiquity, universality, and antiquity—are interesting but unworkable. Yet a careful study of Vincent reveals that he is very cautious about precisely how one achieves both the preservation of doctrine (the Pauline injunction "Guard the deposit, Timothy!" is always uppermost in his mind; 1 Tim. 6:20) and its proper development over time. The Lérinian's work offers not only a serious treatment of doctrinal development but also a carefully balanced and multicentered hermeneutics of doctrine, deeply concerned with the proper interpretation of God's Word.

It is sometimes said that the contemporary ecumenical movement wallows in stagnation. Although it is true that there have been few stunning breakthroughs toward unity, it is also true that the Holy Spirit works through continuing theological initiatives and through the church's performative appropriation of Scripture. Serious discussions continue. Theology advances in its historical and doctrinal investigations. Progress may come slowly, but there are many reasons for hope in the continuing ecumenical quest. Although this work is from the hand of a Roman Catholic author, and so undoubtedly bears the distinctive marks of its origin, it is my intention to have written a book that not only elucidates Vincent's thought but also helps to foster growth toward Christian unity.

A few final notes on the style of the book: I had originally thought about offering an entirely new translation of Vincent's *Commonitorium* but quickly came to realize that translations abound in all the major European languages. Translations into English are particularly abundant because of the high regard in which the Lérinian has been traditionally held in the Anglican Communion. Such works are readily available both in printed editions (often bilingual) and on the internet. In this volume I will be offering my own translation of sections of the *Commonitorium*. However, it became my firm conviction that what is most urgently needed is not still another translation of Vincent's short book but a theological commentary explaining why Vincent's thought is still vibrant and robust some sixteen centuries later.

I have usually translated Scripture quotations from Vincent's text; often I compared against the Revised Standard Version, the New American Bible, or another published translation.

Readers should be aware that throughout the *Commonitorium*, Vincent consistently refers to the church of his day as the Catholic church. In accordance with one common ecumenical practice, I will keep his usage of Catholic when referring to the ancient, undivided Christian church, the church of the early centuries, for which Vincent had such great love and singular devotion. I will use the terms Roman Catholic, Eastern Orthodox, Anglican, evangelical, Lutheran, Presbyterian, and so on when referring to contemporary Christian communions.

Introduction

The Life and Works of Vincent of Lérins

Before embarking on a theological analysis of Vincent's chief work, the *Commonitorium*, I here discuss some of the major issues surrounding his life and times. Little is directly known of the Lérinian's life or of the precise theological context in which his magnum opus was written. Indeed, for centuries scholars have debated the exact circumstances giving rise to the *Commonitorium*. Those discussions continue today. In my judgment, these controversies do not have a significant bearing on the theological value of Vincent's work. They do, however, help us to understand the Christian world of the early fifth century and the debates then taking place. While making no pretense of exhausting every theory that has been advanced, or of finally deciding certain disputed questions, I hope to offer some insight into the theological context of Vincent's life and thought.[1]

In the remarks that follow, I will proceed in three steps: the life of Vincent of Lérins; the controversies that exist over the exact number and nature of his works; and most disputed of all, Vincent's precise relationship to Augustine's thought and to the movement later known as semi-Pelagianism.

Life of Vincent of Lérins

Adolf von Harnack describes the *Commonitorium* well: "We really breathe freely when we see the attempt of this man to introduce light and certainty into the question [of tradition]."[2] But while Vincent's work does indeed allow us to breathe pure theological air, it gives us little indication of his identity. In the *Commonitorium* itself, the Lérinian hides behind a pseudonym (as was often the custom for monks), calling himself *Peregrinus*—pilgrim or journeyman—no doubt indicating, as a resident of a monastery in southern Gaul, that he regarded himself primarily as one on a pilgrimage toward the kingdom of God.[3] Right at the outset of his book, he says that he is dwelling in the seclusion of a monastery, far from crowded cities, so that he may better follow the advice of the psalmist, "Be still and know that I am God!" (Ps. 46:10).[4]

All of what we know of Vincent comes from the early Christian writer Gennadius and his book *De viris illustribus*.[5] Gennadius tells us that Vincent was a presbyter of Gaul who lived at the monastery on (one of) the Lérins Islands, and who died in the reign of Theodosius and Valentinianus (allowing us to conclude that he did not live beyond 450). Vincent is described as learned in Holy Scripture and in doctrine, referring to himself pseudonymously in his book, *Peregrinus against the Heretics*. Gennadius adds that this work (which we have subsequently come to know as the *Commonitorium* since Vincent refers to it as such) was in two parts, the second of which was stolen, leading the author to write a mere summary of the second book, appending it to the first. We shall return to this last point in a moment.

Vincent lived at the monastery at Lérinum (Lérins), which was founded around 410 by Honoratus (later the bishop of Arles, France). This particular island, now known as Saint Honorat, in honor of the founder, is off the coast of southern France and close to the present-day city of Cannes.[6] As Moxon remarks, the monastery at Lérins was a famous center of learning in the fifth century, sending out numerous bishops to the church of Gaul and producing important theological treatises.[7] It was here that Vincent wrote his *Commonitorium*, probably around the year 434.[8]

Textual and Historical Remarks on Works Attributed to Vincent

Commonitorium

While Gennadius denotes the title of Vincent's book as *Peregrinus against the Heretics*, it has been speculated that the Lérinian himself may have called the volume *Commonitorium peregrini adversus haereticos* (Reminder of the Pilgrim against the Heretics).[9] No one disputes the authorship of this work; it is universally attributed to Vincent.

As we shall see, Vincent's *Commonitorium* shows him to be a precise thinker on many subjects, and impressively so. He clearly outlines the christological and trinitarian foundations of the Christian faith, and he devotes serious thought to how the Spirit works in the church over the course of time. How is there true development in Christianity? And how is authentic growth distinguished from the pernicious adulteration of the faith? Vincent also has a detailed knowledge of the heresies of his day, indicating that he was a keen student of all theological attempts to understand the person of Christ and the nature of God. Thus Gennadius rightly refers to him as learned in matters of Holy Scripture and church doctrine. Gennadius mentions Vincent as the author of no work other than this celebrated aide-mémoire. Nonetheless, successive research has concluded that Vincent was surely the editor of at least one more book and may have been involved with other productions as well.

Excerpta Vincentii

The *Excerpta Vincentii* is a florilegium of phrases about the Holy Trinity and the incarnation, largely drawn from the writings of Augustine.[10] This short piece was entirely unknown until it was discovered by the noted Spanish scholar of Vincent's work, José Madoz, among the manuscripts in the archives of the Crown of Aragon in Catalonia. It was first published in 1940.[11] Madoz convincingly argues that the *Excerpta* is from Vincent's hand, fulfilling the promise the monk makes at the end of chapter 16 of the *Commonitorium* that, should God allow, he would return again to the subject of the Trinity in the future (16.9). In support of Vincentian authorship, Demeulenaere adds that both the prologue and conclusion of the work are clearly from the pen of the Lérinian. Even the extracts chosen from Augustine, illustrating the bishop of Hippo's trinitarian and christological doctrine, perfectly correspond to Vincent's doctrinal interests.[12] In the past, some historians have argued that the Athanasian Creed constituted the fulfillment of Vincent's promise to provide further trinitarian investigations, but as we shall see, this position is no longer accepted by contemporary scholarship.

The *Excerpta* certainly reveals Vincent as an enthusiastic admirer of Augustine's trinitarian and christological work. The noted patrologist Basil Studer says that even though Vincent is reserved about Augustine's teaching on grace, "he does not fail to acknowledge Augustine's authority as a theologian in dealing with the Trinity and Christology."[13] Indeed, this florilegium, which is today attributed to Vincent without controversy, shows the monk of Lérins to be a great admirer of Augustine's thought. Is it possible that such an ardent devotee of Augustine in one area, going so far as to collect and publish his comments, would issue a vitriolic attack on him as well? This is the question that surrounds the next work, which is often attributed to the Lérinian.

Objectiones Vincentianae

Until recently, a work usually assigned to Vincent has been the *Objectiones Vincentianae*, or *Vincentian Objections*. This text—whose content is found only in its confutation by Prosper of Aquitaine (a fifth-century defender of Augustine's thought)—lists a series of objections to Augustine's work, particularly on the questions of grace and predestination.[14] Prosper's refutation both attributes the objections to Vincent and convicts him of views later called semi-Pelagian. Some writers argue that there exists a deep congruency between certain passages in the *Commonitorium* and the fifth and sixth of the *Objectiones Vincentianae*.[15]

Most historians are also convinced that the atmosphere at Lérins and through-out southern Gaul was profoundly semi-Pelagian in tone. Moxon, for example, an astute historian, states that the monastery of Lérins was "a stronghold of Semipelagian views."[16] Such an atmosphere lends credence to the traditional claim that Vincent was indeed the author of the polemical *Objectiones*.

Despite this evidence, there has emerged a strengthening consensus that the monk of Lérins may not be the author of the objections cited by Prosper's confutation. A well-known translator of a French edition of the *Commonitorium* rejects the Vincentian authorship of the *Objectiones*, arguing that the attribution of this text to the Lérinian "suffers from difficulties and so remains very problematic."[17] In an exhaustive study, surely the most influential to date, William O'Connor contends that the *Objectiones* certainly did not come from the pen of the Lérinian.[18] Among his many arguments (and refutations of coun-terpositions), O'Connor states that the author of the objections clearly did not understand Augustine's thought. Could this really be Vincent of Lérins, the master of historical rigor, who himself was intimately familiar with (and deeply appreciative of) Augustine's work—to the point of publishing a florilegium of the African's trinitarian theology—and who carefully outlines the fateful missteps of heresies in the *Commonitorium*?[19] Could Vincent, who in his *Excerpta* speaks of Augustine's insights into the Trinity as "pearls and diamonds of priceless value," really be the author of the polemical objections? And is not the elegant Latin style of the Lérinian's authentic work missing from the artless *Objectiones*?[20] Can this be the same man who gives us such an extraordinarily insightful treatise on the nature of doctrine and its proper development?

An Italian commentator on Vincent's book similarly argues that the author of the *Objectiones* attributes absurd opinions to Augustine, clearly contradic-tory to the African's theology, whereas the *Commonitorium* reveals a precise and serious mind.[21] Finally, the editor of the most recent critical edition of the *Commonitorium* insists, largely on the basis of O'Connor's detailed work, that one can no longer attribute the *Objectiones* to Vincent.[22] The crucial question remains: Is it likely that the author of the *Excerpta*, so laudatory of Augustine's christological and trinitarian work, is the same man who turns so strongly against Augustine on grace and predestination in the *Objectiones*? If the authorship of the *Objectiones* has not been definitively settled, then the door is at least closer to being finally closed.[23]

Athanasian Creed

Vincent of Lérins has at times been regarded as the author of the Athanasian Creed, the statement of faith that has had so much influence in the Western church and was originally thought, as the name indicates, to have come from the pen of that resolute champion of Nicaea, Athanasius himself. Moxon observes that Vincent's comments on the Trinity in the *Commonitorium* so closely parallel those found in the Athanasian Creed that it was natural to regard him as the author of the famous symbol.[24] This suspicion was intensified by the fact that Vincent himself says, "If it pleases God, the author will explain this matter [the Trinity and incarnation] more fully at another time" (16.9). Some saw in the deeply trinitarian *Quicunque* (Athanasian Creed) Vincent's fulfillment of just this promise.

In the seventeenth century, for example, Joseph Anthelmi marshaled a strong case for Vincentian authorship of the Athanasian symbol. Two centuries later A. E. Burn, in a very solid study, argued for the monastery of Lérins as the definitive source of the creed, but with the founder, Honoratus, as the likely author. Burn contended that the strong parallels between the creed and the *Commonitorium* could be accounted for by Vincent's already having the creed ready at hand in the monastery.[25] More recently J. N. D. Kelly, in his exhaustive examination of the Athanasian symbol, concedes that the resemblances between Vincent's *Commonitorium* and the creed are "so striking that the theory [of Vincent's authorship] cannot be rejected without further scrutiny."[26]

The Vincentian hypothesis was further strengthened with Madoz's publication of the *Excerpta* in 1940, where one finds even more resemblances between Vincent's work and the *fides Athanasii*. This similarity leads Kelly to aver that a "relationship between the *Quicunque* and Vincent's writings cannot reasonably be doubted" even if it is difficult to determine the precise nature of that relationship.[27] He finally concludes that Vincent was not likely the author of the creed, primarily because the tone of the symbol is "relatively unpolemical" and Vincent was something of a controversialist. If Vincent had been the author, Kelly speculates, then surely, with his fiercely anti-Nestorian sensibility, he would have included the *Theotokos* (Mary as the Mother of God) in the creed itself.[28] At the same time, Kelly recognizes the creed's "direct and large-scale indebtedness to Vincent," finally agreeing with Madoz's earlier judgment that if Vincent is not the author of the creed, than he is an "immediate precursor" to it.[29]

Is the *Commonitorium* One Book or Two?

Frequently one sees references to the *Commonitoria* (plural) or to citations listing either the first *Commonitorium* or the second. In fact, the *Commonitorium* originally existed in two separate books, but we now possess only a portion of the second appended to the first. As Moxon says, at the end of chapter 28 all of the existing manuscripts contain the statement (which is clearly a later gloss) that the second book of the *Commonitorium* has been lost, with only a summary remaining (chaps. 29–33).[30] Gennadius explained this in 490 by saying that the second book was stolen, forcing Vincent to compose a short summary of its contents. But this, Moxon rightly says, is no more than a guess on Gennadius's part. The *Commonitorium* itself says nothing at all to support this claim.[31]

On the basis of internal evidence, one may believe that Vincent had both books before him when he wrote his summary. As he says, "The time has now come, at the end of the second commonitory, to recapitulate what has been said in both books" (29.1). But if he had both books before him, why did Vincent prepare for publication only a short summary of the second book and not the second book in its entirety? Moxon speculates that Vincent may have been concerned about the "dull and tedious nature" of the second book, dealing as it does with minutiae from the First Council of Ephesus (431).[32] Rather than provoking his audience with "wearisome reading," Vincent decided to offer a lengthy epitome of his second book, attaching it to the first. Moxon concludes that Vincent probably never published either the first or second book during his lifetime. One of his fellow monks at Lérins published the work, sometime between Vincent's death around 450 and Gennadius's comments in 490, using only Vincent's abstract of the second book (attached to the first) and leaving aside the full version of the second book as unnecessarily ponderous.

In all critical and contemporary editions, the chapters of the *Commonitorium* are now numbered consecutively from 1 to 33. In this book, I will refer simply to the *Commonitorium* as one volume, regarding the older practice of distinguishing two different books when referring to the work as unnecessarily cumbersome.

Vincent and Semi-Pelagianism

Was Vincent a semi-Pelagian? And, if so, should the entire *Commonitorium* be seen as a tract against Augustine's theory of predestination and grace?

This book will concentrate on Vincent's insights into the nature of Christian doctrine and its preservation and development over time. Indeed, it is precisely Vincent's reflections on doctrine that constitute his unique and essential contribution to theology. But we must also treat, at least briefly, the question of whether Vincent was a semi-Pelagian theologian, one deeply dissatisfied with certain theses of Augustine, and thus a writer who was reflective of a notable theological tendency in southern Gaul in the early fifth century. The Lérinian's reputation as a defender of semi-Pelagianism has, over the years, tarnished his standing as a reputable theological guide. As one commentator has noted, the anti-Augustinian aura that has now encompassed the monk of Lérins has obscured the high reputation he enjoyed in earlier centuries.[33]

In what follows, I will offer a brief discussion of this disputed question, with further indications offered for those who wish to pursue the issue at length. The conclusions reached on this matter do not significantly affect either Vincent's reflections on the development of doctrine or the importance of his insights for contemporary theology. If anything—and this is central for our treatment—the lively debates on grace and predestination (along with those on the incarnation and the Holy Trinity) that existed in the church of the early fifth century spurred Vincent to think deeply about precisely *how* doctrine properly develops and precisely *how* the church comes to a decision about disputed theological questions. In this sense the controversies of his day proved to be a salutary stimulus to his hermeneutics of doctrine. And it is the latter issue, along with how the Lérinian may provide theological guidance for the church today, that is of greatest interest for this volume. Vincent's major contemporary contribution is to be found in his attempt to understand how church teaching advances over time under the light of the Spirit and, relatedly, how the entire body of Christ is involved in the twin tasks of preserving the Christian faith and discerning its authentic progression. But let us proceed to the contentious topic at hand.

Probably a good way to begin the discussion of Vincent's role in the controversies of his day is to distinguish Pelagianism from its mitigated counterpart. Classically, Pelagianism refers to the position championed by the monk Pelagius (active in the early fifth century) that humanity's own free will is entirely intact and possesses, even absent divine grace, the innate ability to follow the commandments and to lead a virtuous life. Throughout the *Commonitorium*, Vincent is very critical of Pelagianism, making clear that the position he champions is entirely distinct from Pelagius's highly optimistic assessment of human capabilities.[34]

Semi-Pelagianism is traditionally distinguished from its full-blown counterpart (Pelagianism) thus: semi-Pelagianism insists that grace must aid and strengthen the human will, but it need not first incline the will toward God.[35] For semi-Pelagianism, the initial turn toward salvation, the *initium fidei*, springs not from God's gift of grace but from free will. An example may be found in one of the well-known monks of southern Gaul, John Cassian, who "tried to prove from Sacred Scripture that grace is the reward given us for good beginnings which spring from the will's own natural powers."[36] In this sense, grace is necessary only to complete these good, first (natural) intentions. Human beings, then, are not so unaffected by sin that they can work out their salvation without divine grace (as is the case with the Pelagians), but semi-Pelagians "could not understand that everything in the work of our salvation is a gift of the divine mercy, and that grace always anticipates man's efforts."[37]

In the semi-Pelagian understanding, then, grace is bestowed upon all those who, *with their own disciplined effort*, knock, seek, and ask, as Christ has counseled. But the weakness of this position, its opponents held, is that the renunciation of sin begins through human agency alone rather than through God's unmerited grace. Ultimately, Western Christianity judged semi-Pelagian principles as inadequate because too strong an accent was placed on the human will rather than on divine grace as the absolute prerequisite for the beginning of salvation.

Why is Vincent of Lérins often regarded as a semi-Pelagian thinker, despite the ardent condemnations of Pelagianism strewn throughout his *Commonitorium*? One reason, as noted, is that the monastic communities of southern Gaul had marked semi-Pelagian tendencies. This inclination may be seen, for example, in the writings of the aforementioned Cassian, an esteemed monk and theologian of Marseilles who died in 435, just after Vincent wrote his famous work. Cassian has long been considered the paladin and architect of Gallic monasticism, with his insights shaping the theology of nearby monastic settlements.[38] Thus it is not surprising that Moxon claims the monastery of Lérins was nothing less than "a stronghold of Semipelagian views."[39] Because of the theological atmosphere surrounding the monastic environs of southern France, it is generally held that Vincent was deeply sympathetic with the semi-Pelagian position.[40]

Because of this theological tendency, many scholars have detected a marked anti-Augustinian sentiment in Vincent's *Commonitorium*. Why this opposition to Augustine? Because the great bishop of Hippo placed so much emphasis on the absolute sovereignty of grace that all disciplined human effort seemed to pale in comparison to God's eternal, preordained will. As Weaver says, opposition to Augustine existed because the monks argued for the "relevance of human agency in the process of salvation."[41] Augustine's severe diminution of free will seemed to place all of the emphasis on God's eternal decision, absent human initiative. This leads Ogliari to conclude that the bishop of Hippo (or at least his followers) so exalted the supremacy and sovereignty of divine grace "that there seemed to be little or no room for the action of the human will."[42] Cooper-Marsdin adds that Augustine, particularly in his later works, "almost if not quite maintained the position that, in the Divine dispensation of personal salvation, human co-operation is needless."[43] One can understand the dilemma that Augustine's later theology (or at least certain formulations of it) posed for the monks of Marseilles and Lérins. Why would one adhere to the rigorous discipline of monasticism if it were essentially beside the point, *entirely unrelated to one's salvation*? For this reason, many think Vincent—together with the monks of southern Gaul generally—found Augustine's teaching on grace and free will to be tendentious, novel, and unsupported in the prior tradition. The *Commonitorium*, therefore, has often been considered as a sly polemic against Augustine's innovative views on grace.

Vincent and Anti-Augustinianism

Let us offer a broad outline of the events and debates surrounding the common conclusion that Vincent's magnum opus is, essentially, an anti-Augustinian tract.

The reaction of the monks and other clergy of southern Gaul to the teaching of Augustine on grace and predestination caught the attention of Prosper of Aquitaine and his colleague Hilary, two Christian laymen deeply influenced by

Augustine's thought. Prosper wrote to the bishop of Hippo in 428–29 (some five or six years before Vincent penned his *Commonitorium*) about the complaints of the Massilian clergy. In his letter, Prosper says that many of those who dwell in Marseilles "think your [Augustine's] teaching is a novelty" that reflects neither the teaching of the fathers nor the mind of the church.[44] The clergy of Marseilles are concerned that if predestination is overstated, then "toil is useless" since one who is fallen cannot by any work enter God's kingdom, and one who is chosen cannot, no matter his negligence, fail to enter it. The monks think that if one places such a strong accent on predestination, the concept of "fate" is now introduced into Christianity, while all human effort is rendered meaningless.

The Massilians are convinced, Prosper adds, that we come to the grace by which we are reborn through natural ability—by asking, seeking, and knocking. So the beginning of salvation comes from the one who is saved and not from the one who saves. Prosper humbly recognizes that his opponents often surpass him by the merits of their lives, and some have recently attained to the "highest priesthood" (perhaps thinking of Hilary, a monk of Lérins who had recently become bishop of Arles). But Prosper nonetheless thinks they wrongly locate the beginning of salvation in the selfsame human being rather than in God's unmerited grace.

Prosper's letter moved Augustine, shortly before his death in 430, to write two famous tracts, *De praedestinatione sanctorum* and *De dono perseverantiae*. But Prosper and Hilary did not end their campaign with letters to Augustine. So concerned were they about preserving the proper teaching on grace and predestination that they journeyed to Rome to present their case to Pope Celestine. In response to their concerns, Celestine wrote a letter to the bishops of Gaul (ca. 431) in praise of Augustine. Yet, while lauding the great African theologian, Celestine did not take a strong doctrinal stand on the disputed questions of grace and predestination.[45] Celestine insists, rather broadly, that "novelty should cease to molest antiquity." But Vincent finds this phrase deeply congenial because it is precisely theological novelties of every type, novelties that trespass upon the gospel, that he is determined to expunge.[46]

The most heated moments in this controversy over grace and free will—with contributions by Prosper, Augustine, Cassian, and Celestine—occurred just before Vincent wrote his *Commonitorium* in 434. This has led some to conclude that, as a monk of Lérins, Vincent could not have failed to breathe the thick semi-Pelagian air surrounding the Gallic monasteries. As an astute theologian, surely he desired to make some contribution to this pitched debate with Augustine and his followers. These circumstances have led historians to engage in detailed examinations of Vincent's work in the hopes of finding internal evidence of the anti-Augustinianism endemic to the region of Marseilles.

But this thorny issue is complicated by the fact that scholars have long based Vincent's alleged anti-Augustinianism, at least in significant part, upon certain passages found in the *Objectiones Vincentianae*. As we have seen, this text is now regarded by several important commentators as spuriously attributed to Vincent. So leaving aside the *Objectiones*, the question inevitably arises: What evidence is there in the *Commonitorium*, an undoubtedly authentic work, for the claim that the monk of Lérins was an ardent anti-Augustinian?

The first to argue that Vincent's aide-mémoire was likely an attack on the Doctor of Grace (Augustine) was the humanist Gerardus Vossius (Voss) in 1618. His conclusions were developed by Cardinal Henry Noris in 1673. This charge against Vincent has since been cultivated by various historians and theologians. José Madoz, for example, writing before his discovery of the *Excerpta*, argues that Vincent's celebrated book was preoccupied with nothing other than opposing the innovations of Augustine.[47] Harnack states that Vincent's book is "ultimately aimed at Augustine's doctrine of grace and predestination." Pelikan adds that "the immediate purpose of his [Vincent's] treatise seems to have been to attack the predestinarianism of Augustine."[48]

If one collects the various arguments made throughout the centuries in support of the position that Vincent was writing primarily against Augustine (and so in defense of semi-Pelagianism), they may be enumerated as follows:

1. Vincent never explicitly cites Augustine, the great theologian, although he lists several other eminent thinkers.
2. He engages in ardent attacks on Pelagianism, perhaps intending to distinguish (and even mask?) his own mitigated position.[49]
3. Vincent polemicizes against other eminent theologians who have been mistaken in the past, particularly Origen and Tertullian. Is this intended to suggest that even highly distinguished thinkers can fall into error—possibly Augustine as well?
4. The Lérinian sides with Pope Stephen against Cyprian in the rebaptism controversy of the third century, suggesting this possible parallel: If a bishop of Rome once suppressed the errors of a prominent African, is it not time for the present bishop of Rome to act against another distinguished African's innovations?[50]
5. In an impassioned plea, Vincent warns that an eminent teacher—even if he is a well-known doctor, bishop, confessor, or martyr—cannot be trusted if he deviates from the consensus of the church.
6. Although Vincent cites the aforementioned letter of Pope Celestine to the bishops of Gaul, he fails to mention that the pope warmly praises Augustine, saying that the great doctor has been regarded "by my predecessors as among the best teachers."[51]
7. A final point, taken to be conclusive by some, is the strong parallel between chapter 26 of the *Commonitorium* and a passage in Augustine's *De dono perseverantiae*.

In 429, Augustine states in the *De dono perseverantiae* (23.64):

> Let our adversaries consider how mistaken they are to think that our seeking,
> asking, knocking is from ourselves and is not given to us. . . . For these men
> will not understand that it is also a divine gift that we pray, that is, that we seek
> and ask and knock. For we have received a spirit of adoption as sons by virtue
> of which we cry, "Abba, Father." Blessed Ambrose understood this as well, for
> he says, "To pray to God is due to divine grace, for as it is written: No one says
> that Jesus is Lord but in the Holy Spirit." (citing Rom. 8:14–16; 1 Cor. 12:3)[52]

Just a few years later, in 434, Vincent's *Commonitorium* rails against those
who dare to claim that

> in their church, that is, in the small conventicle of their communion, there is a
> great and unique and fully personal grace of God, so that, *without any difficulty,
> without any effort, without any industry—even though they do not ask, they do
> not seek, they do not knock*—all those who belong to their number are dispensed
> by God and held aloft by angelic hands . . . so that never can they dash their
> feet against a rock, in no way can they fall into sin. (26.8–9, emphasis added)

Vincent opposes the idea of receiving grace without effort, and his sentiments are taken as prima facie evidence of a semi-Pelagian campaign against
Augustinian predestination.[53] Prosper, we remember, had specifically mentioned
that the Massilian clergy think that we can come to the grace by which we are
reborn by asking, seeking, and knocking.

Even though this parallel between Augustine and Vincent is striking, there
also exist good arguments defending Vincent against the anti-Augustinian
charge. Brunetière says straightforwardly, "I do not believe that the *Commonitorium* was directed against St. Augustine."[54] He argues that though Vincent is
often charged with semi-Pelagianism, we know next to nothing of this man's
life. Further, the *Commonitorium* strongly denounces Pelagianism while con-
taining no serious allusion to the controversies on grace and predestination.
On the contrary, it is the polemic against Nestorius's error that dominates the
Lérinian's work from beginning to end. Brunetière warns us not to place too
much confidence in the original conclusions of Vossius. The great scholars of
the Renaissance often engaged in arbitrary speculation.

To the argument that Vincent fails to number Augustine among the great
doctors of the church (precisely because Augustine is his opponent), Cooper-
Marsdin responds that the great paradigm of monastic life in Gaul, John
Cassian, is also absent from the *Commonitorium*. Further, Augustine's name
appears nowhere in the acts of the Council of Ephesus (431), the primary
source for Vincent's recitation of the names of important theologians. Cooper-
Marsdin concludes, "It is far too much to assert that the fact that he was a
monk of Lérins is any evidence of his semi-Pelagian point of view." And his

failure to mention Augustine is "equally little proof." On the contrary, Vincent
may simply have been warning (in his comments about those who require no
effort or industry) against an extreme predestinarianism held by certain sects
agitating the church.[55]

Both Brunetière and Cooper-Marsdin wrote before Madoz's publication of
Vincent's *Excerpta* in 1940. That text, a devoted tribute to Augustine's trinitarian theology, has strengthened the argument that Vincent was not a vitriolic
opponent of the bishop of Hippo. As Basil Studer has observed, Vincent acknowledges Augustine's theological authority, particularly in christological and
trinitarian questions.[56] It should also be remembered that the *Commonitorium*
was written against heresy and in defense of Christian truth. Vincent's book
attacks heresy after heresy, heretic after heretic. Did anyone in Marseilles or
Lérins, even those disagreeing with Augustine on certain disputed points, truly
regard this great champion of the Christian faith as proximate to heresy?

Offering a more specific argument is Élie Griffe, who insists that the *Commonitorium* "lies outside this [semi-Pelagian] controversy."[57] Griffe meets
head-on the charge that Vincent is responding directly to Augustine's famous
chapter in *De dono perseverantiae* (above) where the African doctor says that
any human asking, seeking, and knocking (Matt. 7:7) is necessarily preceded
by divine grace. In the passage in the *Commonitorium* where he addresses
this issue (26.8), Vincent is not rebutting Augustine. He denounces not those
who claim that God's grace precedes our asking and seeking; on the contrary,
he vilifies those who see no need to seek or knock *at all* because simply belonging to their heretical "conventicle" ensures divine favor. In the monastic
communities of both Lérins and Marseilles, Griffe argues, one could disagree
with Augustine on certain points of doctrine, but surely no one thought of
him as a heretic.[58]

Recently the editor of a critical edition of Vincent's work, R. Demeulenaere, has defended the Lérinian, observing that while several scholars have
detected a semi-Pelagian tone in Vincent's work, their arguments are vague
and inferential. Too frequently they base their conclusions on the *Objectiones*,
a text that can no longer be regarded as authentically Vincentian. Further,
the undoubtedly authentic *Excerpta* reveals Vincent not only as a connoisseur
of Augustine's immense oeuvre but also as a fervent admirer of his work.[59]
Finally, William O'Connor, a careful student of the Lérinian, concludes that
"an unbiased reading of the *Commonitorium* betrays no semi-Pelagian traces
or secret darts against St. Augustine and his doctrine."[60]

Conclusions

It has not been my intention, in this brief introduction, to evaluate all of the
evidence adduced regarding Vincent's position on the grace–free will question

that roiled the church in the early fifth century. Nonetheless, even with this broad outline, some tentative conclusions may be drawn. Although a good deal of evidence shows that the monks of southern Gaul espoused positions later called semi-Pelagian, and though some internal evidence shows that Vincent had leanings against (at least) exaggerated positions of Augustinian thought, these elements must not be overplayed in one's evaluation of the *Commonitorium*. As several authors have observed, the question of free will and grace is treated tangentially by Vincent. He is much more concerned about issues relating to Christ and to the Holy Trinity.

If Vincent did indeed have semi-Pelagian leanings, as did most of the monks of southern Gaul, we should be careful not to judge him too harshly on this account. The thorny theological issue of grace and freedom was only partially resolved (in the West) in 529 at the Second Council of Orange. As Ogliari says, the grace–free will controversy ended at this provincial council where Augustine's doctrine was generally accepted by the church; at the same time, "absolute grace was softened and the predestinarian theory left aside."[61] In 531, Boniface II approved the acts of this council, thus giving it wider authority. Just as we now do not harshly judge Justin Martyr or Tertullian or other pre-Nicene writers for not perfectly duplicating the precise formulas of the Council of Nicaea (325), so must this same leniency be extended to the monks of southern Gaul.

And in fact, Augustine's thought still has opponents who think his theology of grace and particularly his understanding of predestination were deeply mistaken, as the Massilians had first suggested. David B. Hart, for example, condemns the African's "hideous theology of predestination and original guilt" and "his conviction that genuine trust in the purity and priority of grace obliged him to affirm the eternal damnation of infants who died unbaptized." Hart further rejects the "arch dismissals of Eastern understandings of grace as 'semipelagian' by doctrinaire Augustinians."[62] As Weaver notes, the Gallic monks, in their struggle with Augustine, constantly appealed to the Eastern tradition as authoritative on these issues.[63] Ogliari adds that the monks of southern Gaul were in continuity "with the traditional (pre-Augustinian) views held by the Church (more specifically by the Church of the *pars Orientis*)."[64] Given the ancient witness of the East, facile condemnations of semi-Pelagianism should be avoided.

More important for this volume is the fact that a careful reading of the *Commonitorium* shows that Vincent was concerned about *several* disputed issues when he wrote his magnum opus. In the first place, he devotes a great deal of time to explaining the natures and personhood of Jesus Christ and to refuting the Arian heresy. The spread of Arian-like beliefs and their seeming sanction by the convocation of Ariminum (Rimini) in 359—in direct contradiction to Nicaea—haunted Vincent. It is this recrudescence of sub-ordinationism, and the betrayal of the Creed of Nicaea, that dominates the Lérinian's work. Because error is strong and powerful, the church needs clear criteria to distinguish truth from falsity. Second, Vincent was deeply troubled by Nestorianism and its misinterpretations of Christ's person. But he rejoices in the conclusions of the ecumenical Council of Ephesus (431) and its bestowal on Mary of the title of *Theotokos* (God-bearer). The unanimous interpretation of Scripture championed by this Ephesine Council would become an important dimension of his theological epistemology. Third, Vincent was concerned that certain ideas about grace and predestination were becoming widespread in sectors of the church. As his comments in chapter 26 of the *Commonitorium* show, some Christians could easily misunderstand the gospel, interpreting it in a way that was foreign to the general and accepted ecclesial sense.

All of these issues, but the christological errors in particular, led Vincent to think deeply about continuity and change, about identity and difference, about progress and adulteration, about antiquity and novelty. How is the precious deposit of faith preserved over time? How are illegitimate innovations identified? Again and again Vincent cites the apostle Paul's warning, "Guard the deposit, Timothy!" He repeats this phrase with such force that we can almost hear him crying out the Pauline admonition. Yet, careful thinker that he was, Vincent knew that guarding the deposit of faith did not forestall continued growth and development. Change inexorably occurs over the course of time. The gospel message is always cast in new formulations. Youthful light is shed on old issues.

But which kind of change is acceptable? And which kind deeply injures the Christian faith? These are the questions that deeply intrigued Vincent and motivated his famous book. Equally important, the church has in its possession clear criteria by which to make judgments on newly ventured positions. These criteria need to be effectively employed so that the development of Christian doctrine may be properly warranted and clearly distinguished from its deadly adulteration. Because of Vincent's sophisticated reflection on these questions, it makes little sense—and is textually unjustified—to reduce his small but incisive *Commonitorium* to a semi-Pelagian manifesto dedicated to attacking Augustine's theory of grace and predestination. The doctrinal value of the Lérinian's work far exceeds the disputed question concerning grace and free will.

What clearly emerges from the *Commonitorium* is that several of the controversies roiling the ancient church served as a *catalyst* for Vincent to think deeply about preserving "the faith once delivered to the saints" (Jude 3), even while carefully husbanding its proper development. Acute theologian that he was, Vincent realized that controversies about the Christian faith involved the entire church, and it was the entire church that was necessarily engaged in their resolution. How does the Spirit allow the church to see the truth in a time of dispute? And how can there be real development over the course of time? Vincent was convinced that the successful preaching of the gospel depended on the answers to these questions.

Let us now enter the rich theological world of the *Commonitorium* and see how Vincent constructs his argument.

1

Key Theological Themes
in the *Commonitorium*

Historical Considerations

Before embarking on a study of Vincent's thought, it may be helpful to speak
briefly about his influence in the history of theology. As Brunetière observes,
although the *Commonitorium* was not entirely ignored in the Middle Ages
(after all, Vincent's work was handed down to us, unlike so many other ancient writings), the book goes unnoticed by medieval theologians. Not even
in that vast collection of patristic scholarship in Thomas Aquinas's *Catena
aurea* does Vincent make an appearance. Indeed, for a thousand years, from
the fifth to the fifteenth centuries, the Lérinian's work goes unmentioned,
enveloped by silence.[1]

But Vincent's slim volume was rediscovered in the sixteenth century, giving
rise to multiple editions and translations. Thirty-five editions of the *Commonitorium* appeared in the sixteenth century, and another thirteen editions
(along with twenty-one translations from the Latin) appeared in the nineteenth.[2] The seventeenth-century Roman Catholic theologian Robert Bellarmine called Vincent's short work "a golden book [*libellus plane aureus*]";
similarly, the nineteenth-century Tübingen thinker Johannes E. Kuhn spoke
of it as a *goldenes Büchlein*. But these encomiums should not lead one to assume that Vincent appealed only to Roman Catholics. For centuries Protestant
thinkers have proclaimed the same admiration for the *Commonitorium*.[3]
For all Christians, Vincent represents a firm insistence on the continuous
preservation of the gospel message in its purity. Continuity in fundamental
principles is a sign of truth, while innovation is a sign of wavering from the

clear teaching of the Bible and the apostolic tradition. Roman Catholic authors were attracted to Vincent's accent on tradition; theologians of Reformation heritage (particularly Anglicans) ceaselessly invoked his well-known canon (*semper, ubique, et ab omnibus*), insisting on the strictly regulative value of the early centuries for authentic Christian doctrine. It is no surprise, then, that the young John Henry Newman, whose thought we shall examine in the following chapter, argued in his Anglican writings that Vincent's book opens an assault on the illegitimate innovations of both Rome and Wittenberg, stating repeatedly that the *Commonitorium*'s demand for antiquity embodied classical Anglican principles.[4]

Despite his renown in earlier centuries, Vincent has been generally ignored by contemporary theology, even at a time when *ressourcement* movements of various types dominate theological reasoning. One reason for this dismissal is that the monk of Lérins has seemed to be a rather regressive figure, even something of a cranky antiquarian, constantly urging preservation rather than progress, entirely out of step with the evolutionary character of contemporary thought.

More important, Vincent's work has been neglected because he has been exclusively connected with what has become known as his "canon" or "first rule": Christians are to hold fast only to that which has been believed "always, everywhere, and by everyone." If taken *sensu stricto*, Vincent's criterion is useless. Almost no teaching of the Christian faith has fulfilled this rule, causing the Lutheran theologian Carl Braaten to say that Vincent's canon "sounds strange" both because no doctrine adheres strictly to its demands and because the rule ignores the fact that doctrine itself is not a static reality.[5] Concerns quite similar to those voiced by Braaten caused antipathy to Vincent at Vatican II (1962–65), with the council's desire to stress the living and dynamic aspects of Christian faith and doctrine. Thus the young Joseph Ratzinger, in his commentary on *Dei Verbum* (1965), says that Vatican II "has another conception of the nature of historical identity and continuity. Vincent de Lérins's static *semper* no longer seems the right way of expressing [this] problem."[6] Similarly, the great ecumenist Yves Congar states, "It is because the principle [Vincent's first rule] is too static that Vatican II avoided quoting it in its constitution *Dei Verbum* §8."[7] Congar had earlier made this same point about Vincent's canon, referring to its "excessively static, not to say archaizing, character, and thus its limited validity."[8]

Vincent's theology has also been disdained by the great Reformed theologian Karl Barth. According to Barth, the Lérinian places entirely too heavy an accent on ecclesial tradition, thereby violating the evangelical purity of *sola scriptura*.[9] In fact, the theologian of Lérins strongly emphasizes the material sufficiency of sacred Scripture, with tradition as a necessary interpretative aid because of wanton and continual misinterpretations. At every turn in Vincent's writing, it is the Bible that is always primary and foundational.

Despite this general neglect of Vincent's thought, and at times outright opposition to it, the contention of this volume is that Vincent has much to teach Christianity today. Indeed, one intention of this book is to challenge the interpretations of Vincent bequeathed by Congar, Ratzinger, and Barth. The Lérinian's work is not only of historical interest; it is also a living guide to understanding more clearly the dynamic tension that always exists in the church between preservation and development, and outlines well the significant resources the church possesses to ensure that any development is in full conformity with prior Christian belief. This volume is intended to show that there is much more to Vincent's hermeneutics of doctrine than simply his endlessly cited canon. Indeed, the Vincentian canon itself must be interpreted according to the Lérinian's broad and capacious vision of the church. It cannot simply be ripped from his text as if it had a life apart from the entire context of his subtle work.

The *Commonitorium*

The major issues for Vincent are these: How is the precious truth of Christianity properly conserved? How is it truly preserved even while admitting that, over the course of the four hundred years since Christ's death (for Vincent is writing in 434), there has been some change and development in Christian belief? How can we be certain that such change leads to a greater understanding of the gospel, and not inexorably to heresy? In the church, do clear criteria exist that allow us to distinguish revealed truth from pernicious error?

To answer these questions, we will divide Vincent's thought into three general categories:

1. The preservation of the gospel is always the foremost task of Christians.
2. The development of doctrine is possible and must be fundamentally preservative in intent.
3. Essential criteria ensure that proper development is not confused with poisonous heresy.

Under each of these numbered headings, we will treat themes integral to Vincent's work.

1. The Preservation of Christian Truth

Vincent's preservative instincts are deeply rooted and clearly dominate his work. These impulses lead to the common accusation that the theologian of Lérins purveys only a static model of doctrine. Throughout the *Commonitorium* he pleads with us, consistently citing biblical warrants: "Guard the deposit,

Timothy!" "Do not trespass upon the landmarks of your fathers!" (1 Tim. 6:20; Prov. 22:28). Again and again he exhorts us not to betray the Christian faith by adhering to blasphemous innovations, which clearly are not founded in Scripture or in the apostolic tradition. For Vincent, "the faith once delivered to the saints" must be guarded and protected as the precious treasure that it is. The selfsame identity of the Christian message is under constant siege by heretical innovations, novelties that Christians must firmly resist.

The apostle Paul clearly instructs the Galatians, "If anyone preaches to you a gospel other than the one we preached, even an angel from heaven, let him be anathema" (Gal. 1:8). Reflecting on Paul's warning, Vincent says to his readers: Perhaps some think this anathema was meant only for former times and not for the present. On the contrary, this precept must be observed by all ages. Preaching to Christians a doctrine other than what was received "never was permitted, is not permitted, and never will be permitted" (*Common.* 9.5).

But how does the church preserve the teaching given in the history of Israel and in Jesus of Nazareth? What are Vincent's theological strategies for avoiding heresy and walking in the light of Christian truth?

Vincent's Canon or First Rule (Overcoming Heresy)

Vincent's primary theological instruction—the one with which he is always associated—is known as the Vincentian canon, or first rule. The canon states that, "in the Catholic church, all care must be taken so we hold that which has been believed everywhere, always, and by everyone" (2.5). As one commentator has observed, the brevity and vigor of this formula has assured its continued success.[10] And indeed, Vincent's memorable words (*ubique, semper, et ab omnibus*) have been endlessly invoked, though usually just as quickly dismissed. Contemporary historians and theologians generally hold that Vincent's catchy maxim represents a good attempt at fashioning a criterion for distinguishing truth from heresy, but that the slogan is rather naive, setting forth criteria that almost no Christian doctrine actually meets.[11] Some have argued that the canon raises more questions than it answers since the rule is so general as to be virtually useless.[12]

What is certainly true is that Vincent is groping for a principle that distinguishes truth from heresy. By his insistence on the threefold criteria, he is precluding wanton innovation (hence his insistence on antiquity) and the novel ideas of a few talented teachers (hence his criteria of universality and ubiquity). But before returning to the exact meaning of Vincent's canon, we should first establish its context. Vincent tells us, Socrates-like, that he has long sought a universal rule in order to distinguish the truth of the Catholic faith from the error of heresy. But why should we need a rule? he rhetorically objects. Surely Holy Scripture itself is entirely sufficient. Indeed, he insists, Scripture *is* sufficient and more than sufficient: "it is complete unto itself [*ad omnia satis superque sufficiat]*" (2.2). However, because of the profundity of God's Word, all do not accept it in exactly the same sense. Thus, he laments, Scripture seems to have as many interpretations as there are interpreters (2.3).[13] One needs only to glance at the long roster of heretics who have plagued the church to see the problem. Vincent then presents us with a rogues' gallery of heretics: Donatus, Arius, Apollinaris, Pelagius, and Nestorius—to name only a few.

Because heresiarchs claim biblical support (indeed, Vincent will argue that a distinguishing mark of heretics is that they always have a thousand citations at hand), we need a rule that helps us discern proper from improper interpretations of Scripture. It is just here that the Lérinian says we can distinguish Christian truth from error by adhering to the faith that has been believed *everywhere, always, and by all.* Truth is that which the whole world has confessed, in continuity with the faith of our ancestors. For Vincent, only the universal consent of the church can assure that a teaching is indeed ancient and well-attested rather than local and idiosyncratic. Particular teachings can never be confined to one geographical area, to one time period, or to a small group of believers.

But two oft-forgotten elements must be accented when thinking about the meaning of Vincent's canon. First and most important, *the canon is not just about the remote past.* It is true that Vincent encourages us to look to the consensus of antiquity. But *when* precisely is antiquity? If it begins with the apostolic age, is there a distinct terminus ad quem? No such terminus is ever invoked by Vincent. And this point is central to a proper interpretation of his theology. Vincent is thinking of antiquity—and the consensus of antiquity— in a unique way. He is not wistfully looking back to some golden age in the church, never again to be recaptured. Vincent is insisting that there already exists a way—always rooted in Scripture as the unshakable foundation—to ensure that the apostolic teaching continues unsullied. For the Lérinian, the Councils of Nicaea and Ephesus, the formal meetings of teachers gathered from the entire church, *themselves* represent the consentient judgment of antiquity. The first rule, then—*semper, ubique, et ab omnibus*—should not be understood as if it represents a utopian dream, some asymptotic (approximate) ideal, drawn from a nebulous and remote age of the church. Vincent is much more hardheaded and practical than that. He looks around at the church of his day and sees Christian truth everywhere under siege, everywhere contending with heretical interpretations, some even purveyed by notable churchmen like Nestorius. He himself resides in a monastery that has recently been a locus of heated theological controversy. To deal with these *living* issues, Vincent is seeking a rule that can be applied in his own time, indeed, a rule that has already been applied to great effect at the Councils of Nicaea and Ephesus.

The church, then, already has the *means and authority* to separate biblical truth from pernicious error. In this sense, the entire *Commonitorium* must be understood simply as an elongated commentary on his canon. The remainder of Vincent's book tells us exactly what "always, everywhere, and by everyone" means and how this criterion is ecclesially instantiated. Vincent spends much of his book in answering a key question: What means do we possess to ensure that our belief is in continuity with the apostolic tradition? As he tells us early on, we adhere to antiquity if we do not discard any interpretations shared by the venerable holy ones and by our fathers (2.6).

A second essential element in interpreting the Vincentian canon is that his first rule must always be taken in conjunction with the Lérinian's "second rule": over time, growth undoubtedly occurs in Christian doctrine. Yet he adds the proviso that such growth is always protective of the meaning found in earlier formulations of the faith. This is why Vincent insists that any further doctrinal understanding must always be "according to the same doctrine, the same meaning, and the same judgment [*in eodem scilicet dogmate, eodem sensu, eademque sententia*]" (23.3) as existed in prior articulations of Christian teaching. We shall discuss this second rule at greater length. For the moment, it is enough to say that the Vincentian canon should never be read outside of its context. And its context always includes the possibility of proper development over time. The Christian church possesses the ability, not simply in the past, but also *today*—in Vincent's own time—to ensure that the faith is carefully husbanded. These two elements—that the canon is not just about the remote past and that it allows for proper development—are too often ignored when the first rule is ripped out of its context and is therefore understood in a truncated and ultimately mistaken way.

We shall return to Vincent's precise understanding of his canon, but let us first examine some of his arguments for ensuring that the faith entrusted to the church is properly preserved, not altered or distorted by poisonous innovations.

Selected Biblical Indications on Preserving Christian Faith

O Timothy, guard the deposit that has been entrusted to you!

1 Tim. 6:20

This passage is the most important biblical text for Vincent's theological purposes and the one to which he returns again and again throughout his work. He reads Paul's warning to Timothy as a cri de coeur, insisting that if we are to avoid heresies, we must faithfully guard the faith that has been entrusted and transmitted to us through the centuries. The Lérinian constantly cries out, "O Timothy, guard the deposit, avoiding profane novelties [*novitates*] and what is falsely called knowledge. Those professing such opinions are far from the faith" (*Common.* 21.3).[14] Vincent tells us that this biblical passage is a spiritual sword by which all heresies have been and always will be decapitated.

The apostle Paul does not tell us to avoid antiquity. It is novelty and innovation that inexorably lead to error. So the Lérinian concludes, "Novelty is to be avoided; antiquity is to be held dear. And if novelty is profane, antiquity itself is sacred" (21.5).

Again and again Vincent reminds us that by holding fast to antiquity, we stand on the sure ground of faith. The only caution to be lodged, once again, is ascertaining Vincent's exact understanding of antiquity. One should not assume that the monk of Lérins is talking about a mythical, utopian past, a remote *aetas aurea* (age of gold). As we shall see, when he invokes antiquity, he is most often talking about the Council of Nicaea (325) and its decrees (which, by Vincent's time, were already over a century old). Indeed, even the recently concluded Ephesine Council legitimately falls within this description, precisely because it represents the faith of the ancient church.

> Transgress not the landmarks that we have inherited from the fathers.
>
> Prov. 22:28

Another preservative biblical passage of which Vincent is deeply enamored is Prov. 22:28, wherein we are counseled not to transgress the landmarks established by our fathers (*Common.* 5.2; 21.2). After lamenting the execrable dangers of Arianism—to which some bishops (at the convocation of Ariminum in 359) and even the emperor Constantius succumbed—Vincent proposes as a remedy this citation from Proverbs, already put to good use by Ambrose some decades earlier.[15] We must never contravene the landmarks fixed by earlier ages. And precisely what is a significant monument or marker for Vincent? It primarily is the faith of Nicaea, which has been fixed and laid down by the entire church.

The creed solemnly defined at Nicaea cannot be abjured by later synods and conventicles, as happened at Ariminum. This is why Vincent rails against those who dare to "unseal the priestly book already sealed by confessors and consecrated by martyrs" (5.2).[16] It is why he insists that one must adhere "to the decrees and definitions of all the bishops/overseers of holy church, heirs of the apostolic and catholic truth" (5.6).[17] For the Lérinian, the ecumenical Council of Nicaea, representing the unified agreement of all the official teachers from every part of Christendom, has properly interpreted Scriptures, thereby establishing an irreversible milestone, just as Proverbs instructs. Indeed, he adds that those who do contravene the church's solemn teachings will suffer consequences. As Scripture teaches, "Who should break through a wall, the serpent will bite" (Eccles. 10:8; *Common.* 21.2). Whether the image is the "wall" or the "landmark," Vincent's intention is the same: ecumenical councils represent the authentic interpretation of Scripture by *all* the official teachers of the church *everywhere*. The solemn judgments they erect cannot be overturned.

Important to observe is Vincent's ecclesial and theological instantiation of his well-known canon. It is obvious that the first rule—always, everywhere, and by everyone—refers not to some ill-defined golden age. Vincent is thinking, rather, of the faith given to the apostles, the faith of the Scriptures, which is clearly found in the *irreversible doctrinal formulations of Nicaea and Ephesus*. These consentient judgments of the entire church are now established as specific monuments that may under no circumstances be violated. Writing in 434, Vincent already sees Nicaea (325) as a venerable council, a solid and enduring lodestar erected by the universal church transmitting the apostolic tradition. This same judgment applies to Ephesus (431).

> But even if we or an angel from heaven should preach to you a gospel other than the one we preached, let him be anathema.
>
> Gal. 1:8

It is not surprising that Vincent, the great defender of "the faith once delivered to the saints," would find the apostle Paul's warning to the Galatians to be a considerable weapon in his arsenal against wanton innovations. Indeed, Vincent devotes almost two chapters to his exegesis of this text. Paul, Vincent tells us, is not content to oppose himself simply to human beings who innovate against the faith. Even if an *angel* from heaven should preach some other gospel, Paul will oppose him (*Common.* 8.3). Vincent quickly adds that the angels of heaven are holy and sinless. But, he insists, if that were to occur which cannot occur (that an angel betray the faith), then Paul would not hesitate to anathematize him.

Notice that the apostle says "even if we" rather than "even if I" (8.2). Why is this? Because he means even if Peter, or Andrew, or John or any of the other apostles should preach a different gospel than the one originally preached, then he should be accursed. In his zeal for the purity of the gospel, Paul spares no one; such is his extraordinary rigor. But perhaps, Vincent continues, Paul, with these excited phrases, is allowing human impetuousness to cloud his judgment? Not at all. For Paul immediately repeats himself (Gal. 1:9), making clear that he is speaking not with human but divine guidance.

Vincent further explains that Paul's message was not intended only for the Galatians. Reading the Bible as if it were simply a history book would be profoundly erroneous. On the contrary, the Pauline injunctions are intended for today and always: "to preach to Catholic Christians any doctrine other than that which they have received never was permitted, is not permitted, and never will be permitted" (*Common.* 9.5). At the same time, anathematizing those who announce anything other than the doctrine that was once received "always was a duty, always is a duty, and always will be a duty." The doctor of the Gentiles, that trumpet of the apostles, cries out to us—to all of us, and always and everywhere (with Vincent here consciously repeating his *omnibus et semper et ubique*): "If anyone preaches a new doctrine, let him be anathema!" (9.7).

The Deposit and Rule of Faith

Two other important terms that make a frequent appearance in Vincent's work—always with the intention of preserving Christian doctrine—are the deposit of faith (*depositum*) and the rule of faith (*regula fidei*).

CHRISTIAN DOCTRINE AS A *DEPOSITUM*

The word *depositum* appears with some frequency in the *Commonitorium* since it is found in the Latin translation of Paul's famous exhortation to Timothy: "Guard the deposit! [*depositum custodi*]" (1 Tim. 6:20). For Vincent, each age must fully adhere to the apostle Paul's command, guarding the deposit "once delivered to the saints" (Jude 3). But what precisely is the deposit? How is it defined? To the inquiry "What is the deposit?" Vincent responds:

> The deposit is that which has been confided to you, not that which you have discovered; it is that which you have received, not that which you invented; it is something not of your personal ingenuity, but of doctrine; not something that is private, but which belongs to public tradition; it is something which has been given to you, not created by you. You are not the deposit's author, but its guardian; you are not its initiator, but its follower; you are not its leader, but its disciple [*non ducens sed sequens*]. (*Common.* 22.4)

Here Vincent makes clear that the precious gospel once received from Christ is something that Christians must guard with care, not harboring the belief that they possess the authority to re-create it or shape it in their own image. Later in this work, we shall see how Vincent answers a similarly crucial question: Who is the Timothy of today who is faithfully guarding the deposit? For the moment, it is clear that "deposit" indicates all the elements of revelation that have come through the history of Israel and Jesus of Nazareth, now preserved in the Christian church. With the word "deposit" Vincent has in mind the entire patrimony of revelation that has been bestowed on Christians. Because this endowment must be handed on in its fullness, Vincent again and again invokes some form of the word *idem*, "the same." There is a unity and continuity in the Christian faith that cannot be betrayed. The *same* faith once transmitted must now be handed on in its complete integrity.

We should not, however, think of the deposit as a lifeless, static element, as the word might suggest. For the Lérinian, the deposit must be guarded yet also nurtured, husbanded, and properly developed. Christians must defend the deposit in its purity and integrity, even while acknowledging that they are able to receive more light and precision (23.12–13). We shall examine this accent on development in a moment.

REGULA FIDEI

Closely and almost synonymously related to the term *depositum* is that of *regula fidei*, "the rule of faith," a term with a rich Christian provenance.[18] For Vincent, the rule of faith has been given once and for all. The patrimony of grace and truth, in its objective fullness, has already been bestowed upon the world in ancient Israel and in Jesus Christ. One must be certain, therefore, that all teachings are in accord with the normative rule of faith that has been transmitted from antiquity. Christians must resist every attempt to change or innovate. As Vincent says, "We are not to lead religion where we please, but rather we are to follow religion where it leads" (6.6).[19]

We gather a more exact sense of the meaning of the rich phrase "rule of faith" and its cognates when we see how Vincent uses the term. The Lérinian invokes the *regula credenda*, or "rule of believing," when contrasting those who live according to the faith handed down with those who "seek new teaching after new teaching, day after day [*sed nova ac nova de die in diem quaerant*]" (21.1). Vincent also invokes a form of the phrase when speaking about the controversy concerning the rebaptism of those who had apostatized during the Roman persecutions and wanted to return to the church. Certain African bishops, Agrippinus and Cyprian among them, had encouraged the practice of rebaptism, but Stephen, an early bishop of Rome, had condemned it, arguing that baptism in the name of the Trinity must not be repeated. Vincent argues that the introduction of rebaptism in Carthage was contrary to Scripture (the divine canon) and to "the rule of the universal church [*universalis ecclesiae regulam*]" (6.4). The rule of faith here constitutes a normative and irreversible Christian norm.

Toward the close of the *Commonitorium*, Vincent discusses the recently held Council of Ephesus, called to deal with Nestorius's misinterpretation of the person of Christ. Commenting on that solemn assembly, he tells us that the "opinions of the holy fathers have been gathered . . . by the decree and authority of a council, so that the rule of the church's faith [*ecclesiasticae fidei regula*] might be fixed" (28.16). He again says of the Ephesine Council that it was a matter of "definitively laying down the rules of faith [*fidei regulis*]" (29.8). Finally, Vincent speaks of Ephesus as having "pronounced on the rules of faith [*de fidei regulis pronuntiavit*]" (30.6). Ecumenical councils, by collecting the teachings of the entire Christian world, represent antiquity, ubiquity, and universality—and therefore possess the authority to determine the precise meaning of the rule of faith. Councils do not innovate (*nihil minuit, nihil addit*). Rather, they interpret the meaning of Scripture as understood by the church universal and thereby make manifest the unchangeable *regula fidei*.

The Ever-Present Danger of Heresy

For Vincent, the first task of all Christians is to preserve the faith that has been handed down to them. Nonetheless, the lure of heresy remains strong and powerful. At the very beginning of his book, Vincent enumerates a long list of heresies besetting the church: Arianism, Donatism, Pelagianism, and the list proceeds on and on. With so many false teachers, how can Catholics identify the truth? And why does God allow heresy at all? Vincent's entire project, we remember, is to offer criteria to separate sound doctrine from erroneous thinking. He now explains how to pinpoint a heretical teacher.

Unlike Christian truth—which is held *semper, ubique, et ab omnibus*—heresy is always an innovation, a blasphemous novelty introduced into the church by talented and even brilliant teachers. This is why heretics say, "Come, O ignorant ones, who are normally called Catholics, and listen to the true faith which no one besides us understands, which for many centuries has remained hidden but has recently been revealed" (21.7). For Vincent, this is *always* the tactic of clever heretics: the faith has been hidden, and only *now*, at this very moment, is it finally coming to light. But this tactic inexorably conceals novelty and error. Instead of what has been taught always and everywhere, we are introduced to some new, previously unheard-of doctrine. Heretics are those who always seek something new, constantly hoping "to add, to change, and to subtract [*addere, mutare, detrahere*]" from true Christianity (21.1).[20]

As opposed to the ancient Christian truth, every heresy, Vincent insists, "burst forth with a determinate name, in a determinate place, and at a determinate time [*certo nomine, certo loco, certo tempore ebulliuit*]" (24.6). Indeed, a distinguishing mark of heresy is that it has a traceable history. We know who started it and at what precise time the heresiarch began to preach, as with Pelagius and Arius. Unlike heresies, which have a clear founder and a clear date of origin, Catholic Christianity is characterized by continuity and substantial identity. That is why heretics urge us to reject the past. They inevitably tell us, "Take us now as your guides and interpreters. Condemn what you used to hold, and hold what you used to condemn. Reject the ancient faith and the dictates of your fathers and the deposits of the ancients" (9.8). In their quest for novelty, heretics condemn previously established landmarks and decrees, particularly those of ecumenical councils. Here again, Vincent's conciliar instantiation of his threefold canon—*semper, ubique, et ab omnibus*—is intended to serve as a bulwark against those who would violate the rule of faith erected by the venerable ancestors.

But other questions trouble Vincent as well. Why does God allow his holy church to be tempted with heresy? Why is revelation subjected to constant attacks, even by respected teachers and churchmen (such as Nestorius)? The Lérinian's biblical answer is twofold. Most prominent is his oft-cited claim, "If there should arise among you a prophet or dreamer, who gives to you a sign or wonder, urging you to follow strange gods, pay no heed to the words of that prophet, even if that sign or wonder comes to pass, for the Lord your God is testing you, to see if you really love him with all your heart and soul" (Deut. 13:1–3). Vincent also cites the well-known comment of the apostle Paul on the same topic: "There must be heresies among you so that those who are approved are known" (1 Cor. 11:19). But it is the citation from the Old Testament that Vincent finds most attractive. He not only invokes it when discussing heretics such as Apollinaris and Nestorius (*Common.* 12.1–3); he also spends an entire chapter showing its applicability to the present day, lamenting that many brilliant prophets and doctors have arisen in the church and have even been esteemed as defenders of truth, yet have introduced errors, causing great trials to the church of God (10.8).[21]

Vincent is also well aware that illegitimate innovations can have very powerful patronage. When speaking of the third-century rebaptism controversy, for example, he says that this theological innovation had impressive support. On its side were the vigor of genius, waves of eloquence, a great number of partisans, an undeniable resemblance to the truth, and even many statements of Scripture—although now understood in a new and defective manner—so that this proposal could barely be defeated, except that it was ultimately seen as a novelty lacking in foundation (6.8). Heresy can even befall bishops, official teachers in the church. Indeed, Vincent tells us that the Arian poison had contaminated almost the whole world (4.3). Virtually all the bishops of the Latin language were seduced, "partly by violence, partly by fraud," at the assembly of Ariminum in 359. Vincent is haunted by this gathering: later he condemns it as the "perfidy of Ariminum" (29.8), and for good reason. It is of this convocation that Jerome famously pronounced, "The world groaned and was amazed to find itself Arian."[22]

All heretics, whether bishops or theological doctors, are far from the secure harbor of the Catholic faith. Vincent does not mince words: Regurgitate the poisonous errors you have swallowed so that you may now receive the living and clear waters of Christian truth (20.7). Let heretics return to the shelter of their placid and good mother, the church, far from the deceit of novelty.[23]

Heresy and Scripture

Although the foundational role of Scripture in Vincent's work will be discussed below, it is worthwhile to note that the Lérinian is well aware that heretics are adept at citing Scripture. As we shall see, it is just this heretical penchant for twisting biblical arguments that leads Vincent to develop a complex hermeneutics of proper scriptural interpretation. Commenting on this phenomenon, he says, "Someone may perhaps ask, Do heretics appeal to Scripture? They do indeed and with great ardor [*vehementer*]" (25.1). "By citing the Bible, heretics come to us in sheep's clothing, when they are, in truth, ravenous wolves [Matt. 7:15]. They wrap themselves in the words of Scripture so that others, deceived by the soft wool of fleece, will not fear their fangs" (25.8).[24]

Like the apostles, heretics bring forth citations from the Psalms and the Prophets. But while they adduce the same citations as orthodox Christians, they "interpret them in very different ways [*similiter, sed interpretari non similiter*]" (25.12). It is just such men that the apostle Paul rebukes when he says that they are "pseudo-apostles, deceitful workers, masquerading as apostles of Christ" (2 Cor. 11:13). Heretics are those who, in their interpretation of Scripture—and here Vincent returns to his favorite Old Testament images—have broken through the hedge (Eccles. 10:8) and overturned the landmarks of the fathers (Prov. 22:28). By their erroneous interpretations, the faith is attacked and ecclesiastical doctrine (*ecclesiasticum dogma*) destroyed (*Common.* 25.9). Only when Scripture is interpreted in accordance with the conciliar definitions (the monuments, the hedge) and the consentient teaching of the doctors, only then is one treading the path of Christian truth. Biblical learning is essential and foundational for Vincent, but there are many who abuse it, starting with Satan himself (26.1). We need to rely, therefore, on the proper interpretation of the divine canon given to us by solid conciliar teaching and in the wisdom of learned and saintly doctors.

The Christian Faith, Preserved and Inviolate

Vincent of Lérins's entire work is devoted to the preservation of the faith found in Scripture, "the faith once and for all delivered to the saints." Substantial continuity of belief is crucial; novelty is a sign of heresy. Without such continuity, we mock the faith of those who preceded us. This is why Vincent places such a strong accent on the earlier "landmarks" established by the fathers. If these are violated, then the faith of earlier Christians is betrayed.

Just here, in a trope that Vincent finds appealing, he invokes the witness of the entire church against innovation:

[Such novelties], were they accepted, would necessarily defile the faith of the blessed fathers. . . . If they were accepted, then it must be stated that the faithful of all ages, all the saints, all the chaste, continent virgins, all the clerical Levites and priests, so many thousands of confessors, so great an army of martyrs, so many populous cities and nations, . . . almost the entire world incorporated in Christ the Head through the Catholic faith for so many centuries, would have erred, would have blasphemed, would not have known what to believe. (24.5)

Vincent pens a similar passage when discussing Arianism and how this poisonous error, like a Fury, had taken captive the emperor and his court, with predictable results: "Wives were dishonored, widows violated, virgins profaned, monasteries destroyed, clerics dispersed, lower clergy beaten, bishops exiled, and prisons, jails, and mines filled with the saints" (4.6). In other words, when heresies reign, the entire church is thrown into grave tumult. Those formerly held in esteem are now persecuted and in disrepute. Heavenly doctrine is replaced with human superstition; esteemed antiquity is supplanted by profane novelty. The result is that the wisdom of former ages, the teaching of the fathers, and the definitions of the ancestors are violated and destroyed (4.7). In his lament over Arianism, Vincent points again and again to established milestones, particularly the affirmations of Nicaea. The acceptance of Arianism by the emperor Constantius—as well as the hoodwinking of bishops at Ariminum—share a common fault: the trading of established antiquity for profane novelty.[25]

It should be pointed out, once again, that "antiquity" in Vincent is hardly equated with some gossamer, indefinable golden age. *Antiquity is properly mediated through the consentient determinations of living tradition, particularly ecumenical councils.* Conciliar definitions constitute the scripturally inspired monuments, the "hedges" that may not be violated or breached by reversals or betrayals of their teaching. This is why Vincent will say that the genuine Christian not only loves the truth of God and the Catholic faith but also believes only what the church has held universally and from antiquity, and will not believe that which has been introduced by someone "other than all, or against all, the saints [*praeter omnes vel contra omnes sanctos*]" (20.2).[26]

2. The Development of Christian Doctrine

What makes Vincent of Lérins a truly fascinating and theologically important writer for our day is not only his decided accent on the preservation of Christian truth but also his theologically inventive attempt to reconcile strict preservation with inexorable development and growth. Even in the early fifth century, Vincent recognized that there had been some modicum of change—at the very least in language—between biblical times and the church of his own day. Nicaea (325) had used the word *homoousios* (same essence) when speaking of Christ's relationship to God the Father, and the recently concluded council of Ephesus (431) had spoken of the Virgin Mary as *Theotokos* (God-bearer). Writing four hundred years after Christ's death, Vincent has seen the church navigate through tumultuous waters, at every turn beset with heresies and novel biblical interpretations. He gratefully acknowledges that the church, particularly in its creedal and conciliar statements, has both repudiated error and drawn out the implications of steadfast Christian belief. Over the course of the church's life, all these events have forced him to think deeply about continuity and change, identity and difference. How does change truly coexist in the church with substantial continuity? And how may the church identify a change that is proper and legitimate as opposed to one that is an adulteration and debasement of the deposit of Christian faith? These are the questions that animate Vincent, and they are questions that remain with us to this day, making the Lérinian's thoughtful answers worthy of our attention.

David Friedrich Strauss famously wrote, "The true criticism of dogma is its history."[27] In Strauss's understanding, Christian dogma is an inevitable casualty of the historical thinking introduced by modern, critical thought. But this position is entirely foreign to Vincent. Properly understood, history is the glory of doctrine, not its enemy. For history allows the church to polish and develop the unchangeable truth given us in ancient Israel and in Jesus of Nazareth. Right at the outset of the *Commonitorium*, the Lérinian gives us a glimpse into his understanding of temporality: "Since time ravages all human things, we should, in turn, seize from it something that will profit us regarding eternal life" (1.3). Vincent here echoes Ovid's well-known teaching "Time devours all things [*tempus edax rerum*]."[28] But time's ravenous appetite is not only a dyslogistic force for the theologian of Lérins. The Christian thinker can also seize something from temporality that is to his theological advantage—something that is highly profitable for eternal life. Vincent, then, is hardly a purveyor of a static and immovable narrative. Indeed, the Lérinian is the only early Christian writer to treat historicity *ex professo*, and he does so with a positive tone.[29]

In his famous chapter 23 of the *Commonitorium*, Vincent daringly tries to reconcile his first rule—true things are true *semper, ubique, et ab omnibus*—with his second rule, that there indeed exists development in the church of God, but development that is always in continuity with what has preceded it. The Lérinian's attempt to harmonize his deeply preservative instincts with the need for continuing development makes him an intriguing theologian. This great champion of the ancient faith speaks excitedly at the beginning of his reflections on development, intending to show that preservation and growth are entirely reconcilable realities, fully congruent with Christian truth.[30] It is worth quoting the crucial selection:

> But someone will perhaps say: is there no progress of religion in the church of Christ? Certainly there is progress, even exceedingly great progress [*plane et maximus*]! For who is so envious of others and so hateful toward God as to try to prohibit it? Yet it must be an advance [*profectus*] in the proper sense of the word and not an alteration [*permutatio*] in faith. For progress means that each thing is enlarged within itself [*res amplificetur*], while alteration implies that one thing is transformed into something else [*aliquid ex alio in aliud*]. It is necessary, therefore, that understanding, knowledge, and wisdom should grow [*crescat*] and advance [*proficiat*] vigorously in individuals as well as in the community, in a single person as well as in the whole church, and this gradually in the course of ages and centuries. But the progress made must be according to its own type, that is, in accord with the same doctrine, the same meaning, and the same judgment [*eodem sensu eademque sententia*]. (23.1–3)

On the basis of his canon, or first rule, Vincent has often been cast as a mere antiquarian. He is guilty as charged if by that term one means he has an abiding interest in preserving the faith given in ancient Israel and in Jesus Christ. But we would entirely misunderstand his attention to antiquity if we did not conjoin to that interest his equally lively concern for development and his belief that antiquity is properly preserved *in and through* the church's own continuing life. If Vincent had never written his chapter on development, then perhaps the charge of naive antiquarianism, of curatorial Christianity, of ecclesial primitivism, would have stuck, although even then a counterargument could be marshaled. But his vigorous comments on growth, with its robust endorsement of development (*plane et maximus*), end all debate.

Vincent's marked accent on authentic growth over time is another reason why the note of "antiquity" in his first rule should not be pulled out of context. Antiquity itself must always be understood within the horizon of legitimate development. Once again we recognize that when Vincent speaks of "antiquity," he is not referring to a belief or practice existing in an already fully formed state in the apostolic age. If that were the case, it would render his entire chapter on development meaningless. It would also render the conciliar teaching he so highly praises—with the church's gradually drawing out the implications of Scripture—entirely unnecessary. Instead, antiquity refers to elements that are present but lying fallow, only to be fully developed in the church's life over time and, importantly, by means of the proper criteria for organic growth.

But Vincent struggles with the crucial issue: How is the integrity of the Christian faith to be conserved and maintained even while allowing for authentic development over time? How can the faith grow—even *plane et maximus*, as he insists it does—without injuring its essence, which must always be transmitted as the precious treasure that it is? Which criteria may be adduced to ensure that there can be proper development over time? Let us first examine precisely how Vincent understands authentic growth.

Vincent's Second Rule

Vincent's two rules—the *semper, ubique, et ab omnibus* and development *in eodem sensu*—present us with a dynamic and productive tension between the immutability of Christian doctrine and its proper, architectonic growth. Christian faith must always be firmly rooted in the Bible. But the church comes to understand the full implications of the Scriptures only gradually—and in opposition to erroneous interpretations. For this reason, Vincent cannot be accused of doctrinal mummification. Christian teaching is alive and dynamic for him, always growing and developing, although with a growth and change that must be organically and architectonically related to that which preceded it. God continues to work in history, guiding the church to a fuller understanding of revealed truth, just as God guides natural human realities. This is the point of Vincent's analogies of a child's growing into an adult and a seed's becoming a fully formed plant.

The Lérinian, then, is not at all shy about or embarrassed by change. But crucially, he asks: Which kind of change is legitimate? How can we distinguish legitimate from pernicious growth? The images he invokes offer a clue to his understanding.

Vincent tells us that the growth of religion is parallel to the growth of bodies, which develop over the years yet remain the same as they have always been (23.4). People change from childhood to maturity, but "their nature and personhood remain one and the same [*eademque natura, una eademque persona sit*]" (23.5). Whatever is found in the fully grown adult already existed virtually, embryonically, in the child (*iam in seminis*), so that nothing truly new appears in old age (*nihil novum . . . in senibus*). Therefore the legitimate "rule of progress [*regula proficiendi*]" and the order of growth is this: What appears in the adult has already been traced by the Creator in the infant (23.7). If this were not the case, if the development bespoke some other kind of nature, then there would be not organic growth but monstrous deformation. Christian doctrine, Vincent concludes, follows the same law of progress. "It is consolidated by years, developed over time, rendered more sublime by age, but it remains without corruption or adulteration so that it is always complete and perfect in all its dimensions and parts, . . . admitting no change, no debasement of its unique characteristics, no variation within its defined limits" (23.9).

Vincent illustrates his point by arguing that what is sown as wheat must be harvested as wheat: "Original doctrine sown as wheat, when developed over the course of time and properly cultivated, must retain the property of the grain and should undergo no change in its character; there may be added change in shape, form, clarity [*species, forma, distinctio*], *but there must remain the same nature according to its fundamental character*" (23.11, emphasis added). In other words, like wheat, doctrine cannot metamorphose into something different in kind. There may be development and growth, since both wheat and doctrine flourish under cultivation. But there can be no change in their fundamental and essential nature.

By means of these images, Vincent makes clear that he is thinking embryonically. Just as a child has all that is needed for the later adult and a seed all that is needed for the later plant, so the revelation offered in Jesus Christ has all that is necessary for later development. Truth here is both entirely given in revelation—and so in some sense immutable—and yet still lying hidden, latent, in potency, released and unfolded in the church over the course of time, just as Vincent himself has seen in the councils that preceded him. This is why the Lérinian uses the phrases "the church's faith is enlarged by time [*dilatetur tempore*]" (23.9), and "the matter grows within itself [*in semetipsa . . . res amplificetur*]" (23.2).

But the monk of Lérins also insists, and vigorously so, that any growth and enlargement must always be "according to the same doctrine, the same meaning, and the same judgment" (23.3). This is the limiting principle for growth that is essential and indefeasible. Growth can never mean the reversal or the distortion of a fundamental truth. The "same meaning [*idem sensus*]" must be maintained from age to age. One cannot, by trading under the banner of development, furtively introduce a teaching that is genetically and architectonically unrelated to what the church has previously taught. This is why he tells us that while both a child and a plant develop over time, neither can change its substantial nature. What has been sown by the father must be zealously cultivated by the children so that it may flourish, mature, and advance toward perfection (23.12). Vincent enthusiastically endorses growth, with the concomitant insistence that any development also preserve the *idem sensus* so that the rose bed does not degenerate to thorns or thistles, so that the child grows to a proper adult and does not become a deformed monstrosity.

Profectus, non Permutatio

For Vincent, temporality is either God's time, during which one polishes the faith delivered to the saints, or it is a time of heretical innovation, sanctioning an unwarranted modification of the faith. But how can one tell the difference? How is a change a true development and not the work of heresy? After all, one person's authentic growth is often another's illegitimate innovation.

The Lérinian tells us that in a proper development, a *profectus*, something is enlarged according to its own nature, without losing its proper substance. But an alteration of the faith, a *permutatio*, occurs when something is transformed into something else entirely, with "an alteration of its very essence [*aliquid ex alio in aliud*]," such as a rose bed becoming mere thorns and thistles. The growth of a child to an adult—just as the growth of doctrine—must be natural, organic, architectonic growth. Can there be true change and development? Yes, unquestionably so. The Lérinian understands that change is intrinsic to natural human life. And he has already seen it enacted theologically, with the language of the conciliar definitions of Nicaea and Ephesus. The church may sanction change, then, allowing for proportional growth over time, but with no alteration in the general structure of the doctrine itself, without changing, so to speak, its genetic type.

Let us revisit the crucial passage cited earlier. Vincent says, "Is there no progress of religion in the church of Christ? Certainly there is progress, even exceedingly great progress [*plane et maximus*]!" The Lérinian's words are forceful and excited, even after sixteen hundred years. Preserving the faith carefully does not mean that the church does not develop. But *how* does the church develop? This is the crucial issue. And this is why he insists that growth can only be of a certain type: it can only be development that is always mindful of the apostle Paul's ringing words "Guard the deposit, Timothy!" and "No other gospel!" For this reason, Vincent insists that any growth, change, and development must be *in eodem scilicet dogmate, eodem sensu eademque sententia*: all growth must be in accord with the same doctrine, the same meaning, and the same judgment.

The phrase "the same meaning [*idem sensus*]" and its cognates are exceedingly important to the Lérinian and appear throughout his work. The term is decisive because Vincent insists that over the course of the centuries, Christian doctrine must protect the original meaning found in Scripture and the early councils. A continual danger is that, under the guise of development, the meaning of the church's faith is illegitimately transformed, allowing heterogeneous ideas to be introduced. Precisely this kind of alteration constitutes the pernicious adulteration of religion that Vincent labels a *permutatio fidei*. If the substantial content of Christian faith and doctrine is changed, one engages not in the development of the faith but in its corruption. Such alteration is no longer *res amplificetur*, doctrine growing within itself; instead, it is a monstrous deformation of Christian belief.

In its objective sense, then, *idem sensus* (*eodem sensu eademque sententia*) intends the continuity of meaning existing over the course of time. Authentic growth can never bespeak the reversal of a fundamental (conciliar) teaching. One may not "contravene the landmarks" (Prov. 22:28) that have been established by the fathers. One may not "break through the wall," as was attempted by the emperor and even by the bishops at Ariminum—although under duress—when they sought to overturn the consentient teaching of Nicaea.

But this phrase *idem sensus*—the same meaning—is also used by Vincent in a way that accents the role of interpreters. In fact, his crucial insight that doctrine must progress according to the same meaning and the same judgment—*in eodem sensu eademque sententia*—is drawn from the Vulgate translation of 1 Cor. 1:10. It has often been overlooked that the provenance of Vincent's second rule is to be found in the apostle Paul's exhortation to the church at Corinth: "I implore you, brothers, that all of you agree in what you say, and that there be no divisions among you, but that you be united in the same mind and in the same judgment [*in eodem sensu et in eadem sententia*]" (*Common.* 28.10). Paul is beseeching the Christians at Corinth to be united in their decisions, to speak with one voice, thereby avoiding divisions. And this is also a major concern of Vincent. Any development must take account of the entire church. When sanctioning a development, there must be unity with regard to the inferred implications. This consentient agreement is intended to ensure that any proposed advance is not actually an idiosyncratic *permutatio* of the faith, sanctioned only by a few and inexorably leading to heresy.

Idem sensus, then, has two aspects. There remains the objective accent on the identity of preserved meaning. And this is joined to Vincent's stress on the subjective agreement and common consensus of the Christian community.

This consensus is buttressed by Paul's comment, also cited by Vincent, that God is "not a God of dissension but of peace" (1 Cor. 14:33). In other words, organic and architectonic development should be recognized by all. Precisely here one finds the biblical root of Vincent's notes of ubiquity and universality. Only consensual agreement will prevent the church's faith and doctrine from illegitimate incursions by a small group of false teachers. To avoid a dangerous corruption, a development that is transformative of doctrine's very nature, the consentient agreement of the entire church is required. Lacking such agreement, one purveys not the proper growth of *res amplificetur*, but actually the debasement of the faith.

While insisting on communal safeguards, Vincent clearly endorses development. In fact, he says, those who deny such growth are "envious of others and hateful toward God." What is the meaning of such forceful words? Vincent does not tell us explicitly, but we may speculate that some are "hateful toward God" because they fail to recognize that God uses time productively, that God acts in the church in order to lead Christians to a fuller knowledge of his truth. Vincent is eager to rebuke those who wish not just preservation—which he completely sanctions—but doctrinal immobility and mummification. The Holy Spirit is at work guiding the church. So Vincent says, "It is necessary, therefore, that understanding, knowledge, and wisdom should grow [*crescat*] and advance [*proficiat*] vigorously in individuals as well as in the community, in a single person as well as in the whole church, and this gradually in the course of ages and centuries" (*Common.* 23.3). Denying that such growth exists, or resisting it, is to deny that God uses time well. And one therefore expresses "hatred toward God."

As we have seen, because of time's inexorable effects, Vincent makes a distinction between using history properly and improperly. A proper understanding of time, guided by the Holy Spirit, results in a progression of the faith, a *profectus*. But an improper use of time leads to innovation and adulteration, which Vincent calls a *permutatio*. The challenge for Vincent of Lérins and for the Christian church of every age is precisely the same: How can the church's faith grow and evolve without countenancing the kind of essential or substantial alteration that actually deforms Christian truth? As we shall see, Vincent offers determinate criteria so that the church may make such decisions wisely. But for the moment, let us continue to examine his fundamental distinction between proper progress (*profectus*) and illegitimate deformation (*permutatio*).

True Growth

Vincent makes it quite clear that one cannot countenance any kind of "development" that would allow a teaching essentially different from that of the Scripture and the church's prior milestones, such as Nicaea (325). Legitimate development is genetic and organic—children growing to adulthood, seeds becoming plants of the same genus—maintaining the essential and fundamental characteristics of "the faith once delivered to the saints." Doctrines must retain their integrity and their distinct character (23.13). Christian doctrine may indeed be enlarged (*res amplificetur; dilatetur tempore*), but this is a growth wherein the fundamental nature of previous teachings is not betrayed.

Vincent's vocabulary is a clue to his understanding. He does not hesitate to use words indicating growth and development: *crescere* (to grow), *proficere* (to advance), *profectus* (advance), *evolvere* (to develop), *florere* (to flourish), and *maturescere* (to mature). Surely these words acknowledge actual growth and change along with precision and polishing. We need only add, once again, that Vincent sanctions homogeneous growth (*idem sensus*) and ardently rejects any kind of "development" that covertly introduces an essential change. This is why he tells Christians, "You received gold, now transmit gold to others" (22.5). Do not substitute lead or brass, something other than and inferior to what was handed on to you.[31]

Once again, it is important to recall that Vincent was haunted by certain events that loom large in the *Commonitorium*. The major occurrence was the synod held at Ariminum in 359, where bishops—as Vincent says, "partly by violence, partly by fraud"—subscribed to a creed with Arian overtones. He mentions that the emperor, too, was caught up in this madness. But seeking to reverse and contravene the landmarks placed by our venerable ancestors, the "hedges" erected by Scripture and then by the Council of Nicaea, is precisely the kind of "development" that is entirely false and must be rejected. Thus the principle of "continuity of type," a phrase normally associated with the work of John Henry Newman, is actually deeply engrained in Vincent's *Commonitorium*. The opposite of true growth is the deformation of Christian doctrine, which occurs when the essence of a teaching is betrayed. This happened not only at the synod of Ariminum but also in the preaching and teaching of Arius, Donatus, Nestorius, Apollinaris, and countless others, even the great theologians Origen and Tertullian.

Vincent tells us that over the course of time, it is necessary that doctrines should be smoothed, cleaned, and polished; it is criminal, however, if they are changed, truncated, or mutilated (23.13). As he says, "No disruption is permitted [*nihil permutationis admittat*]" (23.9). One may never sanction a teaching that betrays biblical and conciliar doctrine. This is why Vincent insists, in a memorable phase, "The same things that you were taught, teach, so that when you speak newly, you do not say new things [*dicas nove, non dicas nova*]" (22.7). This classic insight, abbreviated to the phase *noviter, non nova* (newly, not new things), indicates clearly that Vincent insists on the material continuity of the ancient faith. Indeed, once the integrity and distinctiveness of Christian teaching is compromised, then "one after another the elements of Catholic truth are necessarily abandoned [*abdicate . . . qualibet parte catholici dogmatis, alia atque alia . . . aliae et aliae*]" (23.14).

In service to the twin goals of preservation and authentic development, Vincent offers a beautiful reflection on the continuing task of Christ's body, the church:

> The true church of Christ, the sedulous and cautious guardian of the dogmas entrusted to its care [*depositorum apud se*], changes nothing in them, subtracts nothing, and adds nothing [*nihil minuit, nihil addit*]. The church does not cut off what is necessary nor add what is superfluous. The church does not lose what belongs to it nor usurp what belongs to another. But with all its knowing, the church applies itself to this one point: treating with fidelity and wisdom the ancient doctrine, perfecting and polishing what may, from antiquity, have been left unformed and shapeless. The church's task is to consolidate and to strengthen doctrine, to guard what has already been confirmed and defined. (23.16–17)[32]

Here one sees Vincent's distinction between *profectus* and *permutatio* in full view. The church does not and cannot add to what has been given in the history of Israel and in Jesus Christ. Instead, the church stands custodial guard over that which has been deposited with it. The church does allow growth, but it is an organic development, preserving and confirming what has already been defined. The fact that Vincent is speaking here primarily about the decrees of ecumenical councils is clear from the next line: "For what has ever been the goal of councils, than that what was believed in simplicity, the same can now be believed reflectively; that what was previously preached languorously, can now be preached vigorously; that what was before honored neglectfully, can now be attended to with solicitude?" (23.18).

Vincent's point is that in ecumenical councils the church theologically sharpens and polishes Christian beliefs that may have been somewhat shapeless and inchoate in the past. And precisely this form-giving life allows these beliefs to be preached with new intensity, vigor, and clarity.[33]

Noviter, non Nova

Vincent's argument is that there is substantial continuity—indeed, identity is not too strong a word—between the biblical church and the Christian community of his time. Yet, writing in the early fifth century, Vincent is well aware that the church of his day speaks somewhat differently than does the church of the New Testament. Now the church uses terms such as *homoousios* and *Theotokos*, phrases unknown in the apostolic age. How can the church introduce such terminology yet neither add nor subtract, neither innovate nor mutilate?

The Lérinian is convinced that ecumenical councils, in particular, transmit the faith in its entirety, establishing monuments that are fully reflective of Scripture and early tradition. Councils, therefore, exemplarily fulfill the first rule of *semper, ubique, et ab omnibus*, using a new lexicon to express the ancient faith, thereby fulfilling the Vincentian exhortation *Dicas nove, non dicas nova*:

Here, I say, provoked by the novelties of heretics, the Catholic church has always accomplished by the decrees of its councils—this and nothing more: what was received from the ancients by means of tradition alone has now been consigned to written documents for the sake of posterity. In a few words the church has summed up a great quantity of matter—most frequently, for a clearer understanding—and has designated by new and appropriate words some article of faith that of itself is traditional [*non novum fidei sensum*]. (23.19)

Councils admirably fulfill the *noviter, non nova* by preserving the ancient biblical faith, but expressing it in new ways. Ecumenical councils may indeed change the *form* of the faith, but they can never change its fundamental content or meaning, which remains always the same (*idem sensus*). Although the Christian faith may "grow within itself [*res amplificetur*]" and be "enlarged by time [*dilatetur tempore*]," it can never be adulterated by contravening solemnly established teachings. In any new formulation, gold must be returned for gold, lest the substantial identity of the faith be betrayed.

Heretics, on the other hand, are never satisfied with "the rule of belief [*regula credendi*]." They not only speak newly; they also continually introduce new beliefs (*nova*). As Vincent says, heretics "seek new teaching after new teaching, day after day [*nova ac nova de die in diem quaerant*]" (21.1). Here it is not a matter of casting old teachings in a new form. Instead, it is a profane and blasphemous novelty that is now introduced.

Christology and Trinity

In the middle of his work (chaps. 13–15), Vincent enters into a detailed analysis of the christological questions roiling the church of his day. Since the primary intention of this work is to examine Vincent's understanding of doctrinal development, I will not enter into a long exegesis of the heretical ideas he opposes. Suffice it to say that the Lérinian's reflections, following upon the conciliar decisions of Nicaea (325) and Ephesus (431), are intended to show that such decisions faithfully reflect biblical intentions and clearly show the insufficiencies attending the heresies purveyed by Nestorius, Arius, Apollinaris, and others.[34] It is of particular interest that Vincent sees the christological and trinitarian affirmations of the early church as drawing out the implications found in Scripture itself. His comments in these chapters are important because they clearly display his understanding of development over time. We also do well to attend to Vincent's oft-overlooked sentence wherein he tells us that he is "unfolding, or disclosing, doctrine more distinctly and explicitly [*distinctius et expressius enucleemus*]" (13.5). This is a significant phrase because "unfolding" is precisely what is taking place. The Lérinian is taking the biblical text and displaying how it is understood by the church of his day, particularly with the help of ecumenical councils.[35]

If a brief list of Vincent's christological affirmations is composed, one may see displayed precisely the kind of doctrinal development he sanctions:

1. Jesus is one person, but with two substances (natures) (13.4).
2. The Word of God is immutable (13.4).
3. In the Trinity, there is "another and another [person] but never another and another [substance] [*alius atque alius, non aliud atque aliud*]" (13.5). Here Vincent means that in the Trinity one speaks of distinction of person (hypostasis/subsistence) but never distinction within the one divine nature.
4. In the Savior, on the other hand, the reverse is true: There is another and another nature, but never another and another person. This means that Christ is always one person with a nature both of the Godhead and of humanity; one nature comes from God the Father and the other from the Virgin Mother (13.9). Indeed, Christ is both consubstantial (*consubstantialis*) with his Father and consubstantial with his mother, but "remaining always one and the same Christ [*unus tamen idemque Christus*]."
5. Christ's divine nature is "unchangeable and incapable of suffering" (13.9).
6. In the Trinity, the unity of the divine substance never blocks the distinctiveness of the persons, and the distinctiveness of the persons does not destroy the divine unity (16.2).
7. In Christ, the distinction in natures does not obscure the unity of person, and the unity of person does not destroy the distinction of natures.
8. Because of the unity of Godhood and humanity in Christ, we may confer (in the classic statement of the "communication of idioms") divine attributes to the human and human attributes to God (16.7).
9. After reflecting on the God-human unity in Christ Jesus, Vincent concludes that Christ's unity of person in two natures is similar to the unity of body and soul in human beings. The distinction between body and soul in humans will continue forever, just as in Christ each nature will retain its own distinctive character (13.14–15).
10. The unity of Christ's person (with two natures) is already perfected in the Virgin's womb (15.1). For Christ is not only one now; he was *always* one; the humanity and Godhead in Jesus are united from his very conception.

From these theologically sophisticated statements, one may see that Vincent's canon—*semper, ubique, et ab omnibus*—hardly entails the simple replication of the language and concepts of the Scriptures. The Lérinian invokes advanced theological ideas that have been developed and polished over time, particularly by ecumenical councils and by the consentient agreement of theological doctors. His clear intention is to preserve the meaning of Scripture, even while making it linguistically more precise and drawing out (*enucleemus*) its theological implications.

3. Ecclesial Criteria for Distinguishing Truth from Heresy

In the first numbered section we examined Vincent's understanding of the preservation of Christian doctrine; then in the second we analyzed more closely his understanding of development. In this third section we show the well-developed criteria Vincent offers for enabling the church properly to distinguish truth from error, orthodoxy from heresy.

We have already seen that Vincent insists on guarding the deposit "once delivered to the saints," yet he also acknowledges that growth and development exist over time. How shall the church distinguish a proper *profectus* from a disastrous *permutatio*? This is the issue that animates Vincent's work and for which he offers determinate criteria.

Many have argued that Vincent's canon—Christian truth is that which has been believed always, everywhere, and by everyone—constitutes the monk of Lérins's ultimate rule for distinguishing truth from heresy. This is not untrue; yet too often this rule has been interpreted apart from its context, leading to contorted readings and to a dismissal of the rule's usefulness, given its alleged inadequacy. Yet a careful reading of the *Commonitorium* shows that Vincent's rule is hardly a pithy but indeterminate slogan. Rather, Vincent not only sanctions proper development over time; he also offers specific *loci theologici* so that the antiquity and universality of the Christian faith can be clearly known within the church—of his day and any day. These *loci* are *living* theological warrants, which can be consulted now just as they were consulted in Vincent's time.

My argument, then, is that the Vincentian canon—*semper, ubique, et ab omnibus*—is concretized by, and instantiated in, a series of determinate theological places or warrants wherein one may visibly see *how* Christian doctrine, in its very antiquity, has been preserved always, everywhere, and by everyone.[36] *Precisely by invoking these authorities*, one can make a clear distinction between a development that is a legitimate *profectus* and an interpretation that is a pernicious *permutatio*, or betrayal of the Christian faith. How can we be certain that we have a proper advance rather than a corruption?

Vincent answers this by positing his own crucial question, on which the intelligibility of his entire work turns: *Quis est hodie Timotheus?* (22.2). "Who is the Timothy of today" to whom the apostle Paul addresses his injunction "Guard the deposit, Timothy"? Who ensures *today* that there are no deviations from the faith? Who ensures that any development is a proper *profectus*? Who confirms that a development in the church is always *in eodem sensu* with the prior tradition and not *in alieno sensu*? Who guarantees that gold is exchanged for gold, rather than for brass or lead (22.17–22)? Who preserves inviolate the "talent" of the apostolic faith (Matt. 25:15)? Who ensures that the children of mother church are able "to distinguish truth from error [in the interpretation of] the sacred Scriptures?" (*Common.* 27.1). These are the theological questions that enthrall Vincent and to which he gives a complex and multilayered answer.

The theologian of Lérins has already told us that the apostolic faith must be inviolately preserved. He has also allowed for development of a certain type and shape. Now he tells us precisely how this lofty goal is achieved. The fact that he does not do so systematically, but with various elements strewn throughout the *Commonitorium*, may be a reason that his careful response has often been overlooked.

Sacred Scripture

At the very outset of the *Commonitorium*, when searching for a "universal rule" to distinguish the truth of the Christian faith from the ravages of heresy, Vincent tells us we must strengthen our belief by means of two aids: first (*primum*) by the authority of the divine law (Scripture), and then next (*tum deinde*) by the tradition of the Catholic church (2.1). Both theoretically and practically, Scripture stands at the foundation of Vincent's work and is the primary warrant that he invokes for Christian doctrine. Why, then, is there need to invoke tradition, even secondarily? Vincent himself asks this neuralgic question: "Since the canon of Scripture is perfect and sufficient of itself for all matters—indeed, more than sufficient [*ad omnia satis superque sufficiat*]—why is there need for the authority of the church's interpretation to be joined to it?" (2.2).

Right from the outset of his work, then, Vincent attests to the authority and sufficiency of God's inspired Word. But he acknowledges and regrets that heretics, too, turn to the Bible. So he answers that "because the Bible is so profound, all do not accept it according to the same meaning [*eodemque sensu*]" (2.3). One person interprets it one way and another in a different way, so much so that we can say that there are "almost as many interpretations as there are interpreters [*quot homines, tot sententiae*]" (2.3). And then Vincent offers a long list of heretics who insist that they expound Scripture correctly: Sabellius, Donatus, Apollinarus, Pelagius, Nestorius, and the roster continues. Because of such a variety of errors, Vincent concludes, one should interpret Scripture according to its normative ecclesiastical and Catholic meaning (2.4). We shall attend to exactly how Vincent understands this authoritative meaning; but for the moment, let us continue to examine the foundational authority of Scripture in the life of the church.

At virtually every point in his book, the Lérinian insists that we can identify erroneous teachers, even those of great learning, and correct their errors, "first [*primum*] by the authority of Scripture and then [*deinde*] by some examples from ecclesiastical tradition" (17.1). When Vincent is discussing older heresies that still plague the church (such as Arianism), he tells us that these should be continually refuted "by the sole authority of the Scriptures [*sola scripturarum auctoritate*] . . . or as condemned by the universal councils of Catholic bishops" (28.4). Near the close of his work, where Vincent is recapitulating his earlier themes, he once again states that "it has long been the custom of Catholics, and remains the custom today, to demonstrate the true faith in two ways: first [*primum*] by the authority of the divine canon [Scripture], followed by [*deinde*] the tradition of the Catholic church" (29.2). And he reminds his readers of what he has said at the very outset of his work: "the canon alone [*canon solus*]" suffices for every question. Only because Scripture has been interpreted variously and arbitrarily is it required that its proper understanding must be directed by the one rule of meaning admitted by the church (29.3).

Central for Vincent, then, is the unique place of Sacred Scripture. It is always mentioned as primary and authoritative in dealing with error and in maintaining the truth of the Christian faith. As Madoz rightly says, everything may be found in Scripture, according to the Lérinian. Even the prohibition of rebaptizing those who had apostatized during persecution and later were returning to the church, which had been classically adduced as a teaching known through tradition, is defended by Vincent on the grounds that rebaptism is prohibited not only by the rule of the universal church but also by "the divine canon" (6.4).

Always "next [*deinde*]" in importance is the tradition of the church. Tradition is essential because it ensures that Scripture is not contorted by heresy and that it is interpreted according to the same sense throughout the church. As earlier noted, Vincent is acutely aware that heretics love to cite Scripture in their favor. And because of its profundity, the Bible, he says, is open to a variety of interpretations. Tradition thus is not some new source of information, a secondary source of apostolic teaching known only by oral tradition. Rather, for Vincent, "tradition is always *the ecclesial understanding of Scripture*."[37]

Before turning to the other warrants or criteria Vincent offers to ensure that the deposit is faithfully guarded and that Christian truth is distinguished from heresy, it is worth examining Vincent's comments on the heretical use of Scripture. It is just this problem that surely forces the need for tradition, understood as the church's normative and authoritative interpretation of God's Word.

Heretics and Scripture

The Lérinian has already told us that Scripture is more than sufficient to answer any doctrinal question that arises. But heretics, too, appeal to the protective carapace of the Bible; and they do so with "great ardor [*vehementer*]" (25.1). Vincent tells us, humorously, that one can see heretics "scurrying [*volare*]" through all the volumes of Moses and Kings and Psalms and Epistles and through the Gospels and Prophets as well. Indeed, heretics say almost nothing of their own that they do not obscure with words from Scripture (25.2). By this means, they seek to introduce novelties into the church, citing the Bible in order to shield their error. In a lively image, the Lérinian accuses heretics of offering a cup of their poisonous doctrine, but coating the edge of the cup with the sweetness of Scripture, just as a nurse coats the lip of a cup with honey when coaxing children to swallow bitter medicine (25.5).[38]

Vincent reminds us that Satan himself quoted Scripture, and the Lérinian pertinently asks, "What chance do we miserable men have against him who used the witness of the Scriptures against the Lord of Glory?" (26.2). This example should remind us that when heretics cite the apostles and prophets against the Catholic faith, it is a sign that Satan himself is speaking through them (26.3). It is just this misuse of Scripture that leads Vincent to invoke a striking image: Just as the head of the devils once spoke to the Head of the church, so now the members of Satan's household speak to the members of the church (26.4). Satan once quoted Scripture in order to tempt Christ; now heretics, Satan's minions, cite Scripture in order to lead Christ's disciples into error.

Vincent insists that heretics always have ready at hand "a thousand witnesses, a thousand examples, a thousand authorities [*mille testimonia, mille exempla, mille auctoritates*] drawn from the Law, the Psalms, the Apostles and Prophets, but now subjected to a new and deceitful method of interpretation" (26.7). They are so adept at biblical citations that if you ask them, "How do you explain and prove that I should abandon the universal and ancient faith of the Catholic church?" they immediately reply, "So it is written . . ." (26.6). Just as Satan beseeched Christ to "cast himself down," for "so it is written [*scriptum est enim*]," heretics similarly invoke the Bible, asking us to cast ourselves down from the sure harbor of the church, the temple of God (26.5).

For all these reasons, Vincent is convinced that the Word of God needs to be interpreted correctly. But how does one achieve a correct interpretation, thereby disarming heretics—Arius, Donatus, Pelagius, Nestorius, and others—who think they can cite the Bible for their own cause? The Lérinian is convinced that we can be assured of a correct interpretation of God's Word only by turning to those "places [*loci*]" wherein the church universal judges some interpretation as in accord with the apostolic tradition. As we shall see, Vincent adduces multiple "centers of authority," several purveyors of "landmarks," thereby ensuring that any interpretation of the Scriptures is not idiosyncratic, but solidly rooted in the faith of the entire Christian church.

Ecumenical Councils

When it comes to distinguishing biblical truth from blasphemous error, authentic theological developments from illegitimate ones, Vincent always turns first to Scripture. But next in importance for opposing profane and heretical innovations are the ecumenical councils. By their very nature, these represent the universal church; they are, in other words, the preeminent instantiations of Vincent's canon, ensuring that biblical interpretation is not idiosyncratic and regional but endorsed by the worldwide *catholica*, everywhere and by everyone.

Right from the outset of the *Commonitorium*, Vincent asks, What if a part of the church, even a province, falls into error? He responds that the Catholic Christian will certainly cleave to antiquity. But it is possible that even in antiquity there can be found some who are in error. How then should one proceed? Vincent tells us that the Christian will always adhere to the decrees of an ancient and universal council (3.3). Ecumenical councils serve as the authoritative voice of the church on disputed questions, says Vincent. By marshaling the witness of the official teachers from every locale throughout the Christian world, these councils bear witness to the proper interpretation of the Word of God.

The accent on ecumenical councils is consistent throughout Vincent's work. Their decisions constitute the "landmarks" that must not be transgressed, the "hedges" that must not be broken. Toward the end of his book, the Lérinian is at pains to establish what may be called a "hierarchy of interpretative authority." So, while insisting on antiquity, he says that "within antiquity itself, to the boldness of the opinions of one or a few, there should be preferred before all else the general decrees of a universal council, although if none exists on a particular matter, then that which is next best, the opinion of numerous and important theological masters" (27.4). Vincent later repeats his instructions. Christians wishing to remain free of heresy have two paths: "They should determine whether, from antiquity, something has been decreed by all the bishops of the Catholic church with the authority of a universal council; next [*deinde*], if there should arise some new question where this kind of decision is not found, they should have recourse to the teachings of the holy fathers, that is, of those who remain, in their own time and place, in the unity of communion and of the faith and have been masters of proven value" (29.5–6). When discussing older heresies that still plague the church (such as Arianism), he tells us that their errors should be refuted "by the sole authority of the Scriptures . . . or by the universal councils of Catholic bishops" (28.4).

In these kinds of statements, Vincent's transparent intention is to uphold ecumenical councils as instantiating his canon of "everywhere, always, and by everyone." Indeed, one may argue that for the Lérinian, ecumenical councils provide exemplary and paradigmatic instances of his first rule. Councils are to be trusted because they represent the opinion of all the bishops/overseers of the church in their interpretation of Scripture. Once again, Vincent would insist that Scripture is sufficient—indeed, more than sufficient. But since its meaning is contorted by heretics, disputed interpretations are best settled by conciliar decree since such statements represent the sure judgment of the universal church.[39]

Earlier in this chapter we alluded to the fact that "antiquity" in Vincent's work cannot be understood as some nebulous golden age, without clearly defined borders, when Christian truth was serenely held everywhere and by everyone. In fact, the Lérinian has no such utopian epoch in mind. When Vincent refers to antiquity, he means the ancient faith of the church as mediated through councils. As he says, one must always prefer antiquity to novelty, and within antiquity honor "the general decrees of a universal council" (27.4). It is the councils themselves that re-present the ancient faith of the church. A consentient opinion of the entire church in universal council can only mean what Scripture itself has meant—although in a new form and with new words, as with *homoousios* and *Theotokos*. The Scriptures and the conciliar decrees teach one and the same truth, although differently expressed.

It should be remembered that for Vincent, writing in 434, the Council of Nicaea is already antiquity, having occurred over a hundred years earlier (in 325). But even the Council of Ephesus (431), just three years old, represents the consensus of the church about its ancient doctrine. Only when this understanding is kept firmly in mind does the Vincentian canon—ubiquity, universality, and antiquity—make sense. These characteristics do not belong to some remote *aetas aurea*. They are preserved by the living, ongoing tradition of the church, particularly through ecumenical councils, where one sees the *noviter, non nova* and the *res amplificetur* in act. By the church's universal agreement, doctrine may be properly and organically extended, *in eodem sensu*—while simultaneously resisting profane novelties.

An ecumenical council, then, indefeasibly fulfills the distinctive characteristics not only of ubiquity and universality (as is obvious from the nature of the gathering) but also of antiquity because councils inexorably draw their conclusions from the Sacred Scriptures. When Ephesus declares Mary to be the *Theotokos*, the God-bearer, Vincent is well aware that this title, while not explicitly traceable back to the apostolic age, represents the "drawing out and unfolding [*distinctius et expressius enucleemus*]" (13.5) of the deposit of faith and thus does indeed indicate the sure judgment of antiquity. The same is true for the *homoousios* of Nicaea. Ecumenical councils, then, represent antiquity in content, even if not necessarily in form, which is the essence of Vincent's dictum that when "you speak newly, you do not say new things [*dicas nove, non dicas nova*]."

> Here, I say, provoked by the novelties of heretics, the Catholic church has always accomplished by the decrees of its councils—this and nothing more: . . .

The church has summed up in a few words a great quantity of matter—most frequently, for a clearer understanding—and has designated by new and appropriate words some article of faith that of itself is traditional [*non novum fidei sensum*]. (23.19)

Councils, for Vincent, cannot innovate. It is precisely innovation that is a sign of heresy. But councils do speak newly, re-presenting the ancient faith of the church. The precise role of ecumenical councils becomes clearer when we look again at Vincent's comment: "For what has ever been the goal of councils, than that what was believed in simplicity, the same can now be believed reflectively; that what was previously preached languorously, can now be preached vigorously; that what was before honored neglectfully, can now be attended to with solicitude?" (23.18). This passage may be complemented by a similar one in which Vincent exhorts the "Timothy" of today (i.e., the universal church and the bishops/overseers) to handle doctrine carefully: "By your explanations, let that which was believed obscurely now be understood clearly. What antiquity venerated without comprehension, let posterity now understand" (22.7). With these comments, Vincent underlines that the role of the councils is to clarify the church's teaching, ruling out any ambiguous or erroneous claims, thereby allowing the church's preaching to be precise and pellucid. With a few words, councils bring to sharp expression the implicit faith of the church. Vincent explains this procedure: "But with all its knowing, [the church] applies itself to this one point—treating with fidelity and wisdom the ancient doctrine, perfecting and polishing what may, from antiquity, have been left unformed and shapeless. The church's task is to consolidate and to strengthen doctrine—and to guard what has already been confirmed and defined" (23.16–17).

This is why Vincent so strongly concurs with the Pauline injunction "Guard the deposit, Timothy" and continually invokes the wisdom of Proverbs, "Do not transgress the landmarks of your fathers." The Synod of Ariminum is a horror because it is a violation of antiquity and the consentient teaching preserved in the Council and Creed of Nicaea. Throughout the *Commonitorium*, the synod of 359 is the paradigmatic example of a *permutatio fidei*, attempting to overturn the irreversible monument established by Nicaea. But in transgressing this milestone, it was guilty of nothing less than profane and blasphemous innovation. The solemn teaching of an ecumenical council must not be contravened. So Vincent laments the "Arian poison that contaminated almost the entire world" (4.3).

And what is true for Nicaea is equally true for the recently concluded Council of Ephesus, a council to which Vincent devotes a long excursus, precisely to provide for his readers a concrete example of how his theological criteria function in separating truth from heresy, for ensuring that interpretation proceeds *in eodem sensu* with the prior tradition. The Council of Ephesus was convened

in June 431—three years before Vincent wrote his *Commonitorium*—in order
to deal with the errors purveyed by Nestorius, the bishop of Constantinople.
How does Vincent understand the council's authority? The synod's primary
role, he makes clear, is to condemn novelty and to uphold antiquity. Of course,
Nestorius himself would hardly claim that he sought to disseminate novelty.
As Vincent has already told us, Nestorius preached on the Scriptures every
day and enjoyed the esteem of the faithful as well as of his fellow bishops.[40]

Nonetheless, an ecumenical council had authoritatively condemned his
teaching as novel. And it is the authority residing in a council—the preeminent
example of *semper, ubique, et ab omnibus*—which justifies the condemnation
of this eminent bishop. So Vincent says that at Ephesus it was "a matter of
authoritatively laying down the rules of the faith [*ubi cum de sanciendis fidei
regulis disceptaretur*]" (29.8). The verb *sancio* is important here because it
indicates nothing less than an authoritative defining, which is what Ephesus
intends. Further, Vincent points to the unity of "the universal episcopacy
[*universis sacerdotibus*]," about two hundred in number. By their consentient
agreement, "the rule of divine doctrine was established [*divini dogmatis regula
constabilita est*]" (29.10).[41]

Vincent goes on to cite ten witnesses to the orthodox Christian faith adduced by the Council of Ephesus. Among these are Athanasius, Cyril, and the
great theological masters Basil, Gregory Nazianzen, and Gregory of Nyssa—
Cappadociae lumina (30.3). Two are from Alexandria (where Cyril is bishop)
and three from Cappadocia. But Vincent, insisting on the universality that a
council must represent, also adds two bishops from Rome in order "to make
clear that this teaching is not only Grecian or Eastern, but also that the Latin
or Western world holds the same belief." And not only "the head of the world
[*caput orbis*]," Rome, but also those from elsewhere give witness to this conciliar judgment, citing, from the South, the holy Cyprian of Carthage, and
from the North, blessed Ambrose of Milan.

For the Lérinian, the Council of Ephesus, with its citation of bishops/teach-
ers from throughout the known globe, conveys universal testimony to apostolic antiquity, thereby witnessing against Nestorius's innovations.[42] Bishops/
teachers from Alexandria, Cappadocia, Rome, Carthage, and Milan testify
to the church's solidly united and universal faith. And Vincent observes that
the bishops who took part in the Council of Ephesus were themselves erudite
in doctrine, so they may have been tempted to make determinations of their
own. However, he notes approvingly, they did not innovate. On the contrary,
they carefully transmitted to posterity what they themselves had received from
their forebears in the faith, adhering to the definitions of sacred antiquity and
condemning profane novelty (31.4–5).

Nestorius represents the antithesis of the Ephesine Council. While the
council transmits the faith of the universal church, Nestorius is symbolic only
of idiosyncrasy. His error was to think of himself as "the first and only one to

understand Scripture. All the others before him had misunderstood it: all the bishops, all the confessors, and all the martyrs." The entire church prior to him "was now in error and had always been in error, following ignorant and erroneous teachers [*doctores*]" (31.6–7). Particularly important for Vincent is the unity of the entire church in its stand against error. Although obviously a Westerner, Vincent had a very strong sense of the universality of the church's witness and teaching, a theme that pervades his entire book.[43]

The Lérinian's strongly supportive comments on ecumenical councils should help to cure any lingering misunderstanding about his first rule. The church's faith is to be found in the revelation given once for all in the history of ancient Israel and in Jesus of Nazareth. But that faith comes to its full and clear expression in the consentient conciliar agreement of the universal church. Ecumenical councils, in their interpretation of the Divine Word, serve as definitive witnesses to the truth. Indeed, the doctrine taught by councils *is* the truth of Scripture, for councils themselves are under divine guidance (33.2). The authoritative decisions of ecumenical councils, then, are preeminent examples of *semper, ubique, et ab omnibus*, of the living tradition of the church in its interpretation of the Bible.[44]

At the same time, Vincent is well aware that ecumenical councils have not pronounced on every question. On the contrary, they have issued solemn teachings on only a few crucial issues. This is a concern because new heresies seem to arise daily. To whom should one turn for guidance if councils themselves have not pronounced on a controversy? In this case, one should look to the teachings of holy, wise, and esteemed theological doctors. These have a high standing in Vincent's hierarchy of interpretative authority.

Theological Doctors

Vincent is always concerned that any theological proposal should steadfastly preserve the evangelical faith and, if responding to some new question, constitute a *profectus* and not a *permutatio fidei*, an advance rather than a debasement of Christian truth. But how can we be certain that some teaching stands *in eodem sensu* with the prior tradition and not *in alieno sensu*? Lacking a clear word of Scripture that has not been contorted by heretics, or lacking a definition of an ecumenical council, Vincent advises us to turn to the opinions of "authorized masters [*magistri probabiles*]" who, though living at different times and places, stand united in the communion and faith of the Catholic church (3.4).

Vincent has the highest regard for the authority of esteemed theologians. He tells us that "these doctors hold their unique appointment in the church of God according to times and places" (28.10). Indeed, the apostle Paul himself counts doctors (or expositors) in third place after apostles and prophets (1 Cor. 12:28 Vulg.; *Common.* 28.9). Their ecclesial role is to guard the Christian faith, even while faithfully cultivating it. So, Vincent tells us when establishing his *taxis* (order) of interpretative authority, "in antiquity itself . . . one must prefer above all the general decrees of a universal council, although if none exists on a particular matter, then what is next best [*quod proximum est*], the opinion of numerous and important theological masters" (27.4). If we observe this rule, we will easily detect the dangerous errors of heretics. A reliable opinion, however, is not one held by only a few theologians (Vincent deeply distrusts mavericks); it must be held by all or by most doctors and repeated frequently and constantly (3.4).

Theological masters cannot simply be learned teachers. Rather, they must have remained in the communion of faith and be widely known for both their learning and their holiness of life. As the Lérinian says, they must have been steadfast in their confession of the Catholic faith, living in a manner that is holy, wise, and constant, counted among those worthy to die faithfully in Christ or to be happily martyred for him (28.6). Sanctity and learning are inseparable in theologians who can be reliably consulted by the faithful.

For Vincent, the work of theological doctors is twofold. They are essential for ensuring faithful theological development. If no decision of an ecumenical council is available on an issue, the approved masters are responsible for the *noviter, non nova* and for the *res amplificetur*, for assuring, therefore, that any *profectus* does not degenerate into a *permutatio*. At the same time, they are, with the entire church, responsible for guarding the deposit of faith. For this reason the Lérinian insists that theological doctors are less imaginative authors than they are faithful transmitters. Thus Vincent charges them: "In guarding the treasury of Christianity, you are preserving what you received, not what you discovered. You are guarding what was transmitted to you, not what you devised" (22.4).

As with councils, so too the acceptable judgments of theological doctors must reflect consentient universality. Vincent always remains the ardent champion of consensus in the church. This is why he insists that we can trust "the ancient consent of the holy fathers [*antiqua sanctorum patrum consensio*]," which is a sure sign of true teaching (28.2). That which has been persistently taught by acknowledged doctors can be safely held by all Christians (28.7).[45]

It is in the context of discussing the role of theological doctors that we should appreciate Vincent's comment, often misunderstood, that the "consentient opinions of venerable doctors" is meant "not for every instance of error [*neque semper neque omnes haereses*]" but "for those heresies that are new and recent, . . . before they have poisoned the ancient rule of faith" (28.3). Does this seeming restriction narrow the effectiveness of Vincent's canon, showing that it is of limited usefulness? Not at all.[46] What Vincent intends by this, as he clarifies, is that older heresies must be confuted "by the sole authority of the Scriptures [*sola . . . scripturarum auctoritate*]" or "as condemned by the universal councils of the Catholic episcopacy" (28.4).

The theologian of Lérins knows that some heresies, such as Arianism, have persisted for decades (indeed, for over a century) and continue to trouble the church, even though they have been condemned by both Scripture and by a general council. Vincent certainly realizes that his rule remains true: the Arian heresy has been condemned by the church in antiquity, ubiquity, and universality; a council has witnessed definitively against it. But despite this authoritative condemnation, the heresy persists, and its poison remains in the body of Christ, serving to mislead the faithful and to destroy the unity of the church. For Vincent, then, it is not a matter that his rule (as actualized in councils) has not protected the truth. This it has clearly accomplished: Nicaea has spoken with the highest authority. However, the fact remains that some entrenched heretics audaciously ignore even the clear mandates of Scripture and of ecumenical councils, thereby opposing consensual antiquity. Vincent's point, therefore, is that the "consentient opinion of esteemed masters" is virtually useless against older heresies, which have already been condemned by the very highest authorities, the Sacred Scriptures and an ecumenical council.[47]

The unified opinions of theological doctors are most effective if invoked immediately, before a heresy can gain a solid footing in the church. In telling us this, Vincent is essentially repeating his argument made early in the *Commonitorium*. For he has already told us that if errors are found, we should turn first to Scripture and then to the decrees of general councils. Lacking these, we are to consult "the consentient opinions [*uno eodemque consensu*]" of approved authorities (3.3–4). When discussing the difference between combating older and newer heresies, he is essentially repeating this advice and applying it practically.

As important as theological doctors are for the proper interpretation of Scripture—and so for the defeat of heresy—they can also be severe trials for the church. In a telling statement, Vincent says, "All true Catholics know that they ought to listen to doctors *with* the church, and not, by following doctors, *abandon* the church's faith" (17.2, emphasis added). Theological doctors are reliable only to the extent that they reflect the faith of the universal church. Esteemed masters best serve the church when they arrange the precious jewels of Christian doctrines so that their beauty shines forth or when they show how doctrine develops *in eodem sensu eademque sententia*. Vincent gives us a sense of the role of theologians when he encourages them to exercise the skill of Bezalel (Exod. 31:2–5), forming the precious gems of divine doctrine with skill and wisdom, arranging them in "splendor, grace, and beauty [*splendorem, gratiam, venustatem*]" (22.6).

But Vincent is fully aware that theologians can lead Christians out of the church by engaging in speculation that, far from rooting itself in Scripture and the apostolic tradition, innovates with profane blasphemies, thereby encouraging development *in alieno sensu* with the prior tradition.

Negative Examples of Theological Doctors: Origen and Tertullian

Even with all the trust that Vincent places in the harmonious opinion of venerable doctors, he realizes that theologians, acting alone or in a small group, can easily lead Christians astray. In a chapter dedicated to this question, the Lérinian asks, "Why does God permit even eminent persons, with positions in the church, to announce to Catholics new doctrines [*res novas catholicis adnuntiare*]?" (10.1). Vincent says the answer to this question should be sought in the divine law (Scripture) and the teaching of the church. As is so often the case, he turns to his beloved passage from Deuteronomy, "If there should arise among you a prophet or dreamer who gives to you a sign or wonder, urging you to follow strange gods, pay no heed to the words of that prophet, even if that sign or wonder comes to pass, for the Lord your God is testing you, to see if you really love him with all your heart and soul" (Deut. 13:1–3). In this passage, Vincent insists, God is speaking of a false doctor, leading us to worship strange gods. But why would God permit such an abomination? As Moses says, the Lord God is providing a trial for us. God permits certain teachers to preach new and false doctrines in order to test us (10.7). Vincent goes on to recall eminent masters who have introduced strange teaching. These include bishops such as Nestorius and Apollinaris, who deeply misunderstand the nature and person of Jesus Christ and thus also the nature of the Holy Trinity. Yet singled out for unique treatment are the lustrous theologians Origen and Tertullian.

Perhaps the witness of Origen is most poignant because of his incandescent brilliance. As Vincent says of the third-century scholar, of all the trials sent to the church, nothing compares to Origen, who was so remarkable, so unusual, and so admirable that one naturally had faith in all his assertions (17.3). Vincent continues with a long list of Origen's gifts. There was almost no aspect of learning that he did not master. Was this simply the result of his human ingenuity? Not at all! No doctor ever lived who offered more examples from divine Scripture itself (17.7). And what man ever wrote more books than Origen? How then can we explain his perfidy? Is it possible he was unhappy with his disciples? But who could be happier? From his school came innumerable doctors, bishops, confessors, and martyrs. Vincent says he could not begin to exhaust Origen's talents and contributions. Even Porphyry, that impious enemy of Christianity, recognized his greatness. In fact, cries the Lérinian, "Who would not rather be wrong with Origen than right with anyone else?" (17.12).[48]

But alas, Origen, "this great personality, this great doctor, this great prophet," proved to be a stinging trial for the church. Many were led astray by his teaching. What was the root of his error? Vincent tells us that he indulged his own genius and placed too much confidence in his own talent. He thought he was wiser than the entire world, misinterpreting the traditions of the church and "interpreting certain scriptural passages in a novel way [*novo more interpretatur*]" (17.14).[49] Vincent laments that Origen took the church—which was fully devoted to him; admired his genius, his knowledge, his eloquence; and never once suspected him—from the old religion to profane novelties (17.16). Vincent ends his disquisition on Origen by again reminding us that, as Deuteronomy says, a false prophet may arise and test our faith.[50]

Tertullian is discussed much more briefly than Origen but with the same lesson intended. Vincent tells us that as Origen holds first place among the Greeks, so Tertullian holds this rank among the Latins. Tertullian was philosophically adept, with the logic and rigor of his arguments universally known. So much was this the case that Vincent exclaims, "Every word was a thought, every sentence a victory!" (18.4). Indeed, Tertullian's careful theological works triumphed over the Praxeans, the gnostics, and many other heretical groups. Yet like Origen he was deeply flawed. He was too little attached to Catholic doctrines and to the universal and ancient faith, inexplicably turning to the novel assertions of the heretical Montanists. In the last analysis, Tertullian was more eloquent than he was faithful. The blessed confessor Hilary rightly says of him, "By his final error, his laudable works lost their authority" (18.5). Vincent concludes these chapters on wayward theologians by remarking that if any doctor has erred from the faith, this is because divine Providence, as Deuteronomy teaches, has allowed a trial for the church (19.1).

Bishops/Overseers

Given his strong accent on teaching in communion with the entire church, Vincent treats bishops as a body of teachers, not individually. Several of the theological doctors cited by Vincent were themselves bishops, as was often the case in the early church. But the Lérinian's main emphasis is on bishops/overseers as corporately constituting the Timothy of today, whose primary task is guarding the deposit of "faith once delivered to the saints."[51] Teaching primarily through ecumenical councils, bishops/overseers constitute a significant criterion for the proper interpretation of Scripture and therefore represent an important instantiation of the Vincentian canon. What is definitively decided in ecumenical councils is, necessarily, that which the church believes *semper, ubique, et ab omnibus.*

Witnessing directly to this point is Vincent's answer to the question "Who is Timothy today? [*Quis est hodie Timotheus?*]" The Timothy of today is "either the universal church generally or, specifically, the entire body of overseers/bishops [*vel generaliter universa ecclesia vel specialiter totum corpus praepositorum*]" (22.2). Vincent's use of the word *corpus* is of interest because when discussing the Pelagian bishop Julian of Eclanum, Vincent says that Julian neglected "to unite himself [*incorporare*] to the interpretation [*sensus*]" held by his colleagues and so presumed "to separate himself [*excorporare*] from them" (28.15). When a bishop (such as Julian or Nestorius) gives himself over to idiosyncratic teaching apart from the general consensus of the church, tragedy necessarily ensues. But when bishops/overseers are united in teaching, such as at the Council of Ephesus, Vincent does not shy away from making the very strong claim that "the rule of the church's faith [*ecclesiasticae fidei regula*] may be fixed" (28.16).

In a famous phrase, Vincent says that "even a holy and learned man, even a bishop, even a confessor and martyr" is holding only a personal opinion if he advances some position that is "other than all or even against all [*praeter omnes aut etiam contra omnes*]" (28.8).[52] Vincent remains convinced that interpretations must be grounded in the faith of the entire church rather than simply a part of it. So, for example, when discussing the rebaptism of heretics at Carthage, the monk of Lérins observes that this innovation was not only against Scripture and the rule of the universal church but also against the interpretation of all the other bishops (6.4).

The same unfortunate spirit of innovation characterizes the bishop Apollinaris. Vincent recounts his many gifts: How many errors did he refute? Who else had the ability to rebuke the allegations of Porphyry, the celebrated philosopher and opponent of Christianity? So deeply respected was Apollinaris that his disciples were torn between the authority (*auctoritas*) of the church and the custom (*consuetudo*) of their master (11.9). But the lust for novelty caused him to fall into heresy. And so, instead of being a builder of the church, Apollinaris became one of its major trials.

To the genius of one person—no matter the reputed learning or sanctity—Vincent opposes the "holy and catholic consent of the blessed fathers [*beatorum patrum sanctum catholicumque consensum*]" (28.9). And, it is worth repeating, where does one find this consensus? Not primarily in an ill-defined and gossamer antiquity, as is sometimes thought, but rather in Scripture as interpreted by ecumenical councils—the living exemplar of *transmitted antiquity*—and then in the unanimous and frequent teaching of venerable and esteemed masters. As Vincent says at the outset of his work, "We adhere to consent if, in antiquity itself, we adopt the definitions and doctrines of all, or certainly almost all, the bishops and doctors [*sacerdotes et magistri*]" (2.6).

The Christian Faithful (the Saints)

In separating Christian truth from pernicious heresy, one looks not only to ecumenical councils, or to the consentient agreement of theological doctors. One may rely, too, on the understanding of the faithful in general.[53] As already noted, when identifying the Timothy of today, charged with guarding the deposit of faith, Vincent responds that it is "either the *universal church generally* or the entire body of overseers" (22.2, emphasis added). It is not simply the bishops or doctors who guard the faith, but also the entire body of the faithful, all the saints. The consensus of the entire church, then, constitutes another significant warrant and criterion for ensuring that any development over time is congruous with antiquity, is an evolution *in eodem sensu* and not *in alieno sensu* with the prior tradition.

Vincent's invocation of the role of the entire church in the preservation of Christian belief is also found in his claim that an inauthentic development mocks the faith that is preserved in the bosom of Christ's body:

> [Such novelties], were they accepted, would necessarily defile the faith of the blessed fathers. . . . If they were accepted, then it must be stated that the faithful of all ages [*omnes fideles*], all the saints [*omnes sancti*], all the chaste, continent virgins, all the clerical Levites and priests, so many thousands of confessors, so great an army of martyrs, . . . almost the entire world incorporated in Christ the Head through the Catholic faith for so many centuries, would have erred, would have blasphemed, would not have known what to believe. (24.5)

This invocation of the entire church as a witness against innovation is a trope of which Vincent is fond. He uses it earlier in the *Commonitorium*, showing that the spread of heresy inexorably disrupts the church at large: "Wives were dishonored, widows violated, virgins profaned, monasteries destroyed, clerics dispersed, lower clergy beaten, bishops exiled, and prisons, jails, and mines filled with the saints" (4.6).

For Vincent, all of the saints guard the Christian faith, and the entire church suffers when heresy reigns. A sure mark of error is that it introduces new and unheard-of doctrine, a new understanding, "other than all, or against all, the saints [*praeter omnes vel contra omnes sanctos*]" (20.2; 28.8). Vincent never uses the term "sense of the faithful [*sensus fidelium*]," but there is a very strong accent in his work that the witness of all the faithful—the witness of the saints in general along with the bishops/overseers and doctors—is a significant warrant for ensuring that antiquity is preserved and development is properly cultivated.

The Bishop of Rome

Along with Scripture, ecumenical councils, theological doctors, and Christians generally, so too in Vincent's theological epistemology does the bishop of Rome have some determinate place in guarding the deposit of faith and ensuring that any development occurs *in eodem sensu* with the prior tradition. How does Vincent envision the pope's role?[54]

The bishop of Rome is mentioned several times in Vincent's book. The first time concerns the rebaptism controversy in the third century. When recounting the details of that dispute, Vincent says that the rebaptism of apostates returning to the church, first proposed in Carthage, was resisted as "contrary to the divine canon [Scripture] and the rule of the universal church" (6.4).

Indeed, this innovation was opposed by all the bishops, led by Pope Stephen, "bishop of the apostolic see [*apostolicae sedis antistes*], with his colleagues, but nevertheless in the forefront of them, surpassing the others, I think, by the devotion of his faith, just as he surpassed them by the authority of his see [*loci auctoritate*]" (6.5).[55] Vincent tells us that in his letter to Africa, Stephen "fixed and decreed [*sanxit*]" these words: "Let there be no innovation except what has been handed down [*nihil novandum, nisi quod traditum est*]" (6.6.).[56] Important here is the verb *sancio* with its forceful meaning of "establish" and "fix inalterably." As Madoz says, the word also means to "lay down a decree" or "offer a definitive constitution."[57] This same word is used elsewhere by Vincent to indicate the teaching of the apostle Paul as well as the teaching of the Council of Ephesus, so the forceful sense of authority intended by the word is apparent.[58]

Toward the end of the *Commonitorium*, Vincent turns his attention specifically to the role of the bishop of Rome and his service in preserving the purity of faith. As he says, his earlier comments are sufficient to destroy profane novelties; "however, so that nothing is lacking in the completeness of the argument, we have added, at the end, the twofold authority of the apostolic see" (32.1). The recent pope, Celestine, and his successor, Sixtus, are the twin figures who now occupy Vincent's attention. The Lérinian portrays both of them as defenders of antiquity and opponents of novelty. Already in the third century, Pope Stephen had laid down the rule "No innovation, except what has been handed down." This dictum is echoed by later bishops of Rome. Moreover, Vincent tells us, Sixtus had recently written to the bishop of Antioch concerning the error of Nestorius, stating, "Let no concession be made to novelty since nothing should be added to antiquity" (32.3). Immediately prior to Sixtus, Pope Celestine had expressed "the same judgment [*eadem sententia*]" (32.4). For in his letter to the bishops of Gaul (ca. 431), Celestine had written that failure to restrain novelty is tantamount to connivance with error. And, Celestine insists, if the case be so (in Gaul), then "let novelty cease to molest antiquity" (32.6). Several commentators have speculated that Vincent's citation of Celestine's letter has one purpose only: to argue that it is Augustine's teachings on predestination and grace that constitute the profane innovations.[59] It is not our intention to guess Vincent's target by his invocation of Celestine's letter. Much more important, both doctrinally and hermeneutically, is Vincent's adduction of the bishop of Rome as one significant witness in the attempt both to preserve doctrinal purity and to ensure proper development.[60]

Vincent closes the *Commonitorium* with a roll call of witnesses to the orthodox and unalterable faith of the church: Celestine and Sixtus of Rome, who both insist that antiquity is to be preserved and novelty shunned; Cyril of Alexandria, who has confirmed the ancient dogmas of faith; and the Council of Ephesus (431), with its testimony of "almost all the holy bishops of the East" (33.2). This council only attests to what "the holy antiquity of the blessed fathers held unanimously in Christ [*in Christo consentiens*]" (33.2). Those, on the contrary, who consider Nestorius to have been condemned unjustly, must regard as rubbish "the universal church of Christ and its doctors and apostles and prophets and especially the holy apostle Paul, . . . who wrote, 'Guard the deposit, Timothy, avoiding profane novelties,' and 'If anyone preach to you something other than you have received, let him be anathema'" (33.4–5). The truth is that "neither apostolic definitions nor ecclesiastical decrees may be violated" (33.6).

There is little doubt that by the early fifth century (when Vincent is writing), the bishop of Rome has become a uniquely authoritative figure, at least in the West. While Vincent's comment, "he surpassed them by the authority of his see," clearly indicates this primacy, perhaps something of this may also be found in Vincent's account of Ephesus. When citing the doctors named by the council, the Lérinian mentions the two bishops of Rome, Felix and Julius. He adds, "but that not only the head of the world [*caput orbis*], but other parts as well may witness to this [conciliar] judgment," there were added the names of Cyprian from Carthage and Ambrose from Milan (30.5). The term *caput orbis* to designate Rome may serve here primarily as a political and geographical description, yet it may also illustrate Vincent's accent on the unique authority of Rome.[61] While the bishop of Rome's precise role remains undefined in Vincent, it always involves a certain preeminence in upholding the principles of universality, antiquity, and consensus.

But equally true is that, for the Lérinian, the pope is never regarded on his own as an ultimately determining authority; he always exists within the church at large. The bishop of Rome belongs to a college of bishops/overseers, and it is their consentient judgment that is most important, as is visible in the Lérinian's remarks on the rebaptism controversy where he says that Pope Stephen was in the forefront, but together with his colleagues. Further, when citing the witnesses adduced by Ephesus, although Rome is denominated as *caput orbis*, the bishops of Rome are always and necessarily conjoined to their fellow bishops/overseers and thus deeply linked to "the body of those placed in oversight [*corpus praepositorum*]." Consentient agreement is always the most significant warrant for Vincent, even if the bishop of Rome carries unique weight.

Conclusion

I hope this chapter has shown that when Vincent says that the true and authentic Catholic is the one who believes what the church has held universally and from antiquity, this phrase must be understood in a singular manner. One discovers what the church holds to be ancient, universal, and ubiquitous by attending to the criteria that Vincent carefully outlines in the rest of his book. The celebrated Vincentian canon, then, does not look back to some mythical, utopian time when all Christians everywhere held the same teachings, living in perfect harmony. If that were the case, the canon would be useless and unintelligible since no one can say precisely which boundaries mark "antiquity," and no one can define what exactly is meant by "all." Properly understanding the hallmarks of the Vincentian canon—ubiquity, antiquity, and universality—means understanding these characteristics as *living warrants* through which the *living church* specifies "the faith once delivered to the saints" and determines which developments are congruent with it. The inspired Word of God is properly interpreted through various channels *in actu ecclesiae*. One therefore must conclude that for Vincent *tradition is a living and active process*. The *semper et ubique* has too often been ripped from the context of the *Commonitorium*, leading to a persistent misunderstanding of the Lérinian's fundamental intentions and casting him as something of a perverse and unrealistic antiquarian.[62]

I hope this chapter has further shown that Vincent's two rules work in tandem. One cannot cite the Vincentian canon without adding the second rule as well. To do so—or to take the first rule in a highly restrictive sense—is to misunderstand and truncate the Lérinian's thought. The church preserves the faith and hence properly interprets Scripture by means of councils, doctors, and other *loci*. But the church also develops the faith as well, never *in alieno sensu* but always *in eodem sensu* with the prior tradition.

In the following chapter we turn to the work of the English historian John Henry Newman, who was deeply influenced by Vincent—as shown from his earlier Anglican works to his later Roman Catholic writings—so much so that one may even ascribe to him the title of *Vincentius Redivivus*. How Newman "receives" and appropriates Vincent is characteristic of much of the Christian theological tradition.

2

The Theological Reception of Vincent of Lérins

John Henry Newman

Having reviewed Vincent's major ideas, I now examine one significant instance of the reception of the Lérinian's theological insights. This review, centered on the thought of the nineteenth-century historian John Henry Newman, will be followed by a constructive chapter indicating the theological and ecumenical importance of Vincent's thought for contemporary Christianity.

One may perhaps think that the emphasis on Newman represents an attempt to commandeer the Lérinian's thought for Roman Catholicism. This is not at all the case. It should be remembered that the young (Anglican) Newman consistently used Vincent *against* Rome, while the later Newman used Vincent to *reform* aspects of Roman Catholicism.[1] Yves Congar rightly observes that although, for varying theological reasons, the monk of Lérins has been attractive to Protestants, Gallicans, and Old Catholics, the Vincentian canon "was particularly revered in the Anglican church."[2] Given his pedigree, it is unsurprising that Newman was deeply influenced by Vincent's thought.

Vincent of Lérins and John Henry Newman

What makes John Henry Newman such a singularly compelling figure today is that he defends a strongly dogmatic Christian faith but is, at the same time, fully aware of the inescapable tides of historicity and change. Newman was rooted in the doctrinal faith of the early church (telling us repeatedly that antiquity was his stronghold), while simultaneously acknowledging that we live in a world of scientific discovery, a world sensitive to history, a world of evolutionary mutation. This striking combination of old and new yields a contemporary quality to Newman's thought that remains engaging; he defends Christianity as the same yesterday, today, and tomorrow, while placing a decided accent on temporality's ineluctable effects on both Christians and the Christian faith.

Something of this same mixture of old and new may be found in Vincent of Lérins as well. Like Newman, Vincent is a staunch supporter of the immutability of the faith delivered once for all in the history of Israel and in Jesus of Nazareth. But he is equally alive to growth and development over the course of time. As Vincent says at the very outset of his *Commonitorium*, "Since time ravages all human things, we should, in turn, seize from it something that will profit us to eternal life" (1.3).

One of the ways both Vincent and Newman "seize" on time's ravenous appetite is through the notion of development. Today the term "development of doctrine" is almost universally associated with the eminent nineteenth-century Englishman. Yet this close affiliation mistakenly implies that "development" itself is a modern idea, spawned by historical consciousness and by a critical study of the sources of doctrine. But as we have seen, there are premodern roots to the notion of doctrinal development clearly visible in the thought of the fifth-century monk of southern Gaul.

It is likely that several of Newman's basic ideas may be traced, at least incipiently, to Vincent himself. Certainly the notion of development over time had already been sketched, and more than sketched, by Vincent, as Newman himself readily acknowledged both in his *Essay on Development* and in his *Apologia pro vita sua*. As Newman avers in the latter work, "[The principle of development] is certainly recognized in the Treatise of Vincent of Lérins [the *Commonitorium*], which has so often been taken as the basis of Anglicanism."[3] The Victorian thinker would never say, as is now commonly the case, that the notion of doctrinal development was an innovative idea, sprung to life only in the nineteenth century.[4] On the contrary, Newman recognized how obligated he was to Vincent for the idea of organic growth over time. Indeed, to understand Newman's indebtedness to the theologian of Lérins, one need only glance at his first "note" for distinguishing between truth and heresy, denominated as "preservation of type." This characteristic is deeply Vincentian in origin. Vincent never tires of calling our attention to the *idem sensus* (same meaning), which must govern any proper development. In what follows, I trace certain similarities between Vincent and Newman, indicating the latter's deep familiarity with the Lérinian's work. In so doing, we will limit ourselves to the areas where Newman discusses Vincent's work explicitly, or where his influence is clearly discernible.[5]

In the year 434, the date of Vincent's *Commonitorium*, it had already forcibly dawned upon the theologian of Lérins that the church and its language had changed over the four hundred years since the death and resurrection of Jesus of Nazareth. Despite these adaptations, he was convinced that the church had remained substantially the same, entirely faithful in its witness to Christ. But how were Christians to distinguish between changes in the church that, on the one hand, were proper and faithful to the apostolic tradition, and alterations that, on the other hand, led inexorably to heresy and the corrosion of the gospel? This was the question that animated Vincent, and Newman takes it up again some fourteen hundred years later.

A good place to start our examination of the relationship between Vincent and Newman is the latter's translation in 1834, while still a young man, of significant portions of the *Commonitorium*. These translations were part of a series of annotated selections from early Christian writers, labeled *Records of the Church*, which were published along with the better-known *Tracts for the Times*. It is in *Records* 24 and 25 that Newman takes up Vincent's magnum opus.[6]

Records of the Church

In the *Records of the Church*, Newman titles his annotated (partial) translation of the *Commonitorium* as "Vincentius of Lérins on the Tests of Heresy and Error." Helpful for understanding his appropriation of Vincent's work are the comments accompanying the translation.[7]

Newman first cites the Lérinian's claim that our Christian belief is buttressed in two ways: "first, by the authority of Scripture, next by the teaching of the church Catholic." He argues that, if these two tests are rigorously applied, "it reduces our choice [for a Christian church] to an alternative between two—[either] the Church established among us [the Anglican], [or] the Latin or Roman Catholic communion" (*Records* 24.2). Newman finds Vincent's advice to be quite sensible. Since the apostle Paul calls the church "the pillar and ground of the truth" (1 Tim. 3:15), we should adhere to its advice in the postapostolic period. In this regard, Newman cites infant baptism and episcopal succession as two instances where the church's interpretation of Scripture must be followed.

However, Newman continues, Roman Catholicism has clearly violated Vincent's directives, particularly his canon, or first rule, with its injunction to hold fast to what has been taught always, everywhere, and by everyone. Rome has transgressed this canon by introducing profane novelties: "In our own day, it [novelty] is fulfilled in the case of the Church of Rome," which has to answer for very serious corruptions it has implanted in a great part of Christianity (*Records* 24.3). Newman's plaint is that Rome has introduced profane teachings and practices that, far from being legitimate developments, are actually poisonous adulterations of the Christian faith.

Newman argues that if we apply Vincent's unbending test—the standard of antiquity, the *semper* of his canon—then "the Church of Rome is convicted of unsoundness, as fully as those other [Protestant] sects among us" (*Records* 24.3). For the Newman of 1834, Roman Catholicism (with much of Protestantism) is in wanton violation of Vincent's note of antiquity and so cannot fulfill the tests found in the Vincentian canon. The young Anglican divine continues his assault on Rome under the banner of the first rule: "There has been since his [Vincent's] time a most deplorable and astounding instance of this [error] in the corruptions of the Latin Church, whether they be called heresy or not." Newman does not specifically mention Rome's errors, but on the basis of his other writings, we can deduce that he is thinking primarily of purgatory as well as certain Mariological excesses. These are obvious profanations of the Christian faith that cannot withstand Vincent's rule of having existed *always and everywhere* in the universal church. Newman tells his readers that the corruptions of Roman Catholicism—explicitly warned against by the monk of Lérins—vitiate the gifts and charisms that otherwise belong to the ancient see of Rome. In a famous passage, Newman turns lyrical:

> Considering the high gifts, and the strong claims of the Church of Rome and its dependencies on our admiration, reverence, love, and gratitude, how could we withstand it, as we do; how could we refrain from being melted into tenderness, and rushing into communion with it, but for the words of Truth itself, which bid us prefer it to the whole world? "He that loveth father or mother more than Me, is not worthy of Me." How could we learn to be severe, and execute judgment, but for the warning of Moses against even a divinely-gifted teacher who should preach new gods, and the anathema of St. Paul even against Angels and Apostles who should bring in a new doctrine? (*Records* 24.7)

For the young Newman, Roman Catholicism shamelessly preaches new doctrines and profligately introduces novelties, a turn of events that had been foreseen by both Moses and Paul (in biblical passages repeatedly cited by Vincent) and so should be roundly condemned. At this point in Newman's career, Vincent clearly witnesses against Rome's blasphemy. The Lérinian says in the *Commonitorium*, "When was there ever a heresy that did not burst forth under a certain name, at a certain place and certain time?" (24.6). Newman observes that this sentence is consistently used by Rome against everyone else, but it is entirely applicable to Rome's corruptions as well: "We can give the very year when image worship was first established. . . . We can assign a date to the doctrine of Transubstantiation. Nay, we are willing to receive all doctrines which were in possession of the Church in the sixteenth century, except so far as we can show a time when they were not in possession" (*Records* 25.6).

Newman's challenge is this: How can Rome ask other Christians to accept later historical developments that were not part of the earliest church?

How can one plausibly adhere to a distinguishing hallmark of the Vincentian canon—*semper*—if some contemporary practice has no clear warrant in the early centuries of Christianity? Newman contends that Anglicanism alone is the true heir of Vincent's thought, providing the truly Catholic via media between the insidious corruptions of Rome and the bewildering amputations of the early tradition characteristic of Protestantism.

In pursuit of this Anglo-Catholic via media, Newman eagerly translates the passages in Vincent where the Lérinian compares heretics, who are constantly spouting Scripture, to Satan himself. Vincent, we remember, had warned against false teachers who are always armed with a thousand biblical citations (*mille testimonia*). If you ask heretics why you should leave the ancient faith, they will reply, with Satan, "For it is written" (*Common.* 26.6). Newman comments that England is currently beset by those crying "the Bible and the Bible only is the religion of Protestants" (no doubt thinking of a claim made famous by William Chillingworth in 1637). But, he insists, the claim to biblical religion alone is un-reasonable given the extraordinary number of discordant views allegedly based on the Scriptures. One does much better to cling to the interpretation that the church has ever taught. To the counterargument that the churches themselves teach very different doctrines, Newman responds that Vincent's *Commonito-rium* does not demand unanimity on all points, but only on the *foundations* of doctrine (referring to Vincent's incipient hierarchy of truths, discussed in the next chapter). And these foundations, clearly embodied in the Nicene Creed, represent the proper understanding of biblical teaching (*Records* 25.5, 8).

Newman concludes this early translation of the *Commonitorium* with sig-nificant extracts from Vincent's famous chapter 23 on development over time. Surprisingly, he does not comment on what development might mean for the church of his day. Instead, he simply laments the split that exists in Christ's church and asks only that he may live and die in the church as it existed before the division of East and West (*Records* 25.11).

From this early translation of Vincent's work, we may conclude that the young Newman was deeply familiar with the Lérinian's thought, having per-sonally translated and commented upon significant chunks of the *Commoni-torium*. Further, as is clear from the very title Newman gives to his translation, "Tests of Heresy and Error," in the young thinker we already see germinating a concern for establishing criteria distinguishing proper Christian advances from mere corruptions. Indeed, Newman's *Essay on Development* will serve as a rethinking of Vincent's insights into just this issue.

The Church of the Fathers

At approximately the same time as Newman circulated his annotated trans-lation of the *Commonitorium*, he was also publishing short papers on early

Christian writers for *British Magazine*. Among these is a brief reflection on
the work of Vincent of Lérins.[8]

Newman begins his short article by noting that several bishops of the
early church—Basil, Athanasius, Gregory, and Ambrose—risked their lives
for the sake of Christian truth. Yet in the nineteenth century the man of
the world will respond to their intense determination with this sentiment:
Why put modern society in a fever with an insistence on strict orthodoxy?
Better to advance peace and love, the end of all true religion. But Newman
will have none of this. He argues, rather, that it is the phenomenon of "certainty" that should be of burning interest to us, for the willingness of those
early Christians to adhere to orthodoxy unto death is little understood in
our day. Their actions show that "truth is the first object of the Christian's
efforts; peace but the second" (375). Newman then turns to Vincent, who
offers clear criteria for knowing truth. That which is true, says the Lérinian, is that which has been believed *semper, ubique, et ab omnibus*. The
advantage of this rule is that it "saves us from the misery of having to find
out the truth for ourselves from Scripture on our independent and private
judgment." We believe the things that "have been universally received in
the Church" (381).

The young Anglican divine then offers several extracts from the *Commonitorium*, pointing out that, for Vincent, the fathers of the church were *witnesses*
to the gospel, not independent authorities. They are not, in other words, cre-
ators and inventors of Christianity; rather, they *testify* to what they received
from the origin of the church itself. Newman says that here he is only "stating
strict Protestant doctrine" (386). But he insists that a candid Protestant should
concede that when the fathers bear witness on matters about which Scripture
is silent, they stand as conclusive authorities.[9]

Newman is particularly taken with Vincent's style. The Lérinian takes a
text, such as 1 Tim. 6:20 ("Guard the deposit, Timothy"), and handles it like a
contemporary preacher, asking about the meaning of terms such as "deposit"
and "profane novelties" (388). The deposit is that which has been committed to Christians, not that which has been invented by them. "Profane" is a
description of elements that are contrary to antiquity and which, if accepted,
would mean that the faithful of all ages and times, all the saints, all the chaste
and continent virgins, all the clergy, so many thousands of confessors and
martyrs and nations—all those incorporated into Christ the Head would
have erred. What are "novelties"? They are the opinions and heresies that
divide one from the "consent of the universality and antiquity of the Catholic
Church" (390). Newman ends his short piece abruptly, remarking that Vincent
was no Protestant. By this comment he means that Vincent bears witness to
the faith of Anglicanism, upholding the consensus of antiquity while firmly
resisting the corruptions introduced by Rome and the amputations embraced
by Protestantism. Only the Vincentian canon—always, everywhere, and by

everyone—provides the proper validation for the Anglican via media between Rome and the Reformation.

British Critic

At around the same time when Newman published his early essays on Vincent, he wrote a short article for *British Critic* titled "Apostolical Tradition."[10] In this essay, Newman once again builds a strong case for the importance of the primitive tradition of the church as an essential aid in interpreting divine Scripture. Against writers who ignore tradition or even write against it, Newman invokes several early Christian witnesses, Vincent among them:

> Vincent of Lérins had even gained a name in theological history by appealing to the testimony, not of Scripture, but of antiquity and catholicity, as the warrant for the creed of his day. But it seems, after all, that the celebrated *Quod semper, quod ubique, quod ab omnibus* means nothing more than "The Bible, and the Bible only, is the religion of Protestants." (*Essays*, 117)

Newman's point (against those denigrating tradition) is that one must examine the writings of Christian witnesses from the apostolic age in order to interpret Scripture properly. He approvingly observes that Vincent invokes antiquity and universality as acceptable criteria for the proper interpretation of Scripture. These criteria cannot be reduced, at least not in any naive sense, to Chillingworth's famous cry of "the Bible only." To besmirch primitive tradition, Newman says, "is fatal to the authority of Vincent of Lérins and to the corner-stone of our [Anglican] theology" (119). This statement indicates not only Vincent's personal authority for Newman but also the Lérinian's cardinal significance as a bulwark for Anglo-Catholicism. Indeed, Vincent provides Newman with his very words in defense of tradition:

> O Timothy, says Vincent, guard the *depositum*, avoiding profane novelties of words. Who is Timothy today? Who but the universal Church, or, in particular, the whole body of prelates, whose duty it is both themselves to have the full knowledge of religion, and to instruct others in it? . . . What is "the deposit"? That which hath been entrusted to you, not that which thou hast discovered; what thou hast received, not what thou hast thought out; a matter, not of cleverness, but of teaching, not of private handling, but of public tradition. (125–26, citing *Common.* 22.4)

In this passage Newman opposes Vincent to those writers who offer only "self-authorized interpretations" of Scripture, thereby ignoring the apostolic tradition. But such personal interpretations, apart from the consensus of antiquity, should remind us of Vincent's condemnation of heretics, who always have ready at hand a thousand testimonies from the Law, the Prophets, and the Apostles (*Common.* 26.7). Newman's obvious point is that in their interpretation of the Divine Word, Christians must be guided by the consensus of the early church. The steady teaching of antiquity marks the proper Anglican *via media* between Rome and Protestantism.

In this article from the *British Critic*, there is no mention of Vincent's comments on doctrinal development. If anything, Newman shows himself somewhat hostile to the idea of development. In defending the Nicene Creed, for example, he says:

> Nor can it be successfully maintained that an identity of doctrine, such as is found in AD 325, in such various quarters of Christendom, was the gradual, silent, insensible, homogeneous growth of the intermediate period, during which the vague statements of Apostles, parallel to those in Scripture, were adjusted and completed. This theory of a development into a higher view of our Lord's Person is not tenable. (*Essays*, 129)

The Via Media of the Anglican Church

Just a few short years after Newman's earliest comments on Vincent, we find the monk of Lérins in a commanding role in Newman's important work of 1837, *Lectures on the Prophetical Office of the Church*.[11]

In this essay, Newman once again argues for the uniqueness of Anglicanism as compared to Rome and the Reformation. He observes that both the Anglican and the Roman churches turn to antiquity. But it is just the Vincentian note of antiquity that Roman Catholicism flagrantly violates, substituting "the authority of the Church for that of Antiquity" (*Via Media*, 49). Rome's religion "is not that of the Fathers" (65), while Anglicanism rests on the ancient tradition of the church:

> The Rule or Canon which I have been explaining, is best known as expressed in the words of Vincentius of Lérins, in his celebrated treatise upon the tests of Heresy and Error; viz. that that is to be received as Apostolic which has been taught "always, everywhere, and by all." Catholicity, Antiquity, and consent of Fathers, is the proper evidence of the fidelity or Apostolicity of a professed Tradition. (51)

Newman thinks he has the best of the argument when he says that "universality . . . proves nothing, if it is traceable to an origin short of Apostolic" (53). Indeed, *antiquity* is the immovable ground on which both Vincent and Anglicanism stake their claim. Both Roman Catholics and Protestants are unfaithful to the fathers, the former by their innovations to antiquity, the latter by their dissolution of it. Roman Catholicism, for example, concedes that for centuries there was disagreement on the precise nature of the intermediate state (purgatory). Newman finds it bewildering, therefore, that a point on which the fathers had no clarity has now crystallized, for Rome, into a dogmatic teaching. This is nothing less than "disrespect shown by Roman theologians towards the ancient Fathers" (65). In claiming "to know better than the Fathers" (64), Rome continually and illegitimately "exalts the will and pleasure of the existing Church above all authority, whether of Scripture or Antiquity, interpreting the one and disposing of the other by its absolute and arbitrary decree" (83). *For precisely these reasons*, Newman argues, *Rome can claim no support in Vincent's teaching.*

In fact, Newman ardently insists, a careful examination of Vincent's thought shows that the monk of Lérins has little in common with Roman Catholicism:

> If Vincentius had the sentiments and feelings of a modern Roman Catholic, it is incomprehensible that, in a treatise written to guide the private Christian in matters of Faith [*Commonitorium*], he should have said not a word about the Pope's supreme authority, nay, not even about the Infallibility of the Church Catholic. He refers the inquirer to a triple rule, difficult, surely, and troublesome to use, compared with that which is ready-furnished by Rome now. Applying his own rule to his work itself, we may unhesitatingly conclude that the Pope's supreme authority in matters of Faith, is no Catholic or Apostolic truth, because he [Vincent] was ignorant of it. (54–55)

Newman's point, hammered home insistently, is that Roman theologians cavalierly violate antiquity. And antiquity is surely ignorant of their claims—as Vincent witnesses—for the bishop of Rome. Of course, it is not papal authority alone that constitutes a corruption. Newman specifies other blasphemous innovations, including "transubstantiation, the Mass as a sacrifice distinct from Calvary, . . . Purgatory as a place of torment, . . . traffic in indulgences, the cult of relics and images," and so forth.[12] All of these practices clearly violate Vincent's decided accent on antiquity by introducing elements for which there exist no primitive warrants or testimony. Only the Anglican via media respects both antiquity and universality by refusing Rome's corruptions while simultaneously rejecting the Protestant jettisoning of the early church.

At the same time, Newman acknowledges that Vincent's canon cannot be taken in a literal sense:

> The Rule of Vincent is not of a mathematical or demonstrative character, but moral, and requires practical judgment and good sense to apply it. For instance: what is meant by being "taught *always*"? Does it mean in every century, or every year, or every month? Does "*everywhere*" mean in every country, or in every diocese? And does "the *Consent of Fathers*" require us to produce the direct testimony of every one of them? How many Fathers, how many places, how many instances constitute a fulfillment of the test proposed? It is, then,

from the nature of the case, a condition which never can be satisfied as fully
as it might have been; it admits of various and unequal application in various
instances. (55–56)[13]

In 1877 (and so in Newman's Roman Catholic period), he republished his
Lectures on the Prophetical Office of the Church, adding footnotes to his
earlier work. It will be unsurprising that during this period of Newman's life,
he places more emphasis on Vincent's comments on development, the second
rule, than he did earlier. Thus, in his early essays on Vincent, all dating from
the 1830s, Newman has very little to say about development or about Vincent's
second rule generally. The accent is almost entirely on the Vincentian canon,
with the note of antiquity singled out. Even when Newman translates the
crucial chapter on development, he makes no significant remark on its possible contemporary meaning.

But in the 1877 annotations to the *Lectures*, Newman's use of Vincent takes
a different turn. Newman comments, for example, on the defense of purgatory and indulgences undertaken by John Fisher, an English bishop who had
opposed Henry VIII's Reformation. The early Newman had always regarded
these teachings as innovations and corruptions introduced by Rome *against*
antiquity. In the 1877 edition, he now argues for the legitimacy of their development by appealing to the *Commonitorium*: "[Development's] principle
and defence are found in the Tract of Vincent, . . . so great an authority in
the present controversy." Newman then goes on to quote the entire Latin text
where Vincent says, "Is there no progress in the church of Christ? There is,
indeed, *plane et maximus*. Of course, it must be a true *profectus fidei* and
not a *permutatio*" (72n4).

Newman gives us another example of his later turn to Vincent's second
rule. The Newman of 1837 had insisted that the rule of faith (*regula fidei*) is
unchangeable. He unequivocally states, "We are expressly told by the Fathers
that the Rule does not admit of increase; it is 'sole, unalterable, unreformable';
not a hint [has] been given us of the Church's power over it" (224). But in
the 1877 footnote, the Roman Catholic Newman adds, "But Vincent . . . says
that, though unalterable, it [the Rule of Faith] admits of growth" (224n6).

In Newman's later notes to the *Lectures*, it is Vincent's second rule that
comes to the fore, theologically underwriting his Roman Catholic account
of doctrinal development in contrast to his earlier accent on the Vincentian
canon, particularly its iron insistence on the note of antiquity. We may conclude that as an Anglican Newman determinedly applied Vincent's first rule;
then as a Roman Catholic he made more use of the second rule (while not
totally abandoning the first). In neither stage of life, however, does Newman
fully integrate the first and second rules as Vincent intended. Indeed, in failing
to see clearly how the first and second rules work in tandem, Newman was
representative of his age.

An Essay on the Development of Christian Doctrine

In Newman's well-known *Essay on Development*, written some ten years after his annotated translation of the *Commonitorium*, we find him again reflecting on the meaning of Vincent's work for elucidating the nature of Christian doctrine.[14] Before examining Newman's use of Vincent in his magnum opus, it may be helpful to say a word about the concept of development itself. Newman, in a notion not borrowed from Vincent—or from anyone else it seems—compares Christian revelation to an idea.[15] Like an idea, revelation is an active principle. Any idea assimilates that which is congruent with it while throwing off that which is foreign and alien. An idea comes to fruition and maturity by trial and error, by tests, and by relationships. Newman therefore speaks of an idea's vigor and "[its] powers of nutrition, of assimilation and of self-reparation" (171). He adds that "whatever has life is characterized by growth" (185). To be a living idea, then, is to grow and develop over the course of time and to be constantly but prudently assimilative.

Speaking of growth and development immediately entails the question, "Which kind of growth?" Does invoking the term "development" presage a change with substantial modifications? In a famous passage of the *Essay on Development*, Newman asks just this question. He says in reply, "It is sometimes said that the stream is clearest near the spring." In fact, the stream (or idea) becomes "purer and stronger when its bed has become deep, and broad, and full" (40). In other words, over the course of time an idea becomes more fully itself, realizes itself more completely, and activates its latent potencies. This is the meaning of Newman's famous comment: "It [an idea] changes with them [new situations] in order to remain the same. In a higher world it is otherwise, but here below to live is to change, and to be perfect is to have changed often" (40).

But if an idea changes, grows, and develops over time, and does so precisely in order to remain itself—indeed, to realize more fully its own potential—how is this now applied to Christian faith and doctrine? How does the "idea" of Christian revelation realize itself over time?

Newman's "Demolition" of Vincent's Canon

In order to answer these questions about development, Newman knows that he must meet head-on the famous canon of Vincent of Lérins. Anglican theologians (himself included) had long invoked Vincent's first rule in order to provide an adamantine criterion separating the ancient and primitive tradition of the church from the later (particularly Roman) corruptions of it. Because of this history—both personal and ecclesial—it is no surprise that the theologian of Lérins dominates the introduction to Newman's seminal work. For Vincent has thrown down the gauntlet to Newman and indeed to all Christians. It is Vincent who has offered "a principle infallibly separating, on the whole field of history, authoritative doctrine from opinion" (10). In the introduction to the *Essay on Development*, Newman will slowly and inexorably demolish Vincent's first rule (as he understands it) as a trustworthy guide for distinguishing truth from error. In so doing, Newman thinks he is demolishing a bulwark of Anglicanism as well as of his own earlier theology.[16]

Newman's argument is that the Vincentian canon—*semper, ubique, et ab omnibus*—despite its deep attraction to Anglican theologians, does not offer a serviceable criterion to distinguish truth from heresy. The first rule (*semper*), Newman says, is deeply congenial to the Anglican mind, for it protects the patristic patrimony even while resisting papal authority (11). But by historical examples he intends to demonstrate that the first rule is, at best, a leaky and dubious criterion. As Newman boldly says at the very dawn of the *Essay on Development*, "I do not see in what sense it can be said that there is a *consensus* of primitive divines in its [the doctrine of the Trinity's] favour, which will not avail also for certain doctrines of the Roman Church which will presently come into mention" (14).

Right from the outset, then, Newman indicates his line of assault. He is hardly calling into question the doctrine of the Trinity. He *is* arguing that one cannot *warrant* the Trinity on the basis of the consensus of the most primitive divines, as Vincent's canon (allegedly) intends. On the question of the Holy Trinity, the consensus of the earliest fathers cannot underwrite later Nicene belief. Why is this the case? Because there exists no clear consensus of antiquity on this very cornerstone of Christian faith. And if the first doctors of Christianity do not reproduce the church's later precision on the doctrine of the Trinity, can we really expect to find in these fathers a consensus about other doctrines (particularly those later accepted by Rome)? In other words, if the Trinity must be admitted by Christians on the basis of less-than-perfect primitive testimony, then on what basis does one exclude certain Roman teachings such as purgatory? How can one apply the Vincentian canon rigorously if the canon fails even with regard to the *very foundation of Christian faith*?

Speaking of the doctrine of the Holy Trinity, Newman adds:

> It is true indeed that the subsequent profession of the doctrine in the Universal Church creates a presumption that it was held even before it was professed; and it is fair to interpret the early Fathers by the later. This is true, and admits of application to certain other doctrines besides that of the Blessed Trinity in Unity; but there is as little room for such antecedent probabilities as for . . . the precise and imperative *Quod semper, quod ubique, quod ab omnibus*, as it is commonly understood by English divines, and is by them used against the later Church and the see of Rome. What we have a right to ask, if we are bound to act

upon Vincent's rule in regard to the Trinitarian dogma, is a sufficient number of Ante-Nicene statements, each distinctly anticipating the Athanasian Creed. (15)

Newman here argues against the Vincentian canon by means of a reductio ad absurdum. As presently interpreted, the canon admits the Trinity *if and only if* the fathers are read through the lens of later church teaching. But if this can happen with the doctrine of the Trinity, what is to prevent this same reading from occurring with other doctrines, such as purgatory? Further, does any pre-Nicene father exactly reproduce the later thought of the church on the Holy Trinity? If not, then can the Vincentian *Quod semper* be credibly invoked against Roman doctrines of a later age (18)? How can one expect Rome to meet Vincent's criteria when even the vast majority of ante-Nicene fathers are unable to do so even with the most fundamental teaching of Christian belief?

With his constant invocation of the Vincentian canon, Newman intends to hoist the Anglican divines of his day (including his earlier self) on their own criteriological petard. Pressing his case with prosecutorial zeal, Newman asks, "How much direct and literal testimony [do] the ante-Nicene Fathers give, one by one, to the divinity of the Holy Spirit?" Reminding us that Basil in the fourth century could barely call the Spirit "God," he concludes, "Could this possibly have been the conduct of any true Christian, not to say Saint, of a later age? . . . Whatever be the true account of it, does it not suggest to us that the testimony of those early times lies very unfavourably for the application of the rule of Vincentius?" (18).

Newman's point is that the status of the Holy Spirit as a distinct divine person within the Godhead, while today taken for granted as bedrock Christian orthodoxy, was contested even in the late fourth century, and so it hardly constitutes a teaching that meets the Vincentian criteria of always, everywhere, and by everyone. Yet Newman immediately adds that he is hardly impugning the orthodoxy of the early fathers of the church. But he is placing them on trial according to an *unfair* understanding of Vincent's thought: a strict and unyielding interpretation of the *semper et ubique* that, if taken literally, is not only available against the Roman church but militates against the most fundamental Christian teachings as well.

Offering another example indicating the inadequacy of Vincent's canon, Newman says:

There are two doctrines which are generally associated with the name of a Father of the fourth and fifth centuries, and which can show little definite, or at least but partial, testimony in their behalf before his time—Purgatory and Original Sin. The dictum of Vincent admits both or excludes both, according as it is or is not rigidly taken; but, if used by Aristotle's "Lesbian Rule," then, as Anglicans would wish, it can be made to admit Original Sin and exclude Purgatory. (20)

Newman's argument is that if one interprets Vincent's canon narrowly, then a Christian can admit *neither* the doctrine of original sin nor the doctrine of purgatory since neither teaching is well supported in the earliest fathers. But if one interprets Vincent broadly, he must accept both doctrines. What is entirely unacceptable is the application of Aristotle's "Lesbian Rule" (a notion taken from the *Ethics*, whereby a norm is entirely pliant and malleable, adaptable to a predetermined outcome). Under the rule of Lesbos, one may interpret broadly in one case but narrowly in another. And the application of the Vincentian canon in this manner is precisely what Newman condemns as unacceptable. Hammering home his point, Newman says, "In truth, scanty as the ante-Nicene notices may be of the Papal Supremacy, they are both more numerous and more definite than the adducible testimonies in favour of the Real Presence" (24). One can therefore hardly employ Vincent in favor of the latter teaching while using him as a bulwark against the former.

Having adduced ample evidence to show the inadequacy of Vincent's first rule as understood by the theologians of his day, Newman rests his case: "It does not seem possible, then, to avoid the conclusion that, whatever be the proper key for harmonizing the records and documents of the early and later Church, and true as the dictum of Vincentius must be considered in the abstract, . . . it is hardly available now, or effective of any satisfactory result. The solution it offers is as difficult as the original problem" (27).

Noteworthy here is that in the *Essay on Development*, Newman's writing on the Vincentian canon marks a sea change from his earlier invocation of the first rule. In Newman's early works, the canon provided clear criteria for establishing an Anglican via media between Rome and the Reformation. By 1845, Newman is convinced that the Vincentian canon is unworkable as a sure means to distinguish truth from heresy and opinion.

Newman's Use of Vincent's Rule on Development

Having examined Newman's demolition of Vincent's first rule, at least as it was commonly understood in his day, we may now turn to his use of the second rule, whose appearance increased during his Roman Catholic period. Already in his 1834 translation of the *Commonitorium*, Newman was wrestling with the issue of tests for distinguishing truth from error, as indicated by the very title he gave to his annotated selections from Vincent's work. But perhaps the real difference in the Newman of 1845 is that, like Vincent himself, he starts to view temporality in a positive way. He argues that both the ecclesial determination of the canon of Scripture and the doctrine of original sin developed over the course of time. And as earlier noted, he insists that the orthodox doctrine of the Holy Trinity took centuries to come to its final and precise form. Indeed, this process of growth and development prompts Newman to say that an idea's "beginnings are no measure of its capabilities nor of its scope" (40). And he argues that the Lord "works out gradually what he has determined absolutely" (69–70).

Whereas the young Newman saw later developments as corruptions of the primitive faith—and thus obvious violations of the Vincentian canon—this is no longer the case in the *Essay on Development*. Newman now argues that devotion to Mary and to the saints, practices earlier condemned as unwarranted excesses, were part of the Christian idea from the beginning but needed time to come to fruition. Because human nature has been deified by Christ, who is fully human as well as divine, one may speak of the veneration of human beings such as Mary and the saints. Even the veneration of relics is justified because of Christ's sanctification of human flesh. This is why he will say in a daring statement, "The Church of Rome is not idolatrous, unless Arianism is orthodoxy" (144). By this he means that both orthodox Christology and a full-blown appreciation of Marian devotion only came to be understood gradually, over the course of time. If the process of development is short-circuited and one insists on primitivism (with the earliest as the most true), then Arianism itself possesses a certain logic and orthodox pedigree.

But Newman does not immediately turn to Vincent to elucidate his notion of development or to fortify his newfound evaluation of temporality. On the contrary, he continues his assault on Vincent's canon, even expressing his own understanding of development in opposition to the Lérinian. He says, "A converging evidence in favour of certain doctrines may, under circumstances, be as clear a proof of their Apostolical origin as can be reached practically from the *Quod semper, quod ubique, quod ab omnibus*" (123). This is to say that "hints" of certain doctrines ("converging evidence") in the writings of the early fathers offer criteria just as useful for determining Christian truth as the allegedly narrow strictures of Vincent's canon. Further, while both Protestants and Roman Catholics receive the same New Testament books, "yet among those books some are to be found, which certainly have no right there if, following the rule of Vincentius, we receive nothing as of divine authority but what has been received always and everywhere. The degrees of evidence are very various for one book and another" (124).

As is obvious, Newman's attack on the Vincentian canon is in service to showing that the first rule does not offer the church an adequate principle for distinguishing Christian truth from falsity. It is surely not the case that Newman is unaware of Vincent's accent on development. In fact, he freely takes up Vincent's biological metaphors in the *Essay on Development*. It is likely, however, that Vincent's canon was so deeply embedded in the theology of his day (including his own) that Newman thought a full-scale attack was required to dislodge it from its princely position.

Profectus, non Permutatio

Although Newman is at pains to demolish a certain understanding of the Vincentian canon, he does not hesitate to incorporate Vincent's distinction between a development that is a proper advance of the faith and one that is a corruption of it. This distinction—between a legitimate *profectus* and a corrosive *permutatio*—is an axial theme of Newman's *Essay on Development*, deeply ingrained in the entire work and borrowed directly from Vincent's pen.

In chapter 5 of the *Essay on Development*, "Genuine Developments as Contrasted with Corruptions," Newman takes head-on the question of *profectus* versus *permutatio*. He recognizes that what he has been calling "developments in the Roman Church are nothing more or less than what used to be called her corruptions" (170). Newman acknowledges the force of this objection; to answer it, he embarks on his mission of establishing "notes" that will display the nature of faithful development over time. His Vincentian intention, he says, is to determine "what a corruption is, and why it cannot rightly be called, and how it differs from, a development" (170). He further reminds readers that a corruption is "the reversal and undoing of what went before," but no corruption occurs if an idea "retains one and the same type, the same principles, the same organization" (170). In these comments, one sees the Lérinian's direct influence. An adulteration of the faith transgresses, as Vincent would say, the landmarks laid down by the fathers (Newman's "undoing of what went before"), while a proper development "retains the same type," which is a virtual translation of Vincent's *in eodem sensu*. This direct influence of Vincent often goes unmentioned in Newman's *Essay*, but it is deep and unmistakable.

In place of Vincent's first rule—the *semper, ubique, et ab omnibus*—which has now been (allegedly) unmasked as unworkable, Newman substitutes his seven notes or "tests" to indicate faithful developments as opposed to pernicious corruptions of the Christian faith. In a few of these, Vincent is clearly the inspiration.

In his first note, for example, Newman argues that "identity of type" is a sure characteristic of faithful development. Unsurprisingly, he immediately turns to Vincent for an illustration of this principle, invoking the Lérinian's analogy of the "law of the body": human limbs grow and develop from youth to age, yet remain the same (172). In his second note, "continuity of principles," Newman says that while doctrines "grow and are enlarged, principles are permanent" (178). He concludes his comment with a statement redolent of Vincent's thought: "Thus the *continuity or the alteration of the principles* on which an idea has developed is a second mark of discrimination between a true development and a corruption" (185). In his comment on his sixth note, "conservative action on the past," Newman cites Vincent directly: "Vincentius of Lérins, in like manner, speaks of the development of Christian doctrine, as *profectus fidei, non permutatio*" (201). The Lérinian is the clear inspiration for the distinction between changes that are legitimate developments and those that are corrosive adulterations of the Christian faith. Indeed, this distinction between *profectus* and *permutatio* sounds as a drumbeat throughout Newman's *Essay on Development*. Toward the end of his book, in an unvarnished appropriation of Vincent, Newman says that "a true development is . . . conservative of the original, and a corruption . . . tends to its destruction" (419).

All of the notes, ultimately, are adduced for the purpose of distinguishing a proper *profectus* from an illegitimate *permutatio*. Like the theologian of Lérins, Newman is groping to find criteria for separating the proper growth of Christian truth from its false mutations and corruptions. Even though Newman thinks that Vincent's first rule—as he understands it—is unworkable, he nonetheless appropriates significant elements from the *Commonitorium*.

Identity of Type: *In Eodem Sensu*

Let it first be said that for Vincent, as for Newman, God's historical revelation is given fully in ancient Israel and in Jesus of Nazareth. In that sense, revelation does not and cannot develop. However, the human *understanding* of revelation, plumbing the breadth and depth of its meaning, clearly does grow over time, just as an idea assimilates new dimensions as it becomes more fully rounded. It is just this growth in history that Newman calls development.

But for any development to be a proper advance (*profectus*), the growth that occurs must be a congruent and harmonious unfolding of earlier principles. Development, then, cannot be interchangeable with random or unguided growth, nor can it mean the intrusion of foreign and alien concepts, much less can it be invoked as a covert synonym for "reversal." Rather, what Newman calls the "essential idea" must be preserved. He sums up this crucial principle thus: "The changes which have taken place in Christianity have not been such as to destroy that type: . . . they are not corruptions, because they are consistent with that type. Here then, in the *preservation of type*, we have a first Note of the fidelity of the existing developments of Christianity" (323).

Any "development" over time, then, must always be consonant, in a fundamental and substantial way, with what has preceded it. Newman is entirely aware that an "idea," the metaphor he has been using to speak about revelation, can become "depraved by the intrusion of foreign principles" (39). This is just the pernicious *permutatio* that must be avoided. For this reason, then, "continuity of type" is the note on which Newman spends by far the most time. And with this note or test, Newman clearly has in mind Vincent's second rule: all legitimate development—growth that is worthy of the name—must be *in eodem sensu eademque sententia* with that which preceded it. Vincent had made clear that development over time certainly does occur, offering organic models to explain this, such as a child becoming an adult and the seed becoming a plant. He indicated this growth by using terms such as *res amplificetur* and *dilatetur tempore*. But as these examples indicate, development always implies a fundamental continuity. *Idem sensus* (the same meaning) is the mark of truth and proper progress; *alienus sensus* is the indelible sign of heresy and corruption. Indeed, one may say that for Vincent as for Newman, "identity of type" is the primary warrant for determining that a later development is a proper advance rather than a depravity of the faith now masquerading under the banner of "development."

Just so, toward the close of his *Essay on Development*, Newman returns to Vincent's law of the body, telling us that "manhood is the perfection of boyhood, adding something of its own, yet keeping what it finds" (419–20). He explicitly cites Vincent's comment that "nothing new appears in old age that was not already hidden in the child [*nihil novum postea proferatur in senibus, quod non in pueris iam ante latitaverit*]" (23.6). From the beginning to the end of his essay, the note of "preservation of type" dominates Newman's thought, indicating his close proximity to, and profound reliance on, the theologian of Lérins.

To solidify his argument, Newman offers concrete historical examples with the intention of showing that *the Christian tradition has certainly sanctioned congruent development*, meaning development *in eodem sensu*, over time. One way in which he displays how this homogeneous unfolding occurs is through the case of Eutyches, a historical sketch we will briefly recount.

Eutyches as an Example of Development by Type

Newman notices that Eutyches, a fifth-century monk, insisted that after the incarnation there was only one nature in our Lord. And Eutyches adduced significant warrants for his position. He argued, for example, that his opinion had the support of fathers no less distinguished and saintly than Cyril and Athanasius. Consequently the church could bring no consensus against him. Further, Eutyches heartily subscribed to the decrees of Nicaea (325) and Ephesus (431) and to the claim that "nothing could be added to the Creed of the Church." Most important, Eutyches relied on the Scriptures, saying that they were "surer than the expositions of the Fathers" (303–4).

To the claim of Eutyches that the Creed of Nicaea is held inviolate by the Council of Ephesus, Newman says, "It is remarkable that the Council of Ephesus, which laid down this rule, had itself sanctioned the *Theotokos*, an addition greater perhaps than any before or since, to the letter of the primitive faith" (303).[17] The English historian adds that even Gregory Nazianzen, while appealing to the Creed of Nicaea, acknowledged that the question of the Spirit had not yet been raised—and so additions to Nicaea were necessary. Indeed,

Newman continues, "This exclusive maintenance [of the Nicene Creed] and yet extension of the Creed, according to the exigencies of the times, is instanced in other Fathers."[18] Newman's point is that development necessarily occurs beyond the letter of creeds, which often need supplementation. But any later development must always be a harmonious unfolding, *in eodem sensu* with that which preceded it.

Newman argues that the Council of Chalcedon (451), by refuting the Monophysitism of Eutyches, offers a clear instance of development according to "type." And this development inexorably occurred despite there being weighty warrants against it:

> The historical account of the Council is this, that a formula [Christ "in two natures"] which the Creed did not contain, which the Fathers did not unanimously witness, and which some eminent Saints had almost in set terms opposed, which the whole East refused as a symbol [at the *Latrocinium*, Robber Council, Ephesus II, 449] . . . and refused upon the grounds of its being an addition to the Creed, was forced upon the Council [of Chalcedon], not indeed as being such an addition, yet, on the other hand, not for subscription merely, but for acceptance as a definition of faith under the sanction of an anathema. (312)

Newman's point is that at the Council of Chalcedon, development definitively occurred *in eodem sensu*. Indeed, in order to clarify errors and to draw out the sure implications of the rule of faith, such homogeneous development had to occur. So Newman adds, "At Ephesus it had been declared that the Creed should not be touched; the Chalcedonian Fathers had not literally but virtually added to it" (313). Christ was not simply "of two natures" but also "in two natures." Explanatory clarifications, clear instances of development according to type had been added to the creed—and necessarily so.

Newman and Vincent

To this point it has been argued that Newman adopts several crucial ideas from Vincent, including the notion of development itself—the distinction between a change that is a *profectus* and one that is a *permutatio*—and the insistence that true development must preserve continuity of type.

But there are differences as well between the two thinkers. One major distinction is that Vincent understands his canon—*semper, ubique, et ab omnibus*—not as a bald criterion that stands on its own. The canon, or first rule, is always instantiated in determinate ecclesial structures. This is simply to say that the canon only lives and breathes, only comes to life, *in and through* Sacred Scripture and, particularly on disputed points, Scripture as interpreted by the church. Newman, on the other hand, goes to great lengths in the *Essay on Development* to demolish the Vincentian canon as he understands it, and he never fully integrates Vincent's two rules over the course of his long life.

This lack of integration may explain a mystery surrounding Newman's work. After devoting two-thirds of his most famous book, *An Essay on the Development of Christian Doctrine*, to his notes or tests for distinguishing a true development from a noxious corruption, Newman never returned to the notes for the rest of his life.[19] Why not? Possibly Newman recognized that he needed not just isolated notes but also a stronger accent on ecclesial structures in order to settle the issue of proper development. In other words, the crucial question is this: how does one ascertain that "continuity of type" *actually exists* over time? Vincent would say that one can be certain of proper development *in eodem sensu* because of Scripture, the sure foundation of divine truth, as interpreted by ecumenical councils, theological doctors, the faithful universally, and the bishop of Rome. The Lérinian offers determinate criteria to ensure that proper growth occurs.

Perhaps Newman gradually recognized that his notes, taken in isolation, were weak and ineffective, in need of stronger buttressing. Standing alone, the notes cannot settle the issue of distinguishing a *profectus* from a *permutatio*.[20] Might it have occurred to Newman that "preservation of type" was hardly self-evident, requiring more concrete warrants? As he conceded: "Unity of type [allows for] . . . considerable alteration of proportion and relation, as time goes on, in the parts or aspects of an idea. [Thus] the butterfly is the development, but not in any sense the image, of the grub" (*Essay on Development*, 173).

But if such wide variations can occur over time—as between the butterfly and the grub—then how can one know if unity of type has been properly preserved? While the notes offer hints, is it really possible, given such wide variations, to identify essential continuity without the help of distinct and determinate structures that live under the influence of the Holy Spirit?

Vincent's questions, we remember, are these: *Who* is the Timothy of today who is guarding the deposit? *Who* is ensuring that Scripture is integrally preserved? *Who* is making certain that any proposed development is *in eodem sensu* with the apostolic tradition and therefore is a legitimate *profectus*? These questions animate and vivify the entire *Commonitorium*. And Vincent offers clear warrants by which such questions may be answered—warrants concretely existing in the life of the church. Newman himself will recognize that the notes need to be further strengthened by ecclesial dimensions.

Newman's Criteria for Assuring Proper Development

My argument thus far has been that the celebrated canon of Vincent of Lérins is instantiated in a series of theological places (such as ecumenical councils) wherein one may visibly see how Christian doctrine has been both preserved and properly developed. Thus one dare not take the first rule in isolation from the rest of the *Commonitorium*. Newman, along with many others, tended to read Vincent's canon as narrowly restrictive, although, from the *Essay on Development* onward, he is somewhat more enamored with the Lérinian's second rule. The eminent Victorian certainly recognized that Vincent was an early proponent of doctrinal development and in the *Apologia pro vita sua* he specifically indicated the insights of his predecessor.

But Newman does not show any explicit awareness of how close he is to the theologian of Lérins on the various warrants he adduces for assuring that later Christian doctrine is always *in eodem sensu* with what has preceded it. Like Vincent, Newman presents a dynamic vision of the church, with the entire body of Christ involved in the process of guarding, conserving, and developing the faith. While this may seem a truism, the invocation of the *entire church* was particularly important in nineteenth-century Roman Catholicism, when the specter of centralized papal authority loomed large. Newman's work had the advantage of reviving Vincent's polycentric view of ecclesial teaching authority. For the English historian comes to ask in the nineteenth century what Vincent was assuredly asking in the fifth: *Quis est hodie Timotheus?* (22.2). Who is the Timothy of today charged by the apostle Paul to "guard the deposit"? Who ensures today that there are no deviations from the ancient Christian faith?

We have already seen that Vincent invokes multilayered centers of authority in order to determine if some development is an authentic *profectus*. There is no need to repeat those warrants here. Our present task is to examine how the same warrants are invoked and treated by Newman. In both thinkers, it is primarily Scripture, and especially Scripture as interpreted in the church (the channels of tradition), that protects revelation and ensures that its understanding harmoniously unfolds over the course of time. One adjudges continuity of type—the *idem sensus*—by turning primarily to the Bible and then the Bible as interpreted *in and through* a weblike network of tradition.[21]

Sacred Scripture

Unsurprisingly, the Bible occupies a highly significant role in Newman's theology from the beginning of his life to its end. We recall that, at the outset of the *Commonitorium*, Vincent turns to the authority of Scripture, telling us that we must strengthen our belief by means of two aids: first (*primum*) by the authority of the divine law (Scripture), and then next (*tum deinde*) by the tradition of the Catholic church (2.1; 29.2). The Lérinian further specifies that the canon of Scripture is perfect and sufficient of itself for all matters and indeed more than sufficient (*ad omnia satis superque sufficiat*), but there is need for church authority because the Bible's profundity easily leads to misinterpretation (2.2).

A very similar approach characterizes Newman's *Lectures on the Propheti-cal Office of the Church*, originally published during his Anglican period in 1837.[22] Thus Newman says:

> Holy Scripture contains all things necessary to salvation, that is, either as being read therein or deducible therefrom; not that Scripture is the only ground of the faith, or ordinarily the guide into it and teacher of it, or the source of all religious truth whatever, or the systematizer of it, or the instrument of unfolding, illustrating, enforcing, and applying it; but that it is the document of ultimate appeal in controversy, and the touchstone of all doctrine.[23]

Like Vincent, Newman sees Scripture as materially sufficient for all truths necessary for salvation. It contains within itself all that is necessary to reach eternal life. At the same time, tradition has some role in understanding bibli-cal meaning: "We differ, then, from Roman teaching in this, not in denying that Tradition is valuable, but in maintaining that there is no case in which by itself, and without Scripture warrant, it conveys to us any article necessary to salvation; in other words, . . . [tradition] is not a rule distinct and co-ordinate, but subordinate and ministrative" (310).

Newman's sentiment here is a harbinger of the contemporary position taken by many Roman Catholic and Protestant theologians, sometimes described as *prima scriptura*. For Newman, as for Vincent, no one looks first to tradi-tion to find some article of faith that was hitherto unknown. One looks first to Scripture while using tradition as a supplementary aid. Newman goes on to say that he agrees with the great eighth-century Eastern theologian John Damascene, who affirms, "It cannot be that we should preach, or at all know, anything about God, besides what the divine oracles of the Old and New Testaments have divinely set forth, said, or manifested to us" (320).

Authority on the ancient church that he assuredly was, Newman acknowl-edges that early Christian writers, while singling out the unique value of Scrip-ture, appealed at times to tradition as well. At just this point he invokes Vincent and offers a subtle evaluation of the Lérinian's thought:

> Vincentius is commonly and rightly adduced as the champion of Tradition. He is certainly a remarkable witness of the sense of the Church in his day, that Private Judgment was not to be tolerated in the great matters of faith, which were as clearly determined, as much parts of the foundation of Christianity, as the Scriptures themselves, or their canonicity. He maintains that individuals must yield to the voice of the Church Catholic. But let it be observed after all, what kind of Tradition he is upholding; [is Tradition] an independent witness of Christian Truth? Far from it, merely and solely an *interpretative* Tradition, a Tradition interpretative of Scripture in the great articles of faith. Thus the very treatise [*Commonitorium*], which is so destructive to mere Protestantism, is as fatal to the claims of Rome. Not only is all mention of the Pope omitted

as the Judge of controversies, but [also] all mention of Tradition, except as subordinate to Holy Scripture. (321)

Newman's point is that tradition is always subject to Scripture, "ministrative" to it.[24] Vincent is adduced as a powerful witness precisely because Newman sees the Lérinian's approach as entirely coincident with his own: the Bible is the sui generis inspired Word of God; tradition is an interpretative aid to understanding it. As is so often the case in his early work, Newman finds in the *Commonitorium* a dual assault on Wittenberg and Rome, to the benefit of the Anglican via media. The monk of Lérins's accent on tradition destroys any naive invocation of *sola scriptura*, while tradition's subordinate place under Scripture dismantles Rome's attempt to regard them as two equal sources.

Commenting on Vincent's point that one first rebuts heresy by the authority of the Bible and then by the tradition of the church, Newman says, "Vincentius assumes as undeniable, the very doctrine rejected by the Romanists, the sovereign and sole authority of Scripture in matters of faith, nor has he a thought of any other question but the further one, how it is to be interpreted. His submission even to Catholic Tradition, is simply and merely as it subserves the due explanation of Scripture" (323).

The Lérinian, Newman rightly observes, is a robust and vigorous defender of biblical primacy. Despite his reliance on tradition, Vincent never wavers from Scripture's unique and unsurpassed authority. For Vincent, as Newman says, Scripture is always prior to tradition "in dignity and consideration" (322). Rome therefore has no basis in antiquity for regarding tradition as an equivalent source of revelation separate from Scripture. As a final witness to the Bible's unique status, Newman cites the fifth-century Syrian bishop Theodoret: "To add anything to the words of Scripture is madness and audacity; but to open the text, and to develop its hidden sense, is holy and religious." In response to this lucid comment, Newman says, "Here is the doctrine of the Gallic Vincentius in the mouth of a Syrian Bishop" (327).

The foregoing passages are hardly meant to offer a comprehensive reading of Newman on Scripture and tradition; they are intended to show how deeply Vincent's work influenced the young Anglican thinker in his interpretation of the Bible and on the abiding relationship between Scripture and ecclesial tradition. Similar passages could easily be adduced from his later work *Essay on Development*, where Newman argues that Scripture is the norm and rule of the church. As he says, even Roman Catholic authors do not "deny that the whole Catholic faith may be proved from Scripture, though they would certainly maintain that it is not to be found on the surface of it, nor in such sense that it may be gained from Scripture without the aid of Tradition" (342).

Newman, then, like Vincent himself, is a strong witness to *prima scriptura*, meaning that the Bible is the unique Word of God but ecclesial tradition is a significantly important aid—at times, an authoritative aid—in interpreting it properly. One may fully endorse the comment made by Avery Dulles that Newman's views on Scripture and tradition, developed while he was an Anglican, "proved to be a blessing to the Church that he joined."[25]

Ecumenical Councils

We have already seen that, for the theologian of Lérins, ecumenical councils are a unique locus of authority, the preeminent site for the church's authentic interpretation of Scripture. Councils embody and instantiate *in actu ecclesiae* the famous Vincentian canon. The criteria of *semper, ubique, et ab omnibus* are exemplified by councils that, through their decrees and definitions, manifest the consentient unity of the entire church. Vincent is convinced that such unity necessarily entails antiquity since the bishops/overseers in council are indefeasibly nourished by Scripture and the apostolic tradition. Ecumenical councils therefore play a pivotal role in the interpretation of the Bible and so in the understanding of divine revelation.

For Newman, too, councils are essential for the life of the church. The early Newman was convinced that the first four councils—Nicaea (325), Constantinople (381), Ephesus (431), and Chalcedon (451)—were sure bases of Christian doctrine. Master of the early church that he was, Newman speaks about these first councils on virtually every page of his work. For example, in an early (1836) essay he writes:

> In the second decade of the fourth century a controversy arose in Alexandria about our Lord's proper Divinity. It was brought before the Bishop, and, when his authority was unequal to the settlement of it, it led to the summoning of the first Ecumenical Council at Nicaea, in AD 325, which was attended by 318 bishops from all parts of the world, as representatives of the whole Church Catholic. Out of this number so collected more than 300 at once pronounced that that doctrine concerning our Lord, such as we hold it now—viz., that He was "God of God"—was the doctrine taught by the Apostles in the beginning.[26]

In the same essay Newman argues that the young churches were very jealous of their own traditions, as indicated by early controversies, such as on the date of Easter. But there was no controversy over the christological affirmations of Nicaea. There, in the witness of the church gathered in council, one sees attested the antiquity and ubiquity of the Christian faith. Newman's words are various, but his sentiments replicate Vincent's thought:

> Each Branch of the extended body had its own distinct line of traditional teaching from the Apostles; and each branch was loyally, nay, obstinately, attached to its own traditions. . . . Thus the dispute between Ephesus and Rome related to the time of keeping Easter. Thus there was a question of the authority of the Apocalypse and other books of Scripture, and a more serious question relative

to the baptism of [former] heretics [returning to the church]. In such controversies the one party religiously refused to yield to the other. The unanimity at
Nicaea, then, was not a mutual sacrifice of views between separate churches
for the sake of peace; not merely the decision of a majority; but simply and
plainly the joint testimony of many local bodies, as independent witnesses to
the separate existence in each of them, from time immemorial, of that great
dogma in which they found each other to agree.[27]

Newman's clear point is that the Council of Nicaea witnessed to a faith
that was attested in every local church and thus preeminently fulfilled the
Vincentian criteria of always, everywhere, and by everyone. In an ecumenical
council, one finds the truth of the gospel, the "great dogma" to which all the
churches bear witness.

At the same time, the young Newman is suspicious of all those councils
claimed as ecumenical. He acknowledges the first four as fundamental, with
a possible extension to the fifth and sixth. But he has reservations about Nicaea II, held in 787, claiming that this council "bears upon it various marks of
error, as if to draw our attention to its want of authority."[28] Newman argues,
as had Anglican theologians before him, that Nicaea II was not ecumenical,
because "it was the meeting, not of the whole Church, but of a mere party of
it, which in no sense really represented the Catholic world" (208). Precisely
on this account, its decisions were not recognized in the West for hundreds of
years afterward, and even in the East, some accounted only six general councils
right up until the fourteenth century. Further, Nicaea II was the "first General
Council which professed to ground its decrees, not on Scripture sanction, but
mainly on Tradition" (208). Important here is not Newman's historiography;
it is, rather, that he adheres to the unique status of councils but is concerned
that Nicaea II lacks the essential warrant of universality and seemingly sub-
ordinates Scripture to tradition.[29]

The Anglican Newman was convinced, like Vincent himself, that only
the councils that truly represent the church *in its entirety* ensure a proper
interpretation of the gospel. Unfortunately, over time, the church broke into
pieces, no longer speaking with one tongue. Nonetheless, unity and solidity
in the fundamentals remained. "It would follow that the Ancient Church will
be our model in all matters of doctrine, till it broke up into portions, and for
Catholic agreement substituted peculiar and local opinions; but that since that
time the Church has possessed no fuller measure of the truth than we see it
has at this day, viz. merely the fundamental faith."[30]

Since the beginning of the schisms, Newman says, the church has become
"more and more disunited, discordant and corrupt" (209). One may only turn
reliably to the early conciliar period, when the church was united in its interpretation of the Scriptures. This unified and universal teaching ensures that
the apostolic tradition is transmitted to us in its integral state. Anglicanism,

for the early Newman, respects and reflects the essential Vincentian hallmarks of universality and antiquity. But Rome is idiosyncratic in its invention of new doctrines, unwarranted by the church universal: "Again, both they [Roman Catholics] and we anathematize those who deny the Faith; but . . . the creed of Rome is ever subject to increase; ours is fixed once for all. . . . They cut themselves off from the rest of Christendom; we cut ourselves off from no branch, not even from themselves."[31]

Later as a Roman Catholic, although Newman would accept doctrinal development as continuing in the life of the church, he persisted in placing a decided accent on *the consentient unity that an ecumenical council offers* and thus its crucial role in witnessing to a legitimate *profectus*. An example may be found in Pius IX's 1854 definition of the Immaculate Conception of Mary. This is the claim that, by means of a prevenient grace extended through the merits of her son, Jesus Christ, Mary was conceived without any taint of Adam's sin. Avery Dulles reports that when Pius IX announced that he intended to call a council in 1869 (Vatican I), "Newman expected that the Council would be asked to ratify the definition of 1854."[32] In other words, developments that entailed new definitions of Christian teaching were, for Newman, best ratified by universal councils. By their unified witness, councils provide a unique warrant for both preserving the deposit of faith and for sanctioning a legitimate *profectus*.

For this reason Newman was "somewhat alarmed" when he realized that the newly called Vatican Council would actually address the issue of papal infallibility. As he had written in his *Apologia* of 1864, "It is to the Pope in Ecumenical Council that we look, as the normal seat of infallibility."[33] Even in his Roman Catholic period, then, Newman held to the Vincentian conviction that consentient unity, particularly as found in universal councils, was the authentic touchstone of Christian truth, allowing for an ecclesial marker between a legitimate development and a corrosive *permutatio*. Anything less than the consensus of the *corpus praepositorum* (body of overseers/bishops) was to be distrusted. This is why, when Vatican I defined, under restrictive conditions, the infallibility of the papal magisterium, Newman believed "there were reasons why a Catholic might suspend judgment on the validity of the definition."[34] More than eighty bishops left Rome before the final vote, indicating their opposition to the new dogma. For Newman, this number was ominous since "a mere majority of the Council, . . . rather than a moral unanimity, could not enact dogmatic decrees."[35]

In Newman's doubts on this point, one sees the very strong Vincentian sense that animates his theology. If any development were to be regarded as legitimately *in eodem sensu eademque sententia* with that which preceded it, then such growth must be warranted by the consensus of the entire church, not by a simple majority of bishops. An authentic *profectus* demands the *semper, ubique, et ab omnibus* instantiated *in actu ecclesiae*. Newman was convinced that a conciliar consensus was essential; thus, if the original opposition of the minority bishops had consolidated over time, "Newman might well have doubted the validity of the definition."[36]

In fact, since the minority bishops ultimately submitted to the definition of Vatican I, and since it was received by the Roman Catholic faithful at large, Newman regarded it as having been ratified by the entire church. To the crucial Vincentian question, then, *Quis est hodie Timotheus?* Newman insists, with the Lérinian, that it is "either the universal church generally or, specifically, the entire body of overseers/bishops [*vel generaliter universa ecclesia vel specialiter totum corpus praepositorum*]" (Vincent, *Common.* 22.2). The acceptance of the bishops and faithful of the definition of Vatican I indicated that the defined teaching was not, at least on Roman Catholic terms, a profane corruption of the Christian faith and so could be accepted as a harmonious development *in eodem sensu* with prior ecclesial teaching.[37]

While Newman accents the consensus of bishops/overseers in ecumenical councils, he places an equally strong emphasis on the role of theologians. Like the monk of Lérins, Newman sees theological doctors as having a significant role in assuring that any development is a legitimate *profectus* and not a pernicious *permutatio*.

Theological Doctors

As we have seen, Vincent tells Christians concerned about disputed inter-pretations of Scripture to turn to ecumenical councils. For if a council has pronounced on a contentious issue, the judgment of antiquity is assured. But in truth, councils have definitively taught on only a few issues, while new heresies appear continually. Lacking authoritative decisions, to whom may Christians turn to refute poisonous errors? Vincent here invokes the authority of trusted theological doctors. When establishing his hierarchy of interpretative bodies, he tells us that "in antiquity itself . . . one must above all prefer the general decrees of a universal council, although if none exists on a particular matter, then what is next best [*quod proximum est*] is the opinion of numerous and important theological masters" (27.4). Vincent insists that these masters cannot be simply gifted teachers; they also must have remained within the commu-nion of faith, distinguished themselves by holiness, and shown a willingness to die for Christ. Learning and sanctity are inseparable in Vincent's account of trustworthy theologians.

For Newman, too, theological doctors play an extraordinarily important role both in preserving the Christian faith and in ensuring that any development is *in eodem sensu* with the earlier tradition. Indeed, Newman's vision of the place of theologians within the church could easily warrant a separate study. Here we simply outline some of his significant convergences with the Lérinian. Of signal importance is that both Vincent and Newman invoke the work of theological doctors in response to the same crucial question: *Quis est hodie Timotheus?* Who is the Timothy of today who is charged with guarding the precious deposit of faith and with ensuring that any development is congruent with the apostolic tradition? With their accent on theologians—united together with councils and the faithful—both Vincent and Newman present a multifaceted, polycentric vision of the church's teaching authority.

Nevertheless, Newman could be critical of theologians. Already in his 1834 translation of the *Commonitorium,* Newman took specific note of Vincent's warning about gifted but idiosyncratic teachers who depart from the church's faith. In a pointed passage, the theologian of Lérins had memorably said that no matter if a man is holy, learned, a bishop, a confessor, nay, even a martyr for Christ, his teaching is to be shunned if he does not transmit the ancient tradition (28.8). Commenting on this passage, Newman remarks that if a gifted theologian departs from the ancient Christian faith, then from "that instant Mene and Tekel are written upon his school" (*Records* 24.7–8). In a later essay, Newman discusses the medieval theologian Abelard, who was undoubtedly brilliant and cultured. But, he judges, "vanity will possess the head, and worldliness the heart, of the man, however gifted, whose wisdom is not an effluence of the Eternal Light."[38]

When Newman's writings are taken as a whole, it is clear that he thinks the greatest danger facing theologians is Enlightenment rationalism, a movement, he was convinced, that had already infected much biblical criticism. Newman was a defender of the "mystical interpretation of Holy Scripture," the principle "on which the teaching of the Church has ever proceeded." Literal interpretation, on the other hand—prone as it was to severe minimalism—had been "the very metropolis of heresy."[39] Institutions of higher learning were particularly susceptible to the influence of rationalism and skepticism. Even the medieval university, under the direct vigilance of the church, had harbored theologians such as Abelard and Roscellinus, who were influenced by dangerous currents of thought.[40]

Despite these occasional criticisms of wayward thinkers, Newman's writings much more often praise the work of the *schola theologorum* and the contributions that theologians make to the robust intellectual life of the church. In his *Essay on Development,* for example, Newman refers to "loving inquisitiveness which is the life of the *Schola.*" He adduces Mary as a biblical model for the task of theology, for "she kept these things and pondered them in her heart" (Luke 2:19, 51). And on the occasion of the Annunciation, she asked the archangel, "How can this be?" (1:34), thereby displaying "that there is a questioning in matters revealed to us compatible with the fullest and most absolute faith."[41]

In the important preface to his republished *Via Media of the Anglican Church,* issued in 1877, Newman insists that theologians occupy the prophetic office in the church, just as pastors and people occupy the priestly office, and bishops and pope the governing, or regal, office. Each group in this multilayered complex is essential to the church's life, and each helps the church both to conserve the faith and to develop it properly. At times tension exists among the various bodies, but this can be a healthy tension leading to a deepening of the church's self-understanding. Any development, any legitimate *profectus*, can occur only when there is consentient coherence among the various bodies. Within this interrelationship, however, Newman singles out theology for a unique role: "Theology is the fundamental and regulating principle of the whole Church system. It is commensurate with Revelation, and Revelation is the initial and essential idea of Christianity."[42]

Centrally important to Newman—for both conservation of the faith and for its homogeneous unfolding—is the idea that any growth or development takes time and is best judged by a variety of ecclesial "courts." Newman was attracted to the faculties of theology that existed in medieval universities, when theologians exercised a quasi-magisterial role. He lamented the dissolution of many such faculties after the French Revolution (1789–99) precisely because this disintegration short-circuited the kind of full-bodied reflection that must accompany new theological proposals. Only when a *variety of courts* thoroughly and vigorously debate a theological proposition can some proposed development or interpretation be sanctioned by the entire church. Tradition—and so the proper interpretation of Scripture—is best protected, nourished, and husbanded when theology flourishes. This is why Newman insists, "Nor is religion ever in greater danger than when, in consequence of national or international troubles, the Schools of theology have been broken up and ceased to be."[43]

In his *Apologia*, Newman looks back, somewhat wistfully, on a time when Rome did not simply act with immediacy but waited until the entire church had expressed its opinion on some theological matter:

> All through Church history from the first, how slow is authority in interfering! Perhaps a local teacher, or a doctor in some local school, hazards a proposition, and a controversy ensues. It smoulders or burns in one place, no one interposing; Rome simply lets it alone. Then it comes before a Bishop; or some priest, or some professor in some other seat of learning takes it up; and then there is a second stage of it. Then it comes before a University, and it may be condemned by the theological faculty. So the controversy proceeds year after year, and Rome is still silent. An appeal perhaps is next made to a seat of authority inferior to Rome; and then at last after a long while it comes before the supreme power. Meanwhile, the question has been ventilated and turned over and over again, and viewed on every side of it, and authority is called upon to pronounce a decision, which has already been arrived at by reason.[44]

Only if theology is flourishing, and reasoned debate is vibrant and robust, can the church fully understand the Scriptures. The church is never reduced, in either Vincent or Newman, to decisions of bishops, popes, or even ecumenical councils. The deliberations of theologians are essential to guarantee that ideas are truly ventured, discussed, debated, refuted, or accepted. An idea (Newman's metaphor for revelation) can only develop properly if it is afforded this kind of freedom. This is why Newman insists that the theologian needs liberty; otherwise

> he would be fighting, as the Persian soldiers, under the lash, and the freedom of his intellect might truly be said to be beaten out of him. But this has not been so. . . . Zosimus treated Pelagius and Coelestius with extreme forbearance; St. Gregory VII was equally indulgent with Berengarius; by reason of the very power of the popes they have commonly been slow and moderate in their use of it.[45]

Therefore, to the crucial Vincentian question *Quis est hodie Timotheus?* Newman's answer is clear: the entire church, with theological doctors occupying a significant role. The eminent historian insists that theologians exercise a moderating influence on the church. They read conciliar and papal pronouncements within the long history of the church's teaching, carefully sifting such documents to determine the precise way in which they are *in eodem sensu* with the gospel. For this reason Newman famously states, "None but the *Schola Theologorum* is competent to determine the force of Papal and Synodal utterances, and the exact interpretation of them is a work of time."[46]

To buttress this assertion, Newman cites examples such as the proper understanding of the ancient axiom *extra ecclesiam nulla salus* (outside the church there is no salvation) and the prohibition against usury decreed by the fourteenth-century Council of Vienne (1311–12). When the church teaches with authority, theologians explain the exact meaning of these decrees "in order to make [them] as tolerable as possible." Such an approach, Newman argues, is not minimalism but a doctrinal moderation consistent with sound faith.[47] The decisions of councils and popes are authoritative for Newman. However, such statements also mark the beginning of sustained reflection wherein theologians determine precisely *how and in which exact manner* they are in continuity with the prior tradition. This is why Newman can say that theology "has restrained and corrected such extravagances as have been committed, through human infirmity, in the exercise of the regal [episcopal] and sacerdotal [pastors and the faithful] powers." Even popes can be salutarily corrected, since some (with Newman citing Liberius, Vigilius, Boniface VIII, and Sixtus V) "seem from time to time to have been wishing, though unsuccessfully, to venture beyond the lines of theology."[48] In a private letter, Newman remarks that theological schools protect the church from the encroachments of popes and councils.[49]

In all of these instances, Newman's intention is to display, Vincent-like, the essential office that theologians occupy in determining how some teaching is *in eodem sensu* with the prior tradition. But Newman's organic vision of the church, with its complex of *loci theologici* ensuring both faithful transmission of the apostolic tradition as well as its proper development, is not limited to theologians or to ecumenical councils. The Christian faithful have an important role to play as well.

The Christian Faithful (the Saints)

As we have seen, when asking who might be the Timothy of today who is charged with guarding the deposit of faith, Vincent immediately responds, "Either the universal church generally or, specifically, the entire body of overseers/bishops [*vel generaliter universa ecclesia vel specialiter totum corpus praepositorum*]" (*Common.* 22.2). While the overseers/bishops gathered in ecumenical council have a unique role to play in the proper interpretation of Scripture, and the consensus of learned and holy theologians is esteemed throughout the *Commonitorium*, Vincent likewise extends to the Christian faithful a significant role in guarding the faith and in its proper development.

Newman places a similar accent on the laity's responsibilities and is, at least within Roman Catholicism, known for his (somewhat controversial) insistence on this point. With his emphasis on the essential office of all the Christian faithful, Newman was continuing to explore the interrelated complex of warrants by which Scripture is properly interpreted and theological developments are authentically underwritten. Pride of place among Newman's reflections on this point belongs to his famous *Rambler* article of 1859. In that essay, Newman observes that Pius IX, in his 1854 papal bull *Ineffabilis Deus* (defining the Immaculate Conception of Mary), states that one reason for the suitability of this dogmatic definition is the *singularis conspiratio* (the unique breathing together) of Roman Catholic bishops and the faithful. Newman is deeply attracted to this phrase: "*Conspiratio*; the two, the Church teaching and the Church taught, are put together, as one twofold testimony, illustrating each other and never to be divided."[50] The testimony of bishops and laity must be conjoined "because the body of the faithful is one of the witnesses to the fact of the tradition of revealed doctrine, and because their consensus through Christendom is the voice of the Infallible Church." For Newman, none of the channels of the church's tradition "may be treated with disrespect" since the apostolic tradition, while firmly rooted in Scripture, is variously displayed in ecumenical councils, theological doctors, the faithful, liturgies, and even the events of history. All of these channels must be esteemed, even while acknowledging that "the gift of . . . defining, promulgating and enforcing any portion of that tradition resides solely in the *Ecclesia docens*." Newman goes on to speak of this consensus of the faithful as "a sort of instinct, or *phronēma*, deep in the bosom of the mystical body of Christ."[51]

Although Newman does not adduce Vincent specifically on this matter, we see a strong correlation with the Lérinian's thought. For Newman's point is that the apostolic tradition is variously manifested in Christianity, and so the faithful (the church generally), with their Spirit-led instinct for properly understanding biblical truth, are an important locus both for guarding the deposit and for ensuring harmonious development. The very title of Newman's controversial essay, "On Consulting the Faithful in Matters of Doctrine," is meant to highlight the idea that any doctrinal *profectus* necessarily finds some warrant in the "saints" themselves.

Newman's position on development resonates not only with Vincent's accent on the "universal church" but also with the Lérinian's insistence that the *semper, ubique, et ab omnibus* is instantiated *in actu ecclesiae*, that is, in the living, breathing, and Spirit-led Christian church. The entire church is marked with the Holy Spirit, and so the entire church bears witness to the apostolic tradition. In order to underwrite a proper *profectus*, one should find among bishops/overseers, theologians, and the faithful a "breathing together [*conspiratio*]," meaning a consentient agreement on the interpretation of the gospel.

Newman even argued that in the post-Nicene period the faithful maintained the orthodox faith with a steadfastness that was absent in the hierarchy, famously quoting Hilary's statement that "there is more holiness in the ears of the people than in the hearts of the bishops." In recent years Newman's post-Nicene historiography has been challenged, but his fundamental principle remains essential and is the cardinal point here.[52] Both Newman and Vincent were convinced that the faithful constituted an essential witness to, and channel of, apostolic tradition, needing to be consulted to ensure that any development was *in eodem sensu* with the prior tradition, thereby preserving "identity of type."

The Bishop of Rome

Animating both Vincent and Newman is the crucial question, how is the deposit of Christian truth authentically guarded? With this in mind, we turn to the role of the bishop of Rome. We have already seen that, for Vincent, the pope has a determinate, although hardly solitary, role in ensuring that the gospel is properly husbanded and developed. For the Lérinian, the bishop of Rome's unique place is indicated by his use of the verbal form *sanxit* (authoritatively laying down [a decision]; *Common.* 6.6) when referring to the controversy over rebaptism, and by his statement about "the unique authority of Stephen's see [*loci auctoritate superabat*]" (6.5). Somewhat lesser indications are Vincent's reference to Rome as *caput orbis* and his adduction of Popes Celestine and Sixtus as witnesses to the tradition transmitted from the apostles.

It may be remembered that Vincent, when turning to the specific role of the bishop of Rome, says that the *loci theologici* up to this point are sufficient of themselves to destroy profane novelties. That is to say, the inspired Word of God—as understood by the interpretative consensus of ecumenical councils, theological doctors, and the faithful generally—is fully capable of demolishing errors and ensuring proper progress. He adds, however, "so that nothing is lacking in the completeness of the argument, we have presented, at the end, the twofold authority of the apostolic see" (32.1). Vincent turns to Rome, then, only at the end of a long process. This method should remind us of Newman's favored procedure. As we have seen, Newman much preferred that disputed theological questions be debated for decades and even centuries before being submitted to the judgment of Rome. A too-quick resolution of an issue would foreshorten necessary theological debate. This is why Newman praised the medieval theological faculties and lamented the demise of many such schools after the French Revolution. When theology possesses a quasi-magisterial role, an important service is rendered to the church. Judging whether some position is harmoniously congruent with the gospel may take centuries of thought, debate, and reflection. The authority of the Roman see is best invoked, Newman believed, at the end of a protracted theological process.

Of course, in his early writings, Newman was convinced that the *Commonitorium* in general, and Vincent's criteria of *semper, ubique, et ab omnibus*, were entirely detrimental to claims made for the bishop of Rome. So in 1837 he does not hesitate to say, "There is this remarkable difference, even of theory, between them [Roman Catholics] and Vincentius, that the latter is altogether silent on the subject of the Pope's Infallibility, whether considered as an attribute of his see, or as attaching to him in General Council."[53]

There is certainly no mention of the infallibility of the Roman see in Vincent's work, and so the young Anglican divine is convinced of Rome's abject failure to adhere to Vincent's criterion of antiquity. This is why Newman, in a passage noted earlier, insists on identifying obvious deviations between Vincent's criteria for truth and those advanced by Rome:

> If Vincentius had the sentiments and feelings of a modern Roman Catholic, it is incomprehensible that, in a treatise written to guide the private Christian in matters of Faith, he should have said not a word about the Pope's supreme authority. . . . Applying his [Vincent's] own rule, . . . we may unhesitatingly conclude that the Pope's supreme authority in matters of Faith is no Catholic or Apostolic truth because he was ignorant of it.[54]

Continuing his assault, Newman argues, "Thus the very treatise [*Commonitorium*], which is so destructive to mere Protestantism, is as fatal to the claims of Rome. Not only is all mention of the Pope omitted as the Judge of controversies, but all mention of Tradition, except as subordinate to Holy Scripture."[55]

For Newman, the *Commonitorium* shatters the claims of both Wittenberg and Rome. Protestantism consistently violates the norms of the early church because of its alleged disinterest in tradition. Rome is convicted, not only because of its misunderstanding of tradition's value, but also because in the *Commonitorium* "all mention of the Pope [is] omitted as the Judge of controversies."

The heat of debate here causes the young Newman to overplay his hand. It is entirely true that for the sake of settling theological controversies, Vincent does not simply revert to the judgment of the bishop of Rome, and Vincent hardly regards the pope as the only center of authoritative ecclesial teaching; yet the pope nonetheless has a significant role in Vincent's taxis (order) of authorities.[56] In ecclesial controversies, Vincent does indeed see the bishop of Rome as a judge, indeed quite probably the leading judge. To confirm this, one need only glance at his comments on Pope Stephen and the rebaptism issue, or the force attached to Vincent's use of the word *sancio* when referring to the pope's teaching. Yet it is certain that, for Vincent, the bishop of Rome never acts alone but always within the consentient agreement of the *corpus praepositorum* of East and West.

In his 1845 *Essay on Development*, Newman judges the idea of development more favorably and with it the role of the Roman bishop. In the examples he adduces, pride of place belongs to the controversy over Eutyches's Monophysite teaching and the response of the Council of Chalcedon (451). We have already reviewed elements of that debate. At this point, we only mention that Newman sees the controversy over Eutyches and the subsequent definition of Chalcedon as (1) indicating the necessity of development over time and (2) displaying the important role of the bishop of Rome in sanctioning such development.

Newman states that, for Eutyches, after the incarnation there existed only one nature in our Lord. And Eutyches argued that he had the (linguistic) support of Cyril and Athanasius. Consequently, no determinative *consensus patrum* could be brought against him. Further, Eutyches subscribed to the decrees of Nicaea and Ephesus, and to the claim that "nothing could be added to the Creed of the Church." Dioscorus, the president of the Second Council of Ephesus (later called the *Latrocinium*, or Robber Council, 449), also insisted that nothing could be affirmed beyond the Creed of Nicaea.[57]

To the argument of Dioscorus and Eutyches that the Creed of Nicaea is inviolate, Newman cites, as we have seen, the (virtual) addition of the *Theotokos* at Ephesus and the claim of Gregory Nazianzen that Nicaea needed a supplement concerning the Holy Spirit. Newman then makes his conclusive point: tradition has always maintained the exclusivity of the creed, even while extending it according to the exigencies of the time (303n8).

In recounting this history, Newman argues primarily that development over time is essential even if one insists—as one must—on the inviolate nature of conciliar creeds. But he has another motive as well. He reviews the case of Eutyches and concludes that the heresiarch had formidable support for his error: "Such was the state of Eastern Christendom in the year 449; a heresy, appealing to the Fathers, to the Creed, and, above all, to Scripture, was by a general Council [the *Latrocinium*], professing to be Ecumenical, received as true in the person of its promulgator [the emperor]." If this position were allowed to triumph, "the Monophysite heresy was established as Apostolic truth in all provinces from Macedonia to Egypt" (306).

Newman hardly wishes to discredit the Scriptures, councils, or creeds, Christian witnesses on which he had staked his entire life. His point is that the assent of the bishop of Rome was also needed to assure that some teaching was indeed in material continuity with the prior tradition. The pope's assent is here regarded as an essential criterion in distinguishing truth from heresy. So Newman continues, "Much might be said on the plausibility of the defence, which Eutyches might have made for his doctrine from the history and documents of the Church before his time." But while Eutyches could plausibly argue that there existed weighty warrants for the truth of his position, in lacking the confirmation of the bishop of Rome, the *idem sensus* of Monophysitism (its legitimate interpretation of the gospel message) could not be assured.

In contrast to the *Latrocinium*, Newman recounts the doctrinal development that the Council of Chalcedon sanctioned a few years later: "The historical account of the Council is this, that a formula [Christ "in two natures"] which the Creed did not contain, which the Fathers did not unanimously witness, . . . [was] forced on the Council by the resolution of the Pope of the day, acting through his Legates and supported by the civil power" (312). Newman concludes, somewhat exultantly, that "Leo's augury of success, which even Athanasius had not, was this, that he was seated in the chair of St. Peter and the heir of his prerogatives" (307).[58] Though couched in triumphant prose, his point is that at a highly significant moment in the history of the church, the bishop of Rome is an essential witness—indeed, the lead witness—for development *in eodem sensu*.[59]

With the criteriological importance that Newman bestows on the bishop of Rome, Vincent would largely agree. But Vincent would undoubtedly insist—as Newman does generally—that this authority must be exercised in conjunction with the entire *corpus praepositorum*. After all, it is only when the affirmations of Leo (together with those of Cyril) were accepted by the entire Council of Chalcedon that they became decisive and binding for the church. To ensure that some development is *in eodem sensu*, that it meets the Vincentian criteria of *semper, ubique, et ab omnibus*, it needs the broad agreement of the channels of apostolic tradition. For the Lérinian, consensus is always a better barometer of proper development than the insights of one man, as he tells us insistently, no matter his authority, sanctity, learning, or even martyrdom (*Common.* 28.8). Vincent places a decided accent on the *agreement* of ecumenical councils, on the *consensus* of theological doctors, and on the *instinctus* of the faithful generally. In the *Commonitorium*, the bishop of Rome is singled out as having unique authority, but even then he teaches authoritatively *together with* the college of bishops/overseers.

Newman is not far from Vincent's position. Scripture is the repository of all divinely revealed truth and is properly interpreted by ecumenical councils, by theologians, and by the *phronēma* for truth residing in the bosom of the faithful. All have an essential role in guarding the deposit of faith and in ensuring that any development over time is congruent with the gospel. In the *Essay on Development* Newman places a decided accent on the bishop of Rome, yet he nevertheless remains Vincentian in stressing the relationship of the Petrine ministry to the wider body of bishops/overseers. As earlier noted, he says in his *Apologia*, "It is to the Pope in Ecumenical Council that we look, as the normal seat of infallibility."[60] For it is the ecumenical council that best provides the guarantee of consentient universality as opposed to idiosyncratic singularity. Buttressing this point is the fact that Newman was "somewhat alarmed" when learning that Vatican I would take up the theme of papal infallibility. As we have seen, he was hoping that this council had been convoked solely for the purpose of ratifying the Marian definition of 1854.[61]

As it turned out, when Vatican I ended in 1870, Newman was relieved to learn that the actual definition of papal infallibility had been framed in moderate terms. Nonetheless, given that a significant number of bishops had left Rome before the final vote (thus signifying their opposition to the definition), he believed that one might legitimately suspend judgment on the decree's validity. For several years Newman refrained from commenting publicly on Vatican I's decree on infallibility. But his theological concerns about this matter slowly dissolved as the minority bishops (and the faithful at large) came to accept this (Roman Catholic) conciliar judgment. Nevertheless, Newman's theological reticence on this matter indicates his traditionally Vincentian concern that the consensus of the universal church is the best indication of a proper development over time. His later writings always seek to interpret the 1870 definition in a moderate way, avoiding any ultrapapal, unilateral approach. For Newman as for Vincent, a true *profectus* requires consentient unity if one is to judge that it is a development actually congruent with the deposit of faith.

Conclusion

The thesis of this chapter is not that Newman is simply a nineteenth-century *Doppelgänger* of Vincent of Lérins. To argue such would be to display a kind of theological Stockholm syndrome, with Newman mimicking the thought of the monk of Lérins. The argument, rather, is that Newman was deeply influenced by Vincent over the course of his theological career. The Vincentian canon had long been authoritative with English divines, providing the theoretical foundation for the Anglican via media against the alleged innovations to the tradition sanctioned by Rome and the alleged amputations of the tradition permitted by the Reformation. Newman, then, was continually forced to engage

Vincent's thought not only because of his personal interest in antiquity but also by force of the Anglican theological tradition.

Newman, who translated large sections of the *Commonitorium* as a young man, shows signs of having deeply imbibed Vincent's thought. He adopts and expands the Lérinian's idea of development, and he very closely—almost literally—adheres to his distinction between a proper *profectus* and an adulterated *permutatio*. Like the theologian of Lérins, Newman has a strong and persistent desire to answer the question *Quis est hodie Timotheus?* His Vincent-like answer is that the Timothy of today is found in a variety of "channels" of apostolic tradition. Scripture certainly has pride of place, followed by the "ministrative" *loci* of ecumenical councils, the *schola theologorum*, the faithful generally, and the bishop of Rome. All the channels together constitute the universality and ubiquity of the church, through which the apostolic tradition—the *semper*—is properly conserved and developed. It is this complex and polycentric vision of the body of Christ that gives the church its strength, allowing it to husband and nurture the Christian faith and to carefully discern any legitimate and architectonic growth.

When Newman explicitly discusses the Vincentian canon, particularly in his earlier days, he interprets it in a narrow sense, as did most thinkers of his time. Logically enough, he concludes that the first rule is "difficult, surely, and troublesome to use."[62] Nevertheless, the canon is only troublesome and difficult when one thinks that universality, ubiquity, and antiquity can somehow be validated apart from *living* ecclesial structures. If that were actually the case, then the first rule is not only troublesome but also entirely useless, a pithy slogan impossible to apply. But as we have seen, this is not at all what Vincent intends. The Vincentian canon is a testament neither to primitivism nor to naive utopianism, looking back to a nebulous *aetas aurea*. I doubt that Newman ever clearly saw how Vincent deftly integrates his first and second rules; he tends to leave them in an uneasy juxtaposition. But his theological genius was such that he wrought better than he (fully) knew.

Both Vincent and Newman are interested in the substantial identity of the Christian faith over time. This is the point of Vincent's *idem sensus* and of Newman's "identity of type." Both see that this identity and continuity can only be preserved *in actu ecclesiae*, in the complex of elements that constitute the church: Scripture as having a unique position as the inspired Word of God—and then as authentically interpreted by ecumenical councils, theological doctors, the faithful generally, and the bishop of Rome (with his colleagues). Taken together, this complex of *loci theologici* can reliably judge that which is truly a development—*profectus fidei*—and that which is actually a corruption of the faith. While in his earlier days, Newman used Vincent against the Roman church; later he employed the Lérinian's thought to repristinate and reform certain elements of Roman Catholic theology. Aspects of his theological "reformation" include his insights into the relationship between Scripture and tradition, his strong accent on the relative autonomy of theologians, his recovery of the importance of the faithful as a theological source, his emphasis on the bishop of Rome within the college of bishops/overseers, and in general his weblike vision of the church's interpretative authority.[63] Indeed, it is Newman who is often credited (along with the nineteenth-century theologians from Tübingen) with having restored to Roman Catholic theology a notion of tradition that is active and dynamic as well as properly preservative. Many of these elements found voice at Vatican II (1962–65), so much so that Paul VI in 1975 declared Vatican II to be "Newman's hour."[64]

The conclusion, then, is not only that Newman was influenced by Vincent of Lérins but also that his theological reception of Vincent has borne fruit for the entire Christian church. In the following chapter, I show how Vincent's thought, carefully balancing preservation and development, can offer continuing theological and ecumenical guidance for Christianity today.

3

The Enduring Ecumenical Importance of Vincent of Lérins

Having carefully examined the *Commonitorium* as well as its reception by a major nineteenth-century thinker, we now proceed to the crucial constructive question: How can the thought of Vincent of Lérins help the church today, both theologically and ecumenically? Can we speak of a "performative appropriation" of Vincent's thought for contemporary Christianity?

In this study we have already noticed that a common understanding of Vincent's famous canon is based on a misreading. The theologian of Lérins is not speaking about a long-ago, mythical *aetas aurea* when the only doctrines Christians believed were those held always, everywhere, and by everyone. The Lérinian, rather, is offering determinate criteria that are *concretely* instantiated in the living, performative life of the church. His canon offers a rule, furthermore, that must be fully integrated with his decided accent on development over time, a growth that must always be *in eodem sensu eademque sententia* with the preceding tradition. Tradition, for Vincent, is a dynamic, organic process, deeply rooted in Scripture, while allowing for a harmonious, architectonic unfolding. Taking with grave seriousness the Pauline injunctions "Guard the deposit" and "no other gospel," the theologian of Lérins lays out the warrants for precisely how such preservation occurs, along with concomitant development.

We have also seen that even the great ecumenist and ecclesiologist Yves Congar misunderstood precisely how Vincent was utilizing his famous rule. Without mincing words, Congar states baldly, "It is because the principle [Vincent's canon] is too static that Vatican II avoided quoting it in its constitution

Dei Verbum §8."[1] In this judgment, Congar is perhaps relying on the influential scholar of Vincent's work, José Madoz, who says that Vincent adheres to a "rigid conservativism."[2] Madoz even states that the *Commonitorium*'s groundbreaking chapter on development—a virtual *novum* in early Christian literature—is "a rather vague and negative sketch."[3] Of course, if one does not see clearly how the first rule is intended to function, this conclusion is inevitable. For if one understands the criteria of ubiquity, antiquity, and universality apart from their *living* ecclesial context, then the chapter on development becomes virtually unintelligible, an odd and uneasy addition to Vincent's canon that does not follow logically. One must conclude, then, that the second rule is "vague" because it cannot be integrated with an understanding of the Vincentian canon that, when taken only in a strictly preservative sense, simply looks backward to a utopian apostolic age. While conceding that Christian doctrine is not, for Vincent, a "dead treasure," Madoz concludes that the Lérinian's formulas "look more to the past than to the future."[4] This evaluation, by one of the primary Roman Catholic experts on Vincent, could not have failed to influence men like Congar and Ratzinger, who were themselves influential at Vatican II. In the Vincentian canon, Madoz sees a rigid exclusivism that does not actually exist. Indeed, Madoz does not hesitate to say that Vincent's canon—leveled against Augustine's theories of grace and predestination—is "viciously personal."[5] In my judgment, Madoz's interpretation of the *Commonitorium*, having occupied a leading place in Roman Catholic circles for almost a century, should now be quietly retired.

But Madoz is hardly alone in his interpretation of the Vincentian canon. In the ecumenical discussions that took place between Roman Catholics and Anglicans at Malines in the 1920s, Charles Gore, applying Vincent's first rule in an exclusive sense, stated that in any future reunion between churches, the Church of England should not be required to believe anything beyond the antiquity positively affirmed by Vincent. His Roman Catholic interlocutors replied that Vincent cannot be taken according to the letter, because none of the articles of faith sanctioned by councils strictly meets Vincent's rule. Noteworthy in this exchange is that both the Anglican and Roman Catholic parties interpret Vincent as a strict antiquarian (with one insisting on the regulative status of the canon and the other opposing such a status), thereby equally missing the wider context within which his first rule should be understood.[6]

Misunderstandings of Vincent are not limited to the West. The Eastern Orthodox theologian Georges Florovsky writes:

> The well-known formula of Vincent of Lérins is very inexact, when he describes the catholic nature of Church life in the words *Quod ubique, quod semper, quod ab omnibus creditum est.* . . . First of all, it is not clear whether this is an empirical criterion or not. If this be so, then the "Vincentian Canon" proves to be inapplicable and quite false. For about what *omnes* is he speaking? Is it

a demand for a general, universal questioning of all the faithful, and even of those who only deem themselves such?[7]

Following in the train of Western commentators, Florovsky summarizes well the usual judgment on Vincent's thought: "It appears that the Vincentian Canon is a postulate of historical simplification, of a harmful primitivism."[8] But as has been shown, the Lérinian was interested neither in primitivism nor in curatorial Christianity. His decided accent was on the living tradition of the church, which preserves the apostolic tradition, primarily through the decisions (*decreta*) of ecumenical councils (*Common.* 3.3; 27.4). It is this living tradition that safeguards antiquity, even while properly unfolding it.

Having cleared away some misunderstandings that have traditionally attached themselves to Vincent's thought, the contemporary question is this: How can Vincent's refined hermeneutics of doctrine help us today?

Identity through Time

The theologian of Lérins, that great custodian of Christian truth, insists that there must be substantial identity between "the faith once delivered to the saints" and the faith preached in every age of the church. Indeed, identity in time—without precluding organic development—is one of Vincent's major themes. "Guard the deposit, Timothy!" is the scriptural injunction found on virtually every page of the *Commonitorium*. And undoubtedly, one may argue that substantial identity over time is one of the hallmarks of orthodox Christianity. For this reason, the Lérinian counsels Christians to be "loyal followers of the faith, not imaginative innovators to it [*non ducens sed sequens*]" (22.4).

Of capital importance for Vincent, then, is the stability and material continuity of Christian doctrine over time. "The same things that you were taught, teach [*eadem tamen quae didicisti, doce*]" (22.7). "You received gold, give others gold in return [*aurum accepisti, aurum redde*]" (22.5). Particularly important are the teachings of ecumenical councils, which by definition fulfill the essential warrants of universality and ubiquity—and in drawing upon the apostolic tradition, provide the warrant of antiquity as well. Their solemn decisions (*decreta*) can never be reversed or weakened under some false banner. This is why Vincent is so critical of the assembly of Ariminum (Rimini) of 359. Its creed was nothing less than an attempted reversal of Nicaea. Just here Vincent invokes the teaching of Proverbs (22:28), "Transgress not the landmarks that you inherited from the fathers." Ecclesiastes (10:8) reaffirms this thought: "Break not through a hedge" established by antiquity. The solemn teachings ratified by the entire church cannot be contravened. To Vincent's rhetorical question *Quid est depositum?* (*Common.* 22.4), he unhesitatingly responds, "It is that which you believed, not that which you created."

It is concern for the material continuity and stability of the *tradita*, the solemn decisions handed down by councils, that inspires Vincent's comment: "The true church of Christ, that sedulous and cautious guardian of the dogmas entrusted to its care, changes nothing in them, adds nothing, and subtracts nothing [*nihil minuit, nihil addit*]" (23.16). For Vincent, nothing can be added to the truth "once delivered" in the history of Israel and in Jesus Christ. Revelation has been given once for all. Christian teachings can always receive further elucidation, but they cannot be transformed into something other than they are. Transformation is that dangerous metamorphosis [*aliquid ex alio in aliud transvertatur*] that must at all costs be avoided (23.2). To illustrate the difference, Vincent says, "There may be added shape, form, and lucidity, but the nature of each thing must remain the same" (23.11). It is precisely when one tries to change the very nature or essence of a teaching that fateful betrayal necessarily ensues.

However, this guarding of the deposit, this proscription of adding or subtracting, is never at antipodes with an *authentic* notion of development. Indeed, it is precisely this point that allows for the reconciliation of Vincent's canon or first rule (*semper, ubique, et ab omnibus*) with his second (development *in eodem sensu*). It is for just this reason that the Lérinian adduces his well-known biological metaphors. Like the child reaching full stature as an adult and the seed becoming a plant, there is a dynamism inherent in Vincent's notion of tradition. The gospel is an active, living presence in the world. Its intrinsic power allows Christian teaching to develop organically over time. The rule of faith, then, can never be mummified; it evolves gradually and architectonically and, of critical importance, with the sanction of essential warrants. The fundamental norm for development is always Scripture, as interpreted preeminently by the universal and consentient judgments of ecumenical councils, but also by the consensus of holy and learned doctors, by the faithful generally, and by the bishop of Rome.

Of vital importance is that any doctrinal development must stand *in consonance* with the originally intended meaning. Any *profectus fidei* must always be *in eodem sensu* with the preceding tradition. Growth and change occur over time and indeed must occur, but such development must always be of a determinate type and shape—preserving the original instinct and insight.[9]

Temporality, then, is never seen by Vincent in a purely dyslogistic way, as if the only task of Christians is preservative, battling *against* the effects of history. It is true that Vincent is aware of time's dangerously ravenous appetite, but he also thinks the church may learn from the inexorable advance of history. The Lérinian does not regard time as an enemy against whom one must retain a hermetically sealed purity, with the truth of Christianity entirely resistant to change. At the outset of his work, he says, "Since time ravages all human things, we should, in turn, seize from it something that will profit us regarding eternal life" (1.3). And we may seize something profitable because time, properly used, participates in the work of the Holy Spirit; it allows for a true *profectus*, an advance in the understanding of Christian truth. This is why Vincent uses the phrase *dilatetur tempore*: the church's teaching is enlarged by time (23.9); and again, *in semetipsa . . . res amplificetur*: the matter grows within itself (23.2). If time is used well, the church advances and develops its understanding of the gospel. This is the great advantage of ecumenical councils, which have served to elucidate and clarify the faith: "By your explanations, let that which was believed obscurely now be understood clearly. What antiquity venerated without comprehension, let posterity now understand" (22.7).

Vincent is fully aware, then, that change is intrinsic to human life. Because of this, time can be doctrine's closest ally. For time allows the precious jewels of Christian teaching to be polished and burnished, freed from any impure alloys. Time—imbued with Judeo-Christian teleology—allows the gems of divine doctrine to be arranged with skill and wisdom, with "splendor, grace, and beauty [*splendorem, gratiam, venustatem*]" (22.6). With time, then, the church develops and refines the unchangeable truth given in ancient Israel and in Jesus of Nazareth. With time, the church carefully distinguishes a true *profectus*, which enriches and adorns the church, from a *permutatio fidei*, which depraves it. Time, properly used, is the locus of God's saving plan.

This explains why Vincent ardently insists that those who oppose development are "hostile toward God [*exosus Dei*]" (23.1) and "envious of others [*invidus hominibus*]." Why this strong language? Because by trying to prohibit development, some fail to recognize that it is God himself who endorses progress. Why are opponents of development "envious of others"? To answer this question, we need to remember Vincent's comment that, thanks to councils, "what antiquity venerated without comprehension, posterity now understands" (22.7). The Lérinian is alluding to the fact that a later generation may possess more clarity and depth than an earlier one. The Christian faith, in other words, becomes more lucid and precise over time. There has been growth in "understanding, knowledge, and wisdom [*intellegentia, scientia, sapientia*]" (23.3). Some may be jealous that later ages have a clearer understanding than earlier ones, with the mystery of revelation in Christ now more transparently unfolded. Precisely this jealousy has inspired some to try to overthrow the landmarks of Nicaea (325) and Ephesus (431), councils that have clarified and advanced the faith with their teachings.

For Vincent, if the church is attentive to the channels of tradition that God has provided—always under the Divine Word—it will see that through history itself God's Word gradually comes to fruition.[10]

Development Itself

There are two dimensions to Vincent's notion of development. On the one hand, there is the matter of framing a traditional teaching in a new way. This is the Lérinian's claim that one should "speak newly, but never say new things [*dicas nove, non dicas nova*]" (22.7). On the other hand, there is the issue of organic growth wherein a particular teaching is coherently and architectonically enlarged. One may say, therefore, that the *Commonitorium* endorses both development in expression and (organic) development in the matter itself. We shall treat of each in turn.

Noviter, non Nova

Vincent's assertion that theologians should say things newly without saying new things was born, no doubt, from his knowledge of ecumenical councils. *Homoousios* and the *Theotokos* were terms not found in Scripture, but which, nonetheless, had become normative for the Christian church. This is why Vincent says that ecumenical councils "designate by new and appropriate words some article of faith which is, of itself, traditional [*non novum fidei sensum, novae appellationis proprietate signando*]" (23.19) This is one kind of development sanctioned by the Lérinian: the use of new terms that had not previously existed in the Christian lexicon. Precisely for this reason, the monk of Lérins sanctions a distinction between the content of the Christian faith and its "form" or "context."

In Roman Catholicism, from Vatican II onward, this distinction between a formula and its substantive meaning has borne much enduring fruit, both theologically and ecumenically. Indeed, it may be argued that the reconceptualization of ecclesial teaching—for subjects as weighty as the Eucharist and justification—has led to extraordinary advances in Christian unity. This distinction has become a way to acknowledge, and indeed to honor, differing formulations of the mystery of faith, while avoiding the deconstruction of substantial identity. In Roman Catholic theology the distinction between context and content was at first strongly resisted because it was suspected of calling into question the precise Scholastic formulations that had been used for centuries. A breakthrough occurred at Vatican II when Pope John XXIII, in his opening address to the council (October 11, 1962), said that "the substance of the ancient doctrine of the *depositum fidei* is one thing; the way in which it is formulated is another."[11] Soon after the council ended, Yves Congar stated that all of Vatican II gave witness to these few words.[12] On the other hand, some have criticized this distinction for courting unacknowledged philosophical problems. It is not necessary to rehearse the matter here since elsewhere I have examined the history of the distinction, as well as the objections.[13]

Many Roman Catholic and Protestant theologians of the twentieth century have utilized some form of the *noviter, non nova*. But the distinction is hardly a contemporary one. In Thomas Aquinas, for instance, one finds many examples:

But with the Latins it does not sound right to say that there are three *substantiae*, even though on a purely verbal basis the term *hypostasis* in Greek means the same as the term *substantia* in Latin. The fact is, *substantia* in Latin is more frequently used to signify essence. And both we and the Greeks hold that in God there is but one essence. So where the Greeks speak of three *hypostases*, we Latins speak of three *personae*, as Augustine in the seventh book on the Trinity also teaches. And, doubtless, there are many similar instances. (*Summa theologiae* I.29.2 ad 2)

Even when speaking about the disputed *Filioque*, Thomas is convinced that the Greek and Latin doctors hold the same teaching although expressed in different words. As he says, the Greeks "differ more in words than in meaning [*magis differunt in verbis quam in sensu*]" (*De potentia*, q. 10, a. 5, c.). Finally, Aquinas explains, Vincent-like—even citing the Lérinian's favorite biblical passage, 1 Tim. 6:20—that a new formulation is *not* a novelty, merely an old truth expressed in a new way:

Although the word "person" is not found applied to God in Scripture, either in the Old or New Testament, nevertheless what the word signifies is found to be affirmed of God in many places of Scripture; as that He is the supreme self-subsisting being, and the most perfectly intelligent being. If we could speak of God only in the very terms themselves of Scripture, it would follow that no one could speak about God in any but the original language of the Old or New Testament. The urgency of confuting heretics made it necessary to find new words to express the ancient faith about God. Nor is such a kind of novelty to be shunned; since it is by no means profane, for it does not lead us astray from the sense of Scripture. The Apostle warns us to avoid "profane novelties of words" (1 Tim. 6:20). (*Summa theologiae*, I.29.3 ad 1)

Five hundred years before Aquinas, one sees a very similar idea about *noviter, non nova* expressed by John of Damascus:

Where can you find in the Old Testament or in the Gospels explicit use of such terms as "Trinity" or "consubstantial" or "one nature of the Godhead," or "three persons," or anything about Christ being one person with two natures? But nevertheless, the meanings of all these things are found, expressed in other phrases which the Scriptures do contain, and the fathers have interpreted them for us. We accept them, and anathematize those who will not.[14]

The Reformation also sees itself as embodying the *noviter, non nova*. For example, Karl Barth speaks of the Augsburg Confession thus: "The *Augustana* and the other Reformed confessions did not want to be confessions in so far as they had no new faith to confess—but they were confessions in so far as they did confess the old faith anew."[15]

In contemporary thinking, the *noviter, non nova* has been helpful with ecumenical dialogue, allowing for a measure of plurality while maintaining a fundamental unity. Its use occurs in all bilateral dialogues as the partners seek to overcome language that may be misleading or have negative connotations. In the Joint Declaration on Justification (Lutherans and Catholics, 1999), for example, Roman Catholics use none of the language of causality that strongly marks the Tridentine decree. Such Aristotelian terminology, while allowing for a certain precision, is not essential for conveying the fundamental teaching on interior renewal in Christ. Similar adjustments have been made with the Eucharist and the term "transubstantiation." And John Paul II, in a 1995 encyclical encouraging creative thought on the papal ministry, invoked the conciliar citation of the *noviter, non nova*: "In all this, it will be of great help methodologically to keep carefully in mind the distinction between the deposit of faith and the formulation in which it is expressed, as Pope John XXIII recommended in his opening address at the Second Vatican Council" (*Ut unum sint* §81).

One impetus for the rebirth of the *noviter, non nova* in Roman Catholic thought was the crisis of theological form that occurred in the early part of the twentieth century. In France of the 1930s, many Christians were drifting toward Marxism, with its vibrant public accent on justice, brotherhood, and human solidarity. Henri de Lubac, Jean Daniélou, and others were convinced that Roman Catholicism, with its neoscholastic, Aristotelian-tinged theological formulations, was no longer speaking to the people of the day. To remedy this crisis, there was a determined attempt to revive the works of the fathers of the church—the series *Sources chrétiennes* was born of this effort—so that men and women could once again relive the power and majesty of the Christian faith in its original vigor and mystery. In other words, this crisis of form led to an attempt to maintain traditional Christian doctrine—the *idem sensus*—but now reexpressed in a mode of speaking that was more biblical, sacramental, vital, and robust.[16] It was precisely this effort that led Henri Bouillard to say in 1943, in a phrase that caused unending grief in its time but was relatively innocuous in its intention, "A theology which is not contemporary would be a false theology [*une theologie qui ne serait pas actuelle serait un theologie fausse*]."[17] Bouillard had been preceded in this thought by Johann Evangelist Kuhn, a nineteenth-century Tübingen theologian much taken with Vincent's *Dicas nove, non dicas nova*. Kuhn argued that in no age could the Christian faith be monotone and spiritless, simply repeating the same concepts and expressions. Christian doctrine must be *zeitgemäß* and *geistlich*, timely and vigorous, speaking the ancient biblical faith in the language of the times.[18]

This issue remains today: How can there be a healthy plurality of formulations (and so of concepts) without betraying a profound unity of faith? How can a delicate balance be maintained between same and other, unity and multiplicity? Within Roman Catholicism, as noted, the notion of a plurality of formulations mediating a stable meaning triumphed at Vatican II. When speaking of Eastern churches, for example, the council says: "It is hardly surprising if from time to time one tradition has come nearer to a full appreciation of some aspects of a mystery of revelation than the other, or has expressed it to better advantage. In such cases, these various theological expressions are often to be considered as mutually complementary rather than as conflicting" (*Unitatis Redintegratio* §17).

In other words, a true plurality of perspectives (in this case, Eastern and Western) is reconcilable with a unity of meaning and faith. Noniterative formulations may be entirely protective of the *idem sensus*. Yet a new formulation will add fresh light and perspective, throwing formerly hidden dimensions of the mystery of faith into relief. This is simply to say that *traditio* and *tradita*, the process of handing on the faith and the faith itself, are always deeply intertwined and cannot be dichotomized. Surely the worlds of art, music, and literature make clear that form and content can never be naively separated.[19] But this close association between context and content is no reason to deny the possibility of a distinction. *Homoousious* is one canonized way of speaking about the ontological unity between Father and Son, but not the only possible way.[20] So too the term "transubstantiation" brings out clearly the presence of Christ in the Eucharist, but for a long time the church explained the mystery of Christ's presence without reference to this specific term. Vincent's admonition *Dicas nove, non dicas nova* indicates that there must be a performative appropriation and a creative reception of the church's faith in every epoch, an appropriation that uses its own language, culture, and concepts even while always maintaining the *idem sensus* of Christian belief.

At the same time, when Vincent says there should be taught no new things (*nova*), we should not understand this in the sense that there can be no development. If that were the case, then his entire chapter on authentic growth, the "golden chapter" of the *Commonitorium*, would be rendered meaningless. What is at stake, rather, is that there can never be *nova* that transgress the landmarks established by the fathers.[21] The Councils of Nicaea (325) and now Ephesus (431)—which have assuredly transmitted the apostolic faith *semper, ubique, et ab omnibus*—have already established the *regula fidei* in accordance with the gospel. The stable and determinate meaning of the conciliar teachings cannot undergo illicit transformation so that their decrees and definitions "become something else entirely [*aliquid ex alio in aliud transvertatur*]" (*Common.* 23.2). This is why Vincent insists so strongly that we must resist heretics who are wont to say to us, "Condemn what you used to hold, and hold what you used to condemn. Reject the ancient faith and the dictates of your fathers and the deposits of the ancients" (9.8). *This* kind of change, the dreaded *permutatio fidei*, Vincent opposes with every fiber of his being. "Guard the deposit, Timothy!"

How, precisely, does one faithfully guard and protect the deposit of faith while still sanctioning authentic development?

Organic Growth

As we have seen, several theologians regard Vincent as simply captive to tradition, a man with custodial interests who eschews any kind of creativity in order to ensure that the deposit of Christian faith is authentically guarded. There is no doubt that Vincent wanted Scripture and the apostolic tradition preserved. He does not hesitate to tell us *Sequens, non ducens!* (Follow, don't lead!) You received gold; do not dare to transmit brass to others.

However, there also exists in Vincent's thought a palpable accent on development over time, a determinate emphasis that long preceded the work of John Henry Newman (as Newman freely acknowledged). In this aspect of the Lérinian's thought, one sees a dynamic and living notion of growth that organically builds upon preceding affirmations. The word "development" can be taken as nothing more than a synonym for change. But Vincent, astute theologian that he is, carefully distinguishes between *kinds* of change: *profectus* or *permutatio*. In authentic change, with time properly used, the universal church brings to fruition the truth "once delivered" to the saints.

Tradition, then, is a living reality for Vincent. His biological metaphors indicate that he conceived of tradition as a growing, organic process. The Lérinian's understanding is reflective of the notion described by Henri de Lubac: "Tradition, according to the fathers of the church, is in fact just the opposite of a burden of the past; it is a vital energy, a propulsive as much as a protective force, acting within an entire community as at the heart of each of the faithful because it is none other than the very Word of God both perpetuating and renewing itself under the action of the Spirit of God."[22] De Lubac's dyadic linking of "protective" and "propulsive" plus "perpetuating and renewing" reflects Vincent's twin goals of identity and creative development. Tradition conserves the achievements of the past, even while allowing them to grow to full flower over the course of time.

The noted ecumenist Yves Congar's description is quite similar:

> Tradition . . . comprises two equally vital aspects: one of development and one of conservation. This is why some see tradition eminently as a safeguard for the purity of the deposit, at the risk of cutting the present off from the future, while others see it eminently as a way of opening the present to the future, in the search for a total synthesis. There is a sort of tension or dialectic between purity and totality, neither of which should be sacrificed.[23]

As we have already noted, Vincent's vocabulary is a clue to his understanding. He does not hesitate to use words indicating growth and development: *crescere* (to grow), *proficere* (to advance), *evolvere* (to unroll), *florere* (to flourish), *maturescere* (to ripen), and *enucleare* (to unfold). How could he be regarded as merely a cranky antiquarian? We need only add to these words that the growth Vincent sanctions is always homogeneous in kind—*idem sensus*—rejecting change that is simply covert heterogeneity.[24]

At Vatican II, Roman Catholicism sought to come to grips with the idea of tradition as both preservative and propulsive. One sees this, for example, in the Dogmatic Constitution on Revelation, *Dei Verbum* §8, where the council says, "Therefore the Apostles, handing on what they themselves had received, warn the faithful to hold fast to the traditions which they have learned either by word of mouth or by letter (2 Thess. 2:15), and to fight in defense of the faith handed on once and for all (Jude 1:3)." Yet this preservative dimension is complemented by the notion of growth:

> This tradition which comes from the Apostles develops in the Church with the help of the Holy Spirit. There is a growth in the understanding of the realities and the words which have been handed down. This happens through the contemplation and study made by believers, who treasure these things in their hearts (Luke 2:19, 51) through a penetrating understanding of the spiritual realities which they experience, and through the preaching of those who have received through episcopal succession the sure gift of truth. For through the unrolling centuries, the Church constantly moves forward toward the fullness of divine truth until the words of God reach their complete fulfillment in her.

For Vincent and for Christianity today, the questions are these: How can we preserve the purity of the gospel message while allowing for authentic and homogeneous growth? How can we know that a teaching has been developed *in eodem sensu*? If there can be growth, indeed *plane et maximus*, as Vincent firmly insists, then how is this legitimately reconciled with the Pauline injunction "Guard the deposit, Timothy"? Christian doctrines do not consist of abstractions: they are lived truths of salvation. Therefore each age must protect those fundamental biblical teachings that are the norm and measure by which any further development is judged. In a moment, we will examine test cases for growth, considering how Vincent would regard, for example, the teachings on Mary and the papacy as these have developed in the Roman Catholic Church. Are these examples of a harmonious unfolding over time? Or are they, rather, illegitimate and profane innovations? Before undertaking that task, let us again discuss the warrants adduced by Vincent to ensure that proper rather than corrosive development occurs.

Warrants for Proper Development

Essential for determining that any evolution is in full harmony with the prior tradition—*in eodem sensu*—are the ecclesial warrants, or *loci theologici*, that the Lérinian adduces. Earlier we noticed that the source of Vincent's second rule is the Vulgate translation of the apostle Paul's exhortation to the church at Corinth: "I implore you, brothers, that all of you agree in what you say, and that there be no divisions among you, but that you be united in the same mind and in the same judgment [*in eodem sensu et in eadem sententia*]" (1 Cor. 1:10; *Common.* 28.10). Here the apostle is urging Christians to speak with one voice. And this consentient unity is a primary concern of Vincent's. For the universal agreement of the church ensures that any proposed development is not actually a *permutatio* of the faith, sanctioned only by an idiosyncratic few and inexorably leading to heresy. The theologian of Lérins was well aware that one person's development is another's mutation. One person's legitimate reform is another's corrosive transformation. That is why his warrants, in their universality and imbricating, multilayered character, are so important. Only the sanction of several levels of the church's life—under the Spirit—may underwrite a proper development.

Vincent's point, then, is that truly organic and architectonic growth should be acknowledged by significant parts of the church—and this is why he insists, following the apostle Paul, on both universality and ubiquity. Consentient agreement prevents the church's faith and doctrine from illegitimate incursions by a small group of false teachers. In order to avoid a dangerous alteration, a change that is transformative of a doctrine's very nature and essence (*aliquid ex alio in aliud*), the church must seek, as far as possible, harmonious agreement. Lacking such concord, one purveys not the proper evolution of *res amplificetur* but the debasement of the faith.

Turning to the contemporary theological and ecumenical questions facing the church, we ask: How do we ensure a proper *profectus* that enriches the church rather than an adulterative *permutatio* that depraves it? Vincent would surely respond today just as he did in the early fifth century: this can only be accomplished *prima scriptura, deinde traditio*—first through Scriptures and then through the tradition of the church. And as we have seen, this living tradition consists in a variety of ecclesial sources. Indeed, one only understands the Vincentian canon if one sees that the truth of *semper, ubique, et ab omnibus* is known and preserved *in actu ecclesiae*, in the living and dynamic life of the church in all of its constitutive facets.

Which are Vincent's constitutive warrants? As we have seen, they are found in his answer to the question, "Who is the Timothy of today guarding the deposit? [*Quis est hodie Timotheus?*]" (22.2). Pride of place is always extended to Scripture, then to Scripture as properly interpreted by ecumenical councils, theological doctors, the faithful generally, and the bishop of Rome (with his colleagues). How can Vincent's warrants be fruitfully utilized today to fulfill the twin tasks of guarding Christian doctrine even while allowing for authentic development? In other words, how can there be faithful growth under the Holy Spirit?

Prima Scriptura

Vincent has already made clear that the canon of Scripture is "perfect and sufficient for all matters—indeed, more than sufficient [*ad omnia satis superque sufficiat*]" (2.2). But because of its profundity, Scripture needs to be joined to the interpretation of the church. And so the Lérinian insists that we demonstrate the faith in two ways: "first by the authority of the divine canon [Scripture], followed by the tradition of the Catholic church" (29.2). Later in the *Commonitorium*, he returns to his point: after Scripture, we rely on the tradition of the church, but this is "not because the canon alone does not suffice for every issue [*non quia canon solus non sibi ad universa sufficiat*]" (29.3).

In Vincent's work, then, an epistemic primacy is always accorded to Scripture. The Bible is the rule and rock on which all church practices and teachings are based. Even the proscription of the rebaptism of former apostates, classically adduced as an element known only through tradition, is defended by Vincent on the grounds that rebaptism is prohibited not only by the rule of the universal church but also by "the divine canon" (6.4). And even a cursory examination of the *Commonitorium* will demonstrate that the monk of Lérins, like all the early Christian writers, was deeply imbued with both the Old and New Testaments. At the same time, Scripture displays its full meaning in the universal and ancient tradition of the church.

When considering the contribution that Vincent might offer Christian thought today, we can surely say that he would appreciate the Reformation's accent on the unparalleled authority of God's Word as found in Scripture. For Vincent's reliance on the Bible colors every paragraph of the *Commonitorium*. He takes Scripture to be glowingly alive, not simply an ancient document handed down to us. When reflecting on the apostle's Paul's statement to the Galatians—"If anyone preaches to you a gospel other than the one we preached, even an angel from heaven, let him be anathema" (1:8)—he remarks that some think this condemnation is meant only for former times and not for the present. On the contrary, this precept must be carefully observed by every age (*Common.* 9.5). Scripture provides God's plan of salvation for the church and instructs us in a life of Christian discipleship. At the same time, rampant misinterpretations of the Bible have given rise to a rogues' gallery of heretics, whose errors continually plague the church and disrupt its unity. It is precisely because of these continual misinterpretations of Scripture that tradition—a multivalent complex of warrants—offers reliable guidance.

Vincent thus is no advocate of a bare *sola scriptura* and shows himself closer to the position often labeled *prima scriptura*. This latter position has been adopted by several contemporary Protestant thinkers, even if they continue using the traditional phrase.[25] *Sola scriptura* cannot be envisioned simply as an antitradition principle since the Reformers themselves were clearly committed to the apostolic confessions. As Kevin Vanhoozer says, "If *sola scriptura* means 'the Bible alone apart from the church and tradition,' it has no future. But this is not what *sola scriptura* means. *Sola scriptura* is a protest not against tradition as such but against the presumption that church tradition (interpretation) and Scripture (text) necessarily coincide."[26]

The coincidence of text and interpretation will occupy us momentarily. But it is Vanhoozer's description of what may be called *prima scriptura* that is of immediate importance. Any student of the history of doctrine knows that the early christological and trinitarian controversies were settled by Scripture and tradition rather than by Scripture (or by tradition) alone. One may turn, for example, to Basil's book *De spiritu sancto*, in which he roots the affirmation of the Holy Spirit as a divine person in Scripture, undoubtedly and at length, but he also takes full account of the doctrinal and liturgical traditions of the church. Basil pleads with his interlocutors, who regard the Spirit as a divine force or power but not as a unique *hypostasis*, to examine both Scripture and tradition in order to come to a fuller understanding of the Holy Trinity.[27]

Today Roman Catholics and Protestants have, for the most part, surpassed the traditional stereotypes clinging to the Scripture/tradition debate. As far back as the Faith and Order conference at Montreal in 1963, one may see Protestant churches insisting on the importance of tradition, thereby adopting a more complex notion of *sola scriptura*. Roman Catholic responses to Montreal argued that, in light of Vatican II, Rome had a much deeper appreciation of the primary importance of Scripture.[28] One would not likely say today, as Luther said at the time of the Reformation, "My opponents say, *Patres, Patres, statua, statua*. We respond, *Euangelion, Euangelion, Christus, Christus*."[29] This kind of dialectical relationship, with Christ and the Scriptures opposed to the fathers of the church and the foundational decrees of tradition, may exist in certain circles, but it is surely no longer as pronounced.

While ardently defending the sovereignty of Scripture, Vincent advances a subtle understanding of the church's authority in interpreting God's Word. Looking around at the heretics of his day, Vincent is distrustful of those who invoke Scripture too easily, apart from the consentient authority of the church. He tells us, humorously, that heretics say almost nothing on their own without obscuring it with the words of Scripture (*Common.* 25.2). And he warns that heretics always have "a thousand biblical citations at hand [*mille testimonia*]" (26.7) and are ever ready to "scamper" through the writings of Moses, the Prophets, and the apostle Paul. Like Satan himself, they conclude their arguments with the statement "So it is written" (26.6).

The true meaning of Scripture, however, is to be found in determinate but crucially nuanced elements of ecclesial life. This is the crux of Vincent's response to the question "Who is the Timothy of today guarding the deposit?" For the Lérinian, a variety of "courts" are necessary to guard the deposit faithfully, to interpret Scripture correctly. He places great emphasis on the body of bishops/overseers, particularly when gathered in council, as had already occurred at the great synods of Nicaea (325) and Ephesus (431). And he observes that the faithful at large are also bearers of the truth, as they, under the Spirit, preserve the deposit by their natural *instinctus* for Christian truth. This is why Vincent states flatly that the deposit is secured by "the universal church generally or, specifically, the entire body of overseers/bishops [*vel generaliter universa ecclesia vel specialiter totum corpus praepositorum*]" (22.2).

In all cases, Vincent emphasizes the importance of consensus within the interpretative tradition. There must be a *consensus* of bishops in council; a *consensus* of holy, learned, and confessing doctors; and a *consensus* of the faithful generally. The bishop of Rome is dealt with as an individual, but even here, he speaks *with* the other bishops, as Stephen did in the controversy over rebaptism. Popes Celestine and Sixtus speak as individuals, but *individuals bound by the prior tradition*. Idiosyncrasy in interpretation is a sure mark of error. As Vincent insists, "Even a holy and learned man, even a bishop, even a confessor and martyr" is holding only a personal opinion if he advances some position that is "other than all or even against all [*praeter omnes aut etiam contra omnes*]" (28.8). Even the shedding of one's blood for Christ constitutes no conclusive proof of the orthodoxy of one's interpretations.

Let us now return to Vanhoozer's comment above, that the phrase *sola scriptura* is intended as a protest not against tradition but against the presumption that ecclesial tradition and Scripture necessarily coincide. Protestantism has traditionally asked important questions: How may Scripture function as a critical principle *over and against* ecclesial tradition? How can there be an actual *Gegenüber*, a true confrontation of the church with its norm?[30] Is not the power of the Reformation critique precisely its resistance to melting the Bible into ecclesial tradition? And did not Jesus himself express reservations about certain traditions (e.g., Mark 7:7–9)?

Vanhoozer's understandable fears about the presumed identity between Scripture and ecclesial tradition may be somewhat eased by the fact that in contemporary Roman Catholicism, tradition itself must be underwritten, at least implicitly, by Scripture. The essential truth of *prima scriptura*, that the church must always be *ecclesia audiens* in order to be *ecclesia docens*, is never in doubt today. Roman Catholic theologians do not hesitate to speak of the material sufficiency of Scripture for the truths of salvation. In fact, it is commonly held that Scripture is the essential touchstone for all statements, including papal and conciliar decisions.[31] And this is not a new teaching. Thomas Aquinas himself had said, in a famous comment, "Canonical Scripture alone is the rule of faith [*sola canonica scriptura est regula fidei*]."[32] In their own sense, then, Roman Catholics will speak of the articles of faith as needing the warrant of the Word, as the Reformation insisted. And while some Protestant Christians may think that the two-source theory is still hegemonic within Roman Catholicism (with Scripture and tradition placed on entirely equal footing), historical research has shown that the language of two sources is largely a post-Tridentine phenomenon rather than rooted in the Council of Trent itself (1545–63).[33] In fact, the idea of two different but equal sources has long been buried in Roman Catholic thought.

Such elucidations may still not entirely ease traditional Protestant concerns about the enmeshment of Scripture with ecclesial interpretation and the ruling presumption of identity between the two. Vincent's thought may be useful here since, by appealing to a variety of theological "courts," he is insisting on consentient unity as a condition for sanctioning such identity. How can we make continuing sense of the Pauline injunction, "Guard the deposit, Timothy"? Vincent is convinced that the "Timothy" of today is enshrined in several interpretative spheres within the church—all under the Holy Spirit, and each with some pivotal role to play. The Lérinian's multilayered notion of tradition contravenes any naive identity between Scripture and church teaching.

It is true that tradition, taken in a broad sense, provides the normative context within which Scripture is rightly understood. But even this essentially ecclesial context of tradition does not detract from Scripture's uniqueness. As Congar says, "Scripture has an absolute sovereignty; it is of divine origin, even in its literary form; it governs Tradition and the Church, whereas it is not governed by Tradition or the Church."[34]

Similarly, he writes, "Exactly the same value, therefore, should not be attributed to *tradition* and to the holy Scriptures, even if they are paid the same respect. The holy Scriptures have an absolute value that tradition has not. . . . If tradition or the Magisterium claimed to teach something contradicting the Holy Scriptures, it would certainly be false, and the faithful ought to reject it."[35]

Several of Congar's ideas were synthesized in a 1995 encyclical by John Paul II, who sought to cut the Gordian knot complicating the debates on Scripture and tradition. The pope speaks of "Sacred Scripture as the highest authority in matters of faith and Sacred Tradition as indispensable to the interpretation of the Word of God" (*Ut unum sint* §79). This statement is a forceful testimony to the idea of *prima scriptura*, insisting on the primary importance of the Scriptures, even if tradition can never be regarded as inessential.

Any development that takes place in the church, then, must be firmly rooted in the Bible, "the highest authority in matters of faith." Scripture is the most foundational warrant, always determinative in deciding if growth is a *profectus* or a *permutatio*.[36] With this formulation, Vincent would be in full agreement.

Ecumenical Councils

As we have seen, the hallmarks of universality, ubiquity, and antiquity are, for Vincent, not an asymptotic ideal but an actually incarnated reality found in the living tradition of the church, particularly in ecumenical councils. How does one distinguish an illegitimate innovation, a profane novelty, from a *profectus*, a legitimate advance? Vincent's answer, encapsulated in his first rule, is through an ecumenical council, through the *corpus praepositorum*. He cannot imagine that the consentient unity of the bishops/overseers, who represent the church in its universality and ubiquity, will not also teach the apostolic tradition, which has been handed down. As Vincent says, one must always prefer antiquity to novelty; and "within antiquity itself, to the boldness of the opinions of one or a few, there should be preferred, before all, if there be such, the general decrees of a universal council" (*Common.* 27.4). Councils, in their definitive teaching, establish the "landmarks" that cannot be transgressed. The acceptance of Arianism by the emperor Constantius II—as well as the fraudulent hoodwinking of many bishops at Ariminum in 359— displays a common fault: the trading of established antiquity for profane novelty, thereby contravening the boundaries of both Scripture and legitimate tradition. "Profane and novel curiosity refused to contain itself within the chaste limits of a holy and incorrupt antiquity" (4.7).

When gathered in council, the body (*corpus*) of bishops/overseers constitutes a uniquely authoritative group. Vincent's use of the word *corpus* is of interest because, as we have seen, when discussing the heretical and Pelagian bishop Julian of Eclanum, Vincent says that Julian neglected to unite himself (*incorporare*) to the interpretation (*sensus*) held by his colleagues and so separated himself (*excorporare*) from them (28.15). When a bishop gives himself over to idiosyncratic teaching (such as Julian or Nestorius), apart from the general consensus of the episcopal body, tragedy necessarily ensues. This is why Vincent firmly condemns Nestorius, who was convinced of his solitary genius and who therefore challenged the universal teaching of the church: His error was to think of himself as "the first and only one to understand Scripture. All the others before him had misunderstood it: all the bishops, all the confessors, and all the martyrs." The entire church, prior to Nestorius, "was now in error and had always been in error, following ignorant and erroneous teachers [*doctores*]" (31.6–7). But ecumenical councils are just the opposite of maverick and idiosyncratic teaching. They convoke bishops/overseers from the universal church for the sake of confirming the apostolic tradition.

Looking at the contemporary church, Vincent would continue to sanction ecumenical councils and endorse their ability to interpret the Bible in a trustworthy manner, "unfolding/disclosing [Christian teaching] more distinctly and explicitly [*distinctius et expressius enucleemus*]" (13.5).[37] But Vincent would find it difficult to see the notes of universality and ubiquity fully protected today. He would, no doubt, have appreciated the herculean efforts of Paul VI to ensure that the decrees passed by Vatican II did so with overwhelming majorities, thus ensuring consentient unity. For example, the final vote on *Lumen Gentium* (1964), the Dogmatic Constitution on the Church, was passed with over two thousand bishops in favor and with only five opposed, an extraordinary consensus for a document that clearly reformed aspects of the immediately prior tradition. But while Vincent would no doubt appreciate

Paul VI's labors, councils held without significant swaths of the *pars Orientis* would likely be confusing (and even scandalous) to him. Consentient unity is the most important hallmark for Vincent. Only this kind of consensus can properly protect the *depositum* while simultaneously ensuring that any development is organic rather than adulterative. Anything less than a unified church courts the possibility of depraving ecclesial teaching.

For many decades now, theologians have reflected on the nature of universal councils. Ecumenically minded Roman Catholic authors have generally sought to mitigate the authority of at least some (minor) councils recognized as authentic. Even the number of councils traditionally acknowledged by Roman Catholicism has been called into question. As several authors have recognized, the commonly accepted list of councils was established by Robert Bellarmine, a seventeenth-century theologian, but his list has no authoritative status.[38] Vittorio Peri, for example, who had done excellent historical work on the councils, states that at the end of the first millennium, only seven councils were recognized by both East and West. The Fourth Council of Constantinople (869–70), which condemned Photios, was only added (in the West) in the eleventh century. And in the fifteenth century, the Council of Florence, traditionally denominated by Rome as the eighth ecumenical council, was now numbered at sixteen (and later, at seventeen).[39]

Many contemporary Roman Catholic theologians agree with Louis Bouyer's statement: "The Catholic Church of the West and the Orthodox Church of the East have never ceased being *one* church." But if this is truly the case, it inexorably raises the question, "Can the general councils held in the West be considered fully ecumenical?" Bouyer argues that the Latin Middle Ages never put the general Western councils on precisely the same footing as the first seven ecumenical councils of antiquity. Only since Bellarmine have the medieval councils been regarded as ecumenical in nature.[40] This does not mean, Bouyer continues, that a partial council cannot give definitive expression to the "mind of the church [*mens ecclesiae*]," particularly those councils with a substantial episcopal representation, confirmed by the bishop of Rome. Nonetheless, because a considerable part of the episcopate—itself representing an ancient tradition—was absent from these Western councils, Bouyer suggests that these general councils may be in need of supplementation (with Eastern concerns added), even if their dogmatic decisions remain irreformable.

Bouyer's point echoes that of Paul VI, who, in a quiet attempt to further Christian unity, spoke of Western "synods" when referring to certain medieval councils. In a letter to Cardinal Willebrands, his representative at the seventh-centenary celebration (1974) of the Second Council of Lyons, the pope alluded to "the Council of Lyons, which is counted as the sixth among the General Synods celebrated in the Western world in 1274."[41] Here Paul seems to be regarding four of the Lateran councils and the First Council of Lyons as merely Western synods rather than as full-fledged ecumenical councils (a practice common before Bellarmine).

This question of the status of lesser, "general" councils necessarily raises the issue of analogy and participation.[42] Should Roman Catholics, as Congar suggests, recognize that there is a hierarchy of importance among ecumenical councils, just as Vatican II teaches there is a hierarchy of fundamental (doctrinal) truths?[43] The idea of a hierarchy of councils is important and is itself rooted in the earlier tradition. As Newman says, Pope Gregory I, though living after the fifth ecumenical council, does not hesitate to compare the first four councils to the four Gospels.[44] And Congar adduces significant evidence for regarding the first four councils as *principalia concilia*.[45] The young Newman adds that "some councils speak far more authoritatively than others, though all which appeal to Tradition may be presumed to have some element of truth in them."[46]

For the Reformers, the chief warrant for underwriting church doctrine—even those teachings emanating from universal councils—certainly must be Scripture itself, a claim with which Vincent would surely agree.[47] Luther feared that the authority of the inspired Word of God had been replaced by the authority of the church, giving rise to the concern—voiced by Vanhoozer—that the teaching of Scripture was now presumed to coincide with ecclesial teaching, resulting in the loss of Scripture's critical power. But as we have seen, Vincent always exalts the preeminent authority of Scripture and certainly makes no claims for the authority of the church over or against the Word of God. Yet at least on major questions, he does see a circumincession (*perichōrēsis*, reciprocal existence) between the Bible and ecumenical councils. Such councils, in their consentient agreement on the meaning of Scripture, are the living embodiment of Vincent's criteria of always, everywhere, and by everyone. Indeed, the agreement evidenced by such councils—modeled on the apostle Paul's call for unity in 1 Cor. 1:10—prevents idiosyncratic and maverick interpretations of Scripture, interpretations all too prevalent in the early church and still today. Consequently, when Vincent claims, on biblical grounds, that one must not "transgress the landmarks" or "break through the hedge," he is actually arguing that definitive doctrinal markers authoritatively established by the universal church cannot be reversed. The solemn *decreta* of plenary councils—taught at Nicaea and Ephesus—are binding and cannot be contravened (*Common.* 3.6; 27.4; 33.6). In their definitive teachings, then, ecumenical councils represent the universal and ancient faith of the church and thus ensure the faithful interpretation of God's Word.

Luther (and Calvin as well) accepted the four ancient councils—Nicaea (325), Constantinople (381), Ephesus (431), and Chalcedon (451)—as having been warranted by the claims of Scripture. But Samuel M. Powell remarks that, while the Reformers accepted the four early councils, "Luther and Melanchthon had unwittingly driven a wedge between creeds and Bible by insisting that the

creeds are subject to inspection and criticism according to their agreement
with the Bible." The Reformers were convinced that the early creeds restated
biblical teaching, but their subordination of creeds to Scriptures "open[ed]
up the possibility of later theologians finding tension and even contradiction
between creed and Bible."[48] Vincent himself, while agreeing with the Reformers
that Scripture must be the *fons et origo* (source and origin) of every church
teaching, would be extremely hesitant about opening any divide between the
Scriptures and the definitive teachings of a plenary council. Once such division occurs, the consentient unity of the church is thrown into confusion, the
monuments established by the fathers are transgressed, the hedge is broken
through. This is precisely what occurred at Ariminum when the Creed of
Nicaea was called into question on the grounds that *homoousios* was not a
biblical word. It is no surprise, then, that when speaking of the Council of
Ephesus, Vincent does so in solemn tones: the "opinions of the holy fathers
have been gathered . . . by the decree and authority of a council, so that that
the rule of the church's faith [*ecclesiasticae fidei regula*] may be fixed" (*Common.* 28.16). The teachings of Ephesus involved "definitively laying down
the rules of faith [*fidei regulis*]" (29.8). And the council "pronounced on the
rules of faith [*de fidei regulis pronuntiavit*]" (30.6). Ecumenical councils, in
their definitive and formal statements, bespeak the judgment of the universal
church, handing on the apostolic tradition and developing it in a manner
congruous with prior teaching—as *homoousios* and *Theotokos* bear witness. To oppose the universal and definitive teaching of ecumenical councils,
therefore, is to oppose the *semper, ubique, et ab omnibus*. Such opposition
fails to see the profound unity between Scripture and the doctrinal teachings
of the church universal.

Today Christianity faces the challenge of significant divisions. The Roman
Catholic church continues to convoke councils, but as mentioned earlier, Vin-
cent would likely have concerns about an assembly that does not include all
Christians and, most notably, omits certain segments of the ancient East.
For the Lérinian, the *depositum* can be properly protected, and an authentic
profectus warranted, only with the consentient unity of the entire church.
But even with this objection noted, the continual convocations of councils in
Roman Catholicism, particularly the recent Vatican II, allow us to see certain
of Vincent's principles at work. Most important, one sees the essential conflu-
ence of the first and second rules: for Vatican II seeks to vigilantly protect the
deposit of faith even while allowing for legitimate advances—undertakings
equally sanctioned by the Lérinian.

For Vincent, as we have seen, authoritative conciliar teachings and creeds
are binding truths, unimpeachable and irreversible interpretations of Scripture. However, his insistence on the irrevocability of solemn teachings is not
intended to put an end to theological reflection. As Vincent himself comments,
"For what has ever been the goal of councils, than that what was believed in

simplicity, the same can now be believed reflectively; that what was previously preached languorously, can now be preached vigorously; that what was before honored neglectfully, can now be attended to with solicitude?" (23.18). This statement, taken together with Vincent's examples of congruent development— with a child becoming an adult and a seed growing into a plant—testifies not only to the *noviter, non nova* (speak newly, but not new things), but also to the harmonious growth that occurs at councils and is further stimulated by them. Councils sum up definitive teaching even while giving rise to further reflection. Karl Rahner, for example, insists that while the church teaches definitively at ecumenical councils, councils are never exhaustive; they serve, rather, as catalysts for the continued exploration of the mysteries of faith: "The clearest formulations, the most sanctified formulas, the classic condensations of the centuries-long work of the Church in prayer, reflection and struggle concerning God's mysteries: all these derive their life from the fact that they [conciliar formulations] are not end but beginning."[49] There is, then, always room for expansion and counterbalance, for clarifications and reformulations, even while clearly maintaining the stable continuity of fundamental meaning (*idem sensus*). In such comments, one sees displayed the Vincentian teaching that developments newly illuminate some aspect of the Christian faith, yet they must be in organic continuity with the prior *regula fidei*.

Ultimately, for Vincent, ecumenical councils are the primary locus of the church's universal teaching mission. The consentient agreement of bishops/overseers from around the world assures that the Sacred Scriptures are properly interpreted, that apostolic tradition is authentically transmitted, and that developments are *in eodem sensu eademque sententia* with the prior tradition.[50] It has often been suggested that Christian unity may be based on Sacred Scripture, the first councils, and the creeds of the early church. This great shared heritage of faith should never be minimized, even if in our day we have become used to reciting this common patrimony. As the ecumenical movement continues, perhaps the councils of the second millennium offer an opportunity for discussion and even reception (with further supplementation) by the Eastern Orthodox churches and, to the extent possible, by the churches of the Reformation as well.[51]

Theological Doctors

Vincent holds theological masters in great esteem, and they are to be consulted on all questions that have not been decided by ecumenical councils. As he says, "Within antiquity itself, to the boldness of the opinions of one or a few, there should be preferred, before all else, the general decrees of a universal council, although if none exists on a particular matter, then that which is next best, the opinion of numerous and important theological masters" (*Common.* 27.4). What Vincent understands by this is clear when he says that, lacking the teaching of a council, one must consult the authorized masters (*magistri probabiles*), interrogating those who, while living in various places and at diverse times, continue in the communion and faith of the Catholic church. On disputed issues, they must speak frequently, openly, and "with one and the same consent [*uno eodemque consensus*]" (3.4) on a disputed matter. If one finds this kind of universal affirmation among trusted doctors, then one can believe their teachings without hesitation. Vincent offers examples of such masters with his citation of those teachers (and bishops) acknowledged by the Council of Ephesus. He singles out some for admiration: Cyril of Alexandria as well as the "lights of Cappadocia," Basil, Gregory Nazianzen, and Gregory of Nyssa, along with Cyprian and Ambrose from the West (30.3–5). The monk of Lérins insists that theological doctors must be learned, but they must also remain in the confession of the faith, living in a manner that is holy, wise, and constant, counted worthy to die faithfully in Christ or to be happily martyred for the Lord (28.6). For Vincent, sanctity and learning are inseparable in theologians trusted by the church.

As with all Christians, but more intensely because of their unique status, theological doctors are to pass on that which was transmitted to them: "The same things that you were taught, teach [*eadem tamen quae didicisti, doce*]" (22.7). Because of their ingenuity, theologians can be led astray, becoming a trial for the church of God: "All true Catholics know that they ought to listen to the doctors [*doctores*] *with* the church, and not, by following the doctors, *abandon* the church's faith" (17.2, emphasis added). The Lérinian was all too aware of the examples of Origen and Tertullian, to whom he devotes a considerable amount of space. Some of their insights are of great value. Indeed, Vincent poignantly remarks, "Who would not rather be wrong with Origen than right with anyone else?" (17.12). And of Tertullian he exclaims, "Every sentence was a victory!" (18.4). But even the incomparable Origen and the brilliant Tertullian led Christians astray, following their own ideas rather than the faith of the church. Idiosyncratic doctors (no matter their personal genius), like idiosyncratic bishops (Nestorius, Julian of Eclanum), constitute a great trial for Christianity. This is why Vincent insists:

> The deposit (of faith) is that which has been confided to you, not that which you have discovered; it is that which you have received, not that which you invented; it is something not of your personal ingenuity, but of doctrine; not something that is private, but which belongs to public tradition; it is something which has been given to you, not created by you. You are not the deposit's author, but its guardian; you are not its initiator, but its follower; you are not its leader, but its disciple [*non ducens sed sequens*]. (22.4)

Theologians, Vincent avers, must proceed under God's Word as it has been transmitted to them. Timothy himself, with whom the apostle Paul pleads to guard the deposit, is a doctor and interpreter of the faith (*O tractator! O doctor!*) and thus stands as a steadfast example (22.6).

But Vincent's strongly preservative instincts do not militate against authentic development. To claim otherwise would be to render the Lérinian's careful chapter on growth entirely unintelligible (as indeed it is to those who simply stress the Vincentian canon). After all, he was well aware that Origen in the East and Tertullian in the West had helped the church to establish a precise trinitarian vocabulary, with faith in the one God existing in three *hypostases* (Greek), or *personae* (Latin). This terminological precision is evident in Vincent as well, indicating his own status as a faithful theological master. He tells us that in the Trinity there is "another and another person, but not another and another nature [*alius atque alius, non aliud atque aliud*]," just as in the Savior there is "another and another nature, but not another and another person [*aliud atque aliud, non alius atque alius*]" (13.5). He acknowledges that *homoousios* (Christ's same essence with God) is a word superseding anything found in Scripture. And he is well aware that the recently concluded Council of Ephesus (431) had denominated Mary as *Theotokos* (God-bearer), a name indicating theological sophistication about predicates attributable to both the human and divine natures of Christ. As Vincent announces at the beginning of his chapters on the Trinity and the incarnation, he is simply "unfolding/disclosing [doctrine] more distinctly and explicitly [*distinctius et expressius enucleemus*]" (13.5). This is a significant phrase because "unfolding" is precisely what is taking place. The theologian of Lérins is displaying how the biblical texts have been understood and developed over the course of time.

Theological doctors, then, render a great service to the church, helping all to understand the faith delivered in ancient Israel and in Christ. Collectively, they constitute the Bezalel of today (Exod. 31:2–5), shaping the precious gems of divine doctrine with wisdom and skill, arranging them with splendor, grace, and beauty (*Common.* 22.6). Precisely here we need to remember Vincent's challenging comments about development:

> It is necessary, therefore, that understanding, knowledge, and wisdom should grow [*crescat*] and advance [*proficiat*] vigorously in individuals as well as in the community, in a single person as well as in the whole church, and this gradually in the course of ages and centuries. But this progress must be made according to its own type, that is, in accord with the same doctrine, the same meaning, and the same judgment [*eodem sensu eademque sententia*]. (23.3)

But how do "understanding, knowledge, and wisdom" advance, as Vincent insists? Theologians are one of the chief artisans of such growth: the apostle Paul designates them (*doctores*) in third place among the gifts bestowed upon the church (1 Cor. 12:28 Vulg.; *Common.* 28.9). Because of this, they are to be held in high esteem whenever they teach a doctrine with one voice. If someone dares to despise the doctors when they teach unanimously in Christ, that person "condemns not humans, but God himself" (28.10).

The significant role that Vincent envisions for theologians in preserving and developing doctrine has long been a feature of Christian history. In the medieval period, one sees the same approach in Thomas Aquinas, who accented the unique role of theological doctors and distinguished between the *magisterium cathedrae pastoralis* and the *magisterium cathedrae magistralis*—between the pastoral teaching chair of bishops and the magisterial teaching chair of theologians. In our own day, the American theologian Avery Dulles creatively retrieved this distinction, arguing that in the church there is a dual teaching office, that of bishops/overseers, who establish official doctrine, and that of theologians, who investigate the faith with the tools of critical scholarship.[52] Luther launched his reformation of the church on the basis of his expertise both as an exegete and a theologian. He insisted that the clear word of Scripture could repristinate the church by pruning the excesses and illegitimate developments he perceived in his day, all of which distracted from Christ's unique salvific work.[53] And historians have shown the important role that theologians have played in church councils of various kinds.[54]

In the nineteenth century, as we have seen, John Henry Newman bestowed an exalted place on theology and theologians. As a young Anglican thinker, he sought to establish, on the basis of a careful reading of the church fathers, a via media between Protestantism and Roman Catholicism. Later in life, he continually defended the importance of theology, going so far as to say: "Theology is the fundamental and regulating principle of the whole Church system. It is commensurate with Revelation, and Revelation is the initial and essential idea of Christianity."[55] Newman further insisted that before ecclesial authority makes a decision on a serious matter, an issue should be widely discussed—preferably for decades and even centuries—and in a variety of theological courts. Theologians are expected to examine a question from every perspective before some definitive step—a *profectus*—is taken by the entire church. For Newman, then, theologians continually exercise a significant magisterial role, even if not the ultimate one.

Within Roman Catholicism, the important role of theologians was clearly evidenced at Vatican II. For example, the 1928 papal encyclical *Mortalium animos* had appeared to rule out any Roman Catholic involvement with the ecumenical movement. At Vatican II, however, such involvement—which had been widely endorsed by theologians—was sanctioned as legitimate and constitutive. Similarly, the issue of religious freedom had been fervently discussed by theologians for decades before Vatican II took the bold step of insisting on a new relationship between church and state, concluding that while Christians unhesitatingly affirm that Jesus is the universal Savior, the freedom and dignity of humanity is such that they have a right to worship God other than in Jesus Christ. As the young Joseph Ratzinger said soon after the document on religious freedom was approved: "There was in St. Peter's the sense that here was the end of the Middle Ages, the end even of the Constantinian age."[56]

As we all know, in every Christian church today, there is animated discussion over a variety of doctrinal and moral issues as theologians seek to determine to what extent new proposals are *in eodem sensu* or *in alieno sensu* with the gospel and prior authoritative tradition. In just such discernment, one sees the continuing importance of theological doctors who are both learned and faithful to the church. Vincent's multilayered understanding of authority, of the witnesses to be consulted when deciding on any authentic advance, is intended to ensure the consentient unity of the entire church, thereby protecting against an illegitimate and corrosive *permutatio fidei*. As with all matters in Vincent, his accent is on the *consensus* of holy, learned, and faithful theological doctors. Individual masters, like idiosyncratic bishops, can easily go astray. It is the image of a solid body of authorized theologians (*auctores probati*), a unified council of doctors (*magistrorum concilio*) deeply familiar with Christian teaching, that always dominates his thinking (28.7).

Today theologians continue to help the church determine whether some proposal depraves the deposit of faith or whether, in a way not always clearly seen, is congruent with it. Theologians are, as one nineteenth-century author said, "the artisan(s) of the development of dogma."[57] They necessarily propose new ideas that appear to be complementary to, and in harmony with, "the faith once delivered to the saints," developing but never contravening the established landmarks. Deciding whether a new proposal is truly *in eodem sensu* or *in alieno sensu* with the gospel is not always immediately clear; it is a work of time and of the Holy Spirit. Because of some initial vagueness, the creatively faithful task that theologians undertake can lead to friction with ecclesiastical authorities. But since the church is a living, organic body, any friction between theologians and authorities—if not hostile and if expressed within the bonds of *communio*, which must characterize various elements within the church—can lead to a productive and healthy examination of a disputed question.[58]

The Christian Faithful (the Saints)

When Vincent lays down his famous canon—only that is to be believed which has been held *semper, ubique, et ab omnibus*—he is primarily referring to the teachings and creeds of ecumenical councils. Because they hand on the apostolic tradition, councils preeminently establish the "landmarks" that may not be transgressed. However, as we have seen, the "Timothy of today," charged with the Pauline task of guarding the deposit, is not limited to the *corpus praepositorum*, but includes also "the universal church generally" (*Common.* 22.2). With this insight, Vincent is groping for the proper role of the Christian faithful both in guarding the deposit of revelation and in assuring its proper development.

As the Lérinian said, in a crucial passage, "It is necessary, therefore, that understanding, knowledge, and wisdom should grow [*crescat*] and advance [*proficiat*] vigorously *in individuals as well as in the community, in a single person as well as in the whole church*, and this gradually in the course of ages and centuries" (23.3, emphasis added). The Christian faithful, both as individuals and as a community, are involved in the growth of understanding and knowledge, which are the hallmarks of authentic progress. The "saints" possess, one might say, an *instinctus* for the truth of Christian doctrine, an inner sense of whether some proposed development coheres with their firm faith in Christ.

Vincent's conviction that the faithful have a sure grasp of Christian belief is a teaching reiterated in our own times. For example, Eastern Orthodox writers often make reference to the patriarchal letter of 1848 wherein the faithful are referred to as the "shields" of Christian belief, while the bishops are denominated as "judges."[59] A few years later (in 1854), Pius IX, in his bull *Ineffabilis Deus* (proclaiming the teaching that Mary, the Mother of God, was born without taint of sin), writes that one reason for the suitability of this doctrinal definition is the "unique breathing together [*conspiratio singularis*]" of pastors and the faithful. Commenting on just this passage, John Henry Newman says, "*Conspiratio*; the two, the Church teaching and the Church taught, are put together, as one twofold testimony, illustrating each other and never to be divided."[60] Here Newman's accent is on the witness of the faithful: along with their pastors, they ensure that any development of Christian doctrine is a proper *profectus* and not a pernicious *permutatio fidei*.

Newman also assigned an important role to the Christian faithful in the decades immediately following the Council of Nicaea. He argued that while many bishops vacillated in their defense of the council, the faithful displayed fortitude in their firm adherence to orthodoxy. Although Newman's historiography has been challenged in recent decades, his cardinal principle, that the faithful possess an instinct, or *phronēma*, for preserving Christian truth against novelty, remains valid and surely is deeply Vincentian.[61] One essential element in both Vincent's and Newman's theology is that a proposed development can only be authenticated if it has the support of the entire church, with its polycentric warrants. As Newman says, none of the channels of the church's tradition "may be treated with disrespect," since the apostolic tradition, rooted in Scripture, is variously displayed by bishops, theological doctors, people, liturgies, and even the events of history.[62] The consensus of the universal church, proceeding under the authority of Scripture, is the best indication of a proper development over time.

In Roman Catholicism this marked accent on what might be called the epistemological role of the faithful came more explicitly to the fore at Vatican II, which also accents the *conspiratio pastorum ac fidelium*.[63] The council promulgated an ecclesiology highlighting the unity of the baptized, clearly affirming that the people of God participate in Christ's priestly and prophetic offices. It holds that in their witness to the faith, "bishops and [the] faithful display a unique harmony [*singularis . . . conspiratio*]" (*Dei Verbum* §10). Consequently the Christian people, anointed by the Holy One, "are unable to err in matters of belief" and manifest this property "by means of the supernatural sense of faith of all the people, when 'from the bishops to the last of the lay faithful' they show their universal consensus in matters of faith and morals." *Lumen Gentium* (§12) adds that by this *sensus fidei*, itself sustained by the Spirit, the faithful "adhere indefectibly to 'the faith once delivered to the saints,' penetrating it more profoundly with right judgment and applying it more fully to life." These passages clearly emphasize the Spirit-guided instinct, or *phronēma*, of the faithful for Christian truth, their charism for discerning it more acutely, and their catholic consensus, which cannot be ultimately flawed. Yves Congar astutely observes that in every age this consensus of the faithful, along with the consensus of those charged to teach them, has been regarded as a guarantee of truth "not because of some *mystique* of universal suffrage," but because of the gospel principle that unanimity in Christian matters indicates the work of the Spirit.[64] It is precisely this pneumatological understanding of the Spirit at work in the *entire* church that animates Vincent's thought as well as many contemporary ecclesiological developments.

One may see the theological weight of the Christian faithful *in actu* in a 2007 document discussing the fate of infants who die without baptism, published by the International Theological Commission of the Roman Catholic Church.[65] This issue has a long theological history, one that in the West was decisively shaped by Augustine. It was Augustine's teaching that ultimately gave rise to the hypothesis of "limbo," the alleged destiny of unbaptized infants affected by original sin (but innocent of personal sin), who enjoy natural beatitude but not the vision of God. One sentence in the document indicates the crucial role of the faithful in determining whether a proposed teaching is in harmony with the gospel (*in eodem sensu*) or foreign to it (*in alieno sensu*). In reviewing the history of thought on the fate of unbaptized infants, the International Theological Commission states, "An important reason for the failure of attempts to get Vatican II to teach that unbaptized infants are definitely deprived of the vision of God was the testimony of bishops that that was not the faith of their people; it did not correspond to the *sensus fidelium*" (Hope of Salvation §96). This sentence provides a contemporary indication of the kind of interrelationship that must exist among the various warrants that Vincent identifies for properly underwriting doctrinal development. Scripture is authentically interpreted by ecumenical councils, theological doctors, the faithful generally, and the bishop of Rome. It is the entire Christian church, the living body of Christ, that organically hands on the tradition, authenticating any legitimate growth. Vincent would certainly defend the claim that in every age, God's faithful people have a significant role both in preserving and in developing

Christian belief. Contemporary theology similarly acknowledges that all the channels of tradition—including the *instinctus* of the faithful—must be in continual dialogue in order to reach a proper understanding of Christian truth.[66]

The Bishop of Rome

As Vincent tells us, his prior comments (on councils, doctors, and the faithful) are sufficient to destroy profane novelties: "However, so that nothing is lacking in the completeness of the argument we have added, at the end, the twofold authority of the apostolic see" (*Common.* 32.1). Vincent is referring to the recent teaching against innovation advanced by Popes Celestine and Sixtus. Both follow their predecessor, Stephen, who had enunciated the crucial principle about the deposit of faith: "Let there be no innovation except what has been handed down [*nihil novandum, nisi quod traditum est*]" (6.6). Vincent further tells us that Sixtus had written to the bishop of Antioch concerning the error of Nestorius, stating, "Let no concession be made to novelty since nothing should be added to antiquity" (32.3). The theologian of Lérins turns to the bishop of Rome, then, as one significant warrant for guarding the truth of the Christian faith.

As earlier noted, Vincent refers to Pope Stephen, bishop of the apostolic see (*apostolicae sedis antistes*), as "with his colleagues, but nevertheless in the forefront of them, surpassing the others, I think, by the devotion of his faith, just as he surpassed them by the authority of his see [*loci auctoritate*]" (6.5). And the Lérinian uses the strong verbal form *sanxit* (fixed and decreed) when referring to Stephen's dictum "Let there be no innovation." This same verb is used by Vincent when referring to the Council of Ephesus (431) as definitively "laying down the rules of faith [*de sanciendis fidei regulis*]" (29.8). Further, throughout the *Commonitorium* only the bishop of Rome is referred to as "pope" and only Rome as the "apostolic see," although the titles were in wide usage at the time. Of the significant authority of the bishop of Rome in Vincent's work, there is no doubt.

The Lérinian also shows himself to be deeply aware of the proceedings of the Council of Ephesus, as the last chapters of the *Commonitorium* clearly display. Moxon even speculates that the supposedly "lost" second book of the *Commonitorium* likely deals with the proceedings of the Ephesine Council in great detail. Because such minutiae would have taxed the reader's interest, it was not preserved and remained unpublished. If Moxon's surmise is true, then Vincent would likely have been familiar with the well-known passage, read by the papal legate Philip at Ephesus:

> There is no doubt, and in fact it has been known in all ages, that the holy and
> most blessed Peter, prince and head of the apostles, pillar of the faith, and foun-
> dation of the Catholic Church, received the keys of the kingdom from our Lord

Jesus Christ, . . . and that to Peter was given the power of loosing and binding sins: who, even to this time and always, lives and judges in his successors. Our holy and most blessed pope Celestine the bishop is according to due order his successor and holds his place.[67]

Vincent never refers to this statement, but there is no reason to think he would disagree with it. He would surely add, however, that even the bishop of Rome teaches in concert with the other bishops/overseers. Interpretative authority is always best exercised in consentient unity, as 1 Cor. 1:10 makes clear.[68] While leaving the precise role of the bishop of Rome undefined, the Lérinian nonetheless regards the pope as possessing a unique authority in ensuring that the deposit of faith is vigilantly protected and that any *profectus* is in strict accord with the prior tradition. But equally true is that this primacy is always exercised within the universal college of bishops/overseers (the *corpus praepositorum*) and in concert with the other essential *loci* (ecumenical councils, doctors, the faithful) by which a *permutatio fidei* is avoided. After all, when enumerating his warrants for underwriting Christian doctrine, Vincent turns to the bishop of Rome last rather than first. From a *formal* point of view, then, Vincent would likely agree with Luther's well-known statement in the *Babylonian Captivity of the Church*: "Only that which has the approval of the Church universal, and not of the Roman church alone, rests on a trustworthy foundation."[69]

Vincent, we remember, is convinced that the consentient unity of the church offers the best way of interpreting the Scriptures, and thus his criteria of *ubique et omnes*. The "Timothy" who guards the deposit of faith in every age entails a multilayered interpretative approach to the Scriptures. All of the various "channels of apostolic tradition," as Newman says, are invoked. Pride of place goes to the bishops/overseers in ecumenical councils. Theological doctors and the faithful are also important. And the bishops of Rome have a significant role to play, particularly through their leadership within the college of bishops/overseers.

Some may think that Vincent had unique respect for the bishop of Rome because, as a monk of Gaul, he was a Westerner who would normally look to Rome for direction. But while Vincent undoubtedly belonged to the *pars Occidentis* of the church, we should be cautious about too hastily advancing this argument. Outside of bare geography, there is no sense whatsoever in the *Commonitorium* that Vincent thinks of himself as a "Western" Christian. That very term, smacking as it does of a limiting particularity, would likely be anathema to him. The criteria he adduces are concerned with universality and ubiquity, the *catholica*, the *omnes* of the church. Does anyone surpass Vincent in speaking so warmly about the church universal, or about his identity as a truly Catholic Christian? Regionalism, lack of endorsement by the entire church, is an unimpeachable sign of idiosyncrasy and error.

Vincent takes pains to enumerate the characteristics of the "true and genuine Catholic," not the Western Christian: the true Catholic loves the truth
of God and the church, which is the body of Christ (20.1); esteems the faith
above all things, particularly above every attempt at human eloquence and
philosophy; and only believes that which has been held by the church universally and from antiquity, resisting novel doctrine that has been smuggled into
the church "against those beliefs or other than those beliefs that all the saints
hold [*praeter omnes vel contra omnes sanctos*]" (20.1–2).

Certainly Vincent accords the highest respect to Nicaea (325) and Ephesus
(431). He does not regard them as Eastern councils, but as representative of the
church universal, which is always his primary interest. He refers to Ephesus as a
consensus of "almost all the holy bishops of the East" (33.2), showing his deep
respect for the *pars Orientis*. Vincent lists the bishops of Alexandria first when
enumerating the ten doctors of Ephesus. He regards the great Cappadocian
masters as lights for the entire church. Vincent heaps the highest encomiums
on Origen of Alexandria, clearly regarding him as the greatest of theologians,
even if ultimately a trial for the church. And as we have seen earlier, the monks
of southern Gaul, in their controversy with Augustine over predestination,
enlisted the tradition of the East as a witness against the seeming novelties
about predestination and grace purveyed by the great African doctor.

For all these reasons, one must be cautious in assuming that Vincent regards
the bishop of Rome as a uniquely authoritative teacher simply because the
Lérinian resides in Gaul, or because Rome is the only Western apostolic see.
Vincent of Lérins may have been a geographical Westerner, but his theology
is interested only in the universality of faith in Jesus Christ and the witness of
the church throughout the world. Indeed, he does not hesitate to criticize the
West, noting that at Ariminum (359) almost all the bishops of the Latin language—constrained by both violence and fraud, it is true—did not sufficiently
oppose novelty (4.3). As Meslin rightly says, Vincent "is never content to say
that the witness of the churches of the West suffices for the establishment of
healthy doctrine."[70] It is only universality and ubiquity that faithfully transmit
the apostolic tradition and thus ensure orthodoxy. Whatever conflicts may have
existed with Augustine, Vincent would have happily subscribed to the African's
famous phrase "The verdict of the world is conclusive [*securus judicat orbis
terrarum*]."[71] It is difficult to argue the case, then, that the bishop of Rome
is regarded by Vincent as uniquely authoritative because of his place in the
West. The Lérinian is far too cosmopolitan, far too "catholic" for that. One
may even surmise that Vincent had reason to regard the bishop of Rome with
some wariness.[72] At the same time, the primacy of Rome is, for the Lérinian,
always deeply linked to the college of bishops/overseers and particularly to
the authority of ecumenical councils. The Roman bishop always acts *with* the
others, ensuring that the faith he defends is actually sanctioned by the entire
church—councils, doctors, and faithful included.

In contemporary theology, there have been many attempts, theological and ecumenical, to recover the unique office of the bishop of Rome while simultaneously situating his authority firmly within the universal college of bishops/overseers. Vatican II, for example, sought to place the pope squarely within the episcopal college—in Vincent's terms, the *corpus praepositorum*—with the purpose of countering a one-sided and inflated papalism that had emerged from Vatican I.[73] As Avery Dulles says, quite definitively, "Vatican II was to complete the work of Vatican I by stating more explicitly that the pope has no other infallibility than that which was given to the universal Church and is expressed by the consensus of bishops."[74] Vatican II recovered a more Vincentian vision of the church—multilayered, polycentric, and complex—with far less emphasis on papal centralism.[75]

More recently, John Paul II issued *Ut unum sint*, an encyclical letter (of 1995) calling for new ways of exercising the Petrine ministry that might be acceptable to all Christians, thereby allowing the church to breathe again "with . . . two lungs" and "in legitimate diversity" (§54). How may papal authority be envisioned so that its exercise reflects a proper balance of primacy and conciliarity? In contemporary ecumenical discussions, progress has been made toward creatively rethinking the bishop of Rome's role within the body of the church. As Walter Kasper has recently noted, in three of the four major dialogues between Rome and Reformation churches, there has been a "cautious/qualified openness" to the idea of a Petrine ministry.[76] One may further take note of important ecumenical statements such as the Ravenna dialogue on conciliarity and authority of 2007 and the North American Orthodox-Catholic Theological Consultation of 2010.[77] In documents such as these, we see significant attempts to embody the Vincentian ideal of the bishop of Rome's primacy, coupled with a firm commitment to collegiality.

Indeed, in every contemporary ecumenical discussion, there is an attempt to move the papacy away from what is perceived, at times, as an unhealthy centralism, a goal with which Vincent, the great champion of consentient unity, would be in full accord. J. M. R. Tillard cites a poignant statement by an Anglican theologian on just this point: Anglican Christians would like some guarantee that "the most positive fruits in the development of [their] Church, won at the price of much suffering and in the sincere intention of faithfulness to Jesus Christ, should not be devoured by centralism."[78] Vincent would endorse the general intention of this sentiment. Centralism, understood as the exercise of interpretative authority without proper regard for consentient unity, is precisely what he opposed. The *idem sensus* is best maintained by the agreement of the entire church everywhere (*ubique et omnes*), which transmits the apostolic tradition from age to age. The Lérinian always returns to 1 Corinthians (esp. 1:10) and so to that universal consensus that allows the church to make a distinction between a proper *profectus* and an illegitimate *permutatio*.

Having briefly discussed, in a contemporary context, the warrants that
Vincent adduces for underwriting the proper growth of Christian doctrine, let
us now examine two examples of (possible) development that remain a cause
for ecclesial division: Mary and the papacy. To what extent would Vincent
sanction these alleged doctrinal developments?

Examples of Legitimate Development?

Mariology

One hallmark of the Roman Catholic Church has been its devotion to Mary,
the Mother of Jesus Christ. Marian piety exhibits itself in a variety of popular
practices, but one finds this devotion doctrinally expressed in the two defined
dogmas of the Immaculate Conception (1854) and the Assumption (1950). Both
those who adhere to these definitions and those who regard them as ill-advised
or erroneous see them as "developments." The crucial Vincentian question is,
which kind of developments? Do these Marian doctrines, collectively speaking, constitute a legitimate *profectus fidei* or a pernicious *permutatio fidei*?[79]
   There are two aspects to the issue, material and formal. On the material
level, Vincent's thought appears to provide support for a developed Mariology.
As we have seen, the *Commonitorium* places a decided accent on Mary's role
as the Mother of God, although always in direct relationship to Christ the
Savior. Vincent tells us that it is "most Catholic [*catholicissime*]" to believe
that, given the unity of Christ's person, not only the flesh but also God the
Word was born "of the Virgin Mother [*ex integra matre*]" (15.5). Mary has a
special relationship with the Redeemer, and because of this, "no one should
attempt to strip holy Mary [*sancta Maria*] of her privilege of divine grace or
of her unique glory [*speciali gloria*]" (15.6). By the unique gift of her Son our
Lord and God, she indeed is, as the Council of Ephesus had proclaimed her,
the *Theotokos*, the God-bearer, the Mother of God. In her "holy womb the
sacred mystery was accomplished" with the unity of God and man in Jesus
Christ (15.8). And Vincent notes that just as Christ's divine nature proceeds
from his Father, so his human nature comes from "the Virgin, his mother"
(13.9), a point he repeats in his *Excerpta* (Prologue 1.46–48).
   Without tracing all of the intervening theological steps between Vincent
of Lérins and the later Marian definitions, I think it can be plausibly argued
that Vincent's notion of development (with the child becoming an adult and
the seed becoming a plant) could underwrite—always invoking the necessary
warrants—the material development of Mariology found in the doctrines of
the Immaculate Conception and the Assumption. To the legitimate objection that these teachings are not found in Scripture, it could be answered that
the Lérinian, himself a forceful defender of the preeminence of the Bible,
takes a wide rather than a narrow view of the divine Word, seeing its proper

interpretation as guided by the Spirit in the consentient unity of the church. One remembers, for example, that in the controversy over the rebaptism of heretics, Vincent says that repeating baptism is "contrary to the divine canon [Scripture] and the rule of the universal church" (6.4). In other words, the authentic meaning of the sacred Word of God is best known through the prism of the living teaching of the church. The proper exegesis of Scripture is always an act of the entire body of Christ.

But other objections could be raised. The great ecumenist Yves Congar, when commenting specifically on Vincent's thought, says that while one might see certain doctrinal teachings, such as the Creed of Nicaea and the real presence of Christ in the Eucharist, as clarifying the content of Scripture, one can hardly explain the Marian dogmas in this manner.[80] Yet is it not possible to see the Immaculate Conception and the Assumption as developments (*res amplificetur, dilatetur tempore*) commensurable with the *idem sensus* of both Scripture and the early tradition?[81] Can these teachings be understood as consonant with—and so a harmonious unfolding of—the teaching of the Scriptures and apostolic tradition? This is exactly what the Anglican–Roman Catholic International Commission recently concluded.[82]

But while Vincent, one surmises, could have supported the Marian definitions from a material point of view—as examples of authentic and organic growth over time—it is also likely true that he would harbor reservations about the manner or formality under which the definitions were promulgated. For the Lérinian, the accent must always be on the consentient unity of the church. A significant *profectus*, a definition without the concordance of the church's *pars Orientis* in particular, would have struck him as precipitous at best and possibly illegitimate at worst. He was certainly aware of large-scale schisms in the church (such as the Donatists), but he was always at pains to keep together the universal body of Christ, East and West. For any crucial *profectus fidei*, Vincent would certainly have sought to add other warrants, not just the authority of the bishop of Rome alone.

Yet facile conclusions on this point must be avoided since it may be cogently argued that the popes who defined the Marian dogmas were also well aware of the need to adduce significant, indeed universal, theological warrants for their teachings; otherwise the legitimacy of the definitions would be open to doubt. Consequently, the bulls of both Pius IX (1854) and Pius XII (1950) are concerned to marshal all of the traditional *loci theologici* in favor of the Marian definitions. Reading through the documents, one sees that these popes are at great pains to root the teachings in Scripture (typologically understood). They carefully mine the writings of the church fathers in order to establish that the doctrines constitute an organic and architectonic development of earlier insights. They insist that both the bishops and the faithful have been consulted and are in profound accord. As the bull of 1854 explains, there exists a "unique breathing together of both pastors and faithful [*conspiratio singularis pastorum ac fidelium*]" on the issue at hand. Pius IX concludes that the truth of the Immaculate Conception is witnessed by "Holy Scripture, venerable tradition, the constant mind of the church, the desire of Catholic bishops and the faithful," and by "eminent doctors in the science of theology."

Similarly, in the 1950 decree on the Assumption of Mary, Pius XII is eager to cite the work of "outstanding theologians" who have labored to show that the dogma "is contained in the deposit of Christian faith." Greek and Latin fathers are adduced for the slightest evidence. Through the use of analogies and images found in Scripture, theologians are said to "have illustrated and confirmed" the doctrine of Mary's bodily assumption into heaven. Most important, Pius states that "all these proofs and considerations of the holy fathers and theologians are based upon the Sacred Writings as their ultimate foundation."

The simple point is that one sees concerted attempts by the bishops of Rome to marshal the traditionally authoritative warrants when proposing some teaching as a legitimate development. At the same time, Rome has generally considered these crucial warrants, these fundamental criteria, only as they exist within the borders of Roman Catholicism. Vatican II's enhanced recognition of the status of separated churches and ecclesial communities necessarily implies that the theological *loci* considered must themselves become more ecumenical and diverse.[83]

Since Vatican II, and under the strong critique of the Reformation, Roman Catholicism has been at pains to show the relationship of Mary to Christ and indeed to integrate her into ecclesiology as the unique and exemplary disciple of her son. In this sense, Roman Catholicism has come much closer to Karl Barth's position, stated humorously but with a serious theological point: "I said to Balthasar some years ago that I could have no objection in principle to a statue of Mary if, instead of [being] on the altar, it were put on a level with the congregation and had its face turned toward the altar. According to your [Oscar Cullmann's] latest report on the integration of Mariology into ecclesiology [at Vatican II], a development of this kind seems to be under way."[84]

The Papacy

We have already discussed the office of the bishop of Rome at some length, so our comments here will be brief. The role of the Roman bishop was already large in Vincent's time and would soon loom larger, particularly with the collapse of the occidental empire. To what extent would the Lérinian sanction later theological developments surrounding the papacy? Of the bishop of Rome's primacy, Vincent has little doubt. He is deferential to the office in his discussion of Popes Sixtus and Celestine, so much so that it is probably unthinkable that Vincent would reject a definitive teaching of a Roman bishop.[85] We have already reviewed some of the textual evidence for this claim, such as Vincent's statement that the bishop of Rome authoritatively lays down a teaching (*sanxit*) and there is a unique authority connected with his see (*loci auctoritate superabat*). Further, Vincent would likely have been aware of earlier comments, such as Cyprian's reference to Rome as the *ecclesia principalis* and perhaps even of Irenaeus's *potentior principalitas*.[86]

But it is equally true that the Lérinian's marked accent is on the consentient unity of the church, preeminently that of the bishops/overseers. In examining the *Commonitorium*, one sees that the corporate body is always featured: it is the *body* of bishops/overseers who teach authoritatively; it is the *body* of learned and holy doctors who can be trusted; it is the *body* of the faithful who protect Christian truth. The tradition of the Christian faith—and the consensus it exhibits—is maintained by the entire church, reflecting the presence of the Holy Spirit. The proper exercise of teaching authority in the church is not a solitary undertaking. For Vincent, individuality is generally equated with idiosyncrasy and heresy, as in the case of the great theologians Origen and Tertullian and bishops such as Nestorius and Julian.

It is all the more interesting, then, that Vincent discusses the bishop of Rome as an individual who protects the faith from adulteration. Even here, however, Vincent always has the wider college of bishops/overseers in view, with the *Commonitorium* purveying a vigorous theology of communion. The pope teaches "with his colleagues, but nevertheless in the forefront of them [*cum ceteris quidem collegis suis, sed tamen prae ceteris*]" (6.5). And Vincent does not turn simply to Rome to settle questions of orthodoxy and heresy. The Lérinian's canon was developed precisely to offer a criterion for deciding between truth and falsity. And this rule—*semper, ubique, et ab omnibus*—as we have seen, places a distinct accent on the authoritative interpretation of Scripture sanctioned by ecumenical councils. Their definitive teachings constitute the landmarks that may not be transgressed, thereby establishing the *regula fidei*. The Roman bishops certainly have a unique responsibility to guard such monuments of faith. Precisely this is the force of Stephen's original claim, reinforced by later popes and eulogistically cited by Vincent: "Let there be no innovation except what has been handed down [*nihil novandum, nisi quod traditum est*]."

Although Vincent strongly endorses a polycentric web of teaching authority, it is clear that he also supports a primatial ministry for the Roman bishop. Without strong and vigorous leadership, consentient unity would likely be an asymptotic (approximate) dream, a vaporous abstraction never realized. At the same time, one finds no concept of infallibility explicitly attached to the papal teaching office in Vincent's work. This is why the young Newman can say with great ardor: "We may unhesitatingly conclude that the Pope's supreme authority in matters of Faith, is no Catholic or Apostolic truth, because he [Vincent] was ignorant of it."[87] For the Lérinian, infallibility is a charism of the entire church, uniquely instantiated in the solemn teachings of ecumenical councils. Councils establish the irreversible "landmarks" that cannot be contravened, the "hedges" that cannot be breached. Any attempt to transgress such milestones trespasses upon the deposit of faith and thus courts heresy. The theologian of Lérins would likely agree, then, with Newman's statement of 1864: "It is to the Pope in Ecumenical Council that we look, as the normal seat of infallibility."

However, if one sought to develop certain elements in Vincent's thought *toward* the later notion of papal infallibility, one would come close to the position of the "minority" bishops at Vatican I—whose theological concerns later emerged full-blown at Vatican II. They insisted that serious collegial and consensual safeguards must be erected around any claims to infallibility attaching to the papal office.[88] On the material level, Vincent would likely sanction an authentically primatial office for the bishop of Rome; yet formally, he would expect that the exercise of this unique role—and surely any doctrinal claims to an infallible papal magisterium—be confirmed by the entire church, by all of the warrants he has adduced as assuring consentient unity.[89]

Vincent left the precise role of the bishop of Rome undefined, but his entire work attests to the fact that he would find distasteful any kind of overweening centralism. The church does not possess only one center of teaching; many teach with legitimate, even if not final, authority. The teaching authority of the bishop of Rome, therefore, must be firmly placed within the apostolic office committed to the entire church. As Vatican II states, all bishops are "vicars and legates of Christ" (*Lumen Gentium* §27).[90] Tillard sums up Vatican II's reform movement in a statement with which Vincent would have entirely agreed: "The mission and power of the papacy should therefore be understood as inseparable from . . . the college of bishops."[91] One should add that Vincent would also stress a strong circumincession (*perichōrēsis*, reciprocal existence) among the episcopal college, theologians, and the faithful generally. Only these kinds of collective and collegial safeguards ensure that maverick interpretations of the gospel are avoided.

Working out the precise way in which the bishop of Rome should exercise a primatial office for Christendom, within the unity of the entire church, is a continuing theological and ecumenical challenge. Much excellent material has already been written on this question, and it is not our goal to repeat it here.[92] Our more limited intention has been to argue that, on the basis of the principles outlined in the *Commonitorium*, Vincent would certainly sanction doctrinal developments homogeneous with the prior tradition, but with the requirement that such homogeneity is supported by a variety of warrants indicating the consentient unity of the church in its transmittal of Scripture and the apostolic tradition. This accent on universality, increasingly recognized within Roman Catholicism, makes it unlikely that the bishop of Rome, absent a *status confessionis* (confessional status), would again exercise the infallible teaching authority ascribed to him without a significant consensus of the *pars Occidentis et pars Orientis* of Christianity, and indeed without a careful weighing of the mind of all Christians. It is likely that the *conspiratio singularis* noted by Pius IX would now be extended to significant portions of the Christian world.[93]

Doctrinal Development

Vincent treats the idea of the harmonious unfolding of doctrine more fully than any other early Christian writer. The issue is only resumed again, at any length, by Newman in the nineteenth century. But there are hints of it earlier in the tradition. One well-known instance is in the acts of the Council of Nicaea II (787) and the speech of the deacon John on why the iconoclastic convocation of 753–54 at Hieria was not actually an ecumenical council (as had been claimed by some).[94] John makes the point that Hieria could not be a universal council by reasoning thus:

> How can it be the seventh when it does not agree [*non concordavit*] with the preceding holy and venerable six synods? In order to be seventh in numbering, a council must follow upon [*subsequens*] those elements which preceded it. A council cannot be enumerated with other councils with which it has nothing in common. After all, if you lined up six pieces of gold and then added one of bronze, you could not call it seven because of the substantially different material [*propter alterius materiae substantiam*]. Gold is a precious metal while bronze is a dishonorable one. But this council has nothing of precious gold in its dogmas, and in its teachings one finds bronzed falsehood, filled with deadly poison. This council does not merit to be numbered with the six holy synods, which are refulgent with the golden songs of the Spirit.[95]

In this passage one sees some affinity with Vincent, writing some 350 years earlier. Here John hints at the notion of homogeneous development *in eodem sensu*. He states that for any council to be considered "ecumenical," it must agree with the prior six synods. A "seventh" must follow "in those things which preceded it [*in supputatione praecedentium rerum subsequens debet esse*]." Surely John is thinking that a new council cannot contradict any prior solemn teachings; previous "landmarks" cannot be contravened. As Peri says, John the deacon is convinced that one characteristic of an ecumenical council is "the homogeneity of the doctrine taught and the material treated" as compared with the other councils.[96] Further, the theological material treated must be of interest to the entire church. After all, John tells us, a true ecumenical council is one that, like the words of the apostles and the six earlier councils, reaches to the ends of the earth. The simple point is that the notion of homogeneous growth—defending the deposit even while organically developing it—has a long tradition in the Christian church and a distinct bearing on contemporary theology.

One hopes this study has shown that development of doctrine was not a nineteenth-century *novum* suddenly interjected into theology by John Henry Newman as a defensive reaction to the critical judgments of modernity. Development was actually an idea rooted in a theologically sophisticated early Christian writer—one, moreover, who was deeply concerned about preserving the deposit of faith as enshrined in the Scriptures. Vincent offers a careful view of development, allowing only growth that is homogeneous in kind and is underwritten by multiple warrants.

Of signal importance is the fact that mere acceptance by an individual or even by the community cannot, for Vincent, demonstrate the truth of some development, since acceptance is necessarily predicated upon a *material continuity* with prior doctrinal teaching. The problem with Ariminum in 359 was that it did not clearly affirm the teaching of Nicaea (325). The Nicene Creed, while itself requiring further development (at Constantinople in 381), can never be reversed or contravened. Change that is contradictory to the solemn decisions that preceded it would be a corruption of the faith. As the deacon John said of the convocation of 753–54 at Hieria, by teaching something different from the prior six councils, an imposter synod of bronze dared to trade itself as gold. The interpretative consent of the community, then, taken alone, can never be authoritative since the church's interpretation of Scripture is always restricted by a prior *fundamentum in re*, the definitive teachings of universal councils.

Authoritative conciliar teachings and creeds are, for Vincent, binding, irrevocable truths, unimpeachable interpretations of Scripture, sanctioned *semper, ubique, et ab omnibus*. Such solemn decrees cannot be understood, then, as prudential, pragmatic judgments that can later be erased or overturned, as if they offered only the provisional and reversible truth of a particular age or epoch. Understanding solemn doctrinal formulations as merely contingently true is precisely the position that the Lérinian rejects as betraying the *depositum*. Fundamental "landmarks" are irreversible and cannot be transgressed. One abandons the gospel if one seeks to contravene the solemn determinations of the church universal.

At the same time, this insistence on preservative continuity in no way thwarts further development *in eodem sensu*. As we have seen, Vincent sanctions both the reexpression of the faith (*noviter*) as well as its growth according to type (*res amplificetur*). Nonetheless, Christian thinkers have occasionally expressed reservations about the very idea of doctrinal development. The Eastern Orthodox theologian Andrew Louth, for example, says that "development does not seem to be perceived as an available category for Orthodox theology." Indeed, when development is invoked, it is often "the classically Protestant understanding which sees any development as negative—not growth but distortion."[97] One reason for the reluctance of Orthodoxy toward the idea of development, Louth observes, is that it is often thought to be a concept traceable to the

Enlightenment and Romanticism (48). Another reason is the inclination to cite the fathers of the church in a rather flat, ahistorical manner, without careful attention to the actual context of their work (54–55). Despite encouraging a more contextual approach to early Christian writers, Louth concludes that the idea of development "is not an acceptable category in Orthodox theology" (61).[98] Louth himself, while giving us a brisk summary of Newman's position, never mentions Vincent as the eminent patristic thinker on development, who had a profound effect on Newman and indeed on the entire Anglican tradition.[99]

Roman Catholics, too, have had their reservations about the notion of doctrinal development. At Vatican II, for example, the bishops discussed the revised schema on divine revelation in July 1964. The document spoke of a "living tradition [*viva traditio*]" that advances under the Holy Spirit. It added, echoing Vincent, that there is "a growth in the understanding [*crescit intelligentia*]" of the deeds and words that have been handed down. Cardinal Ruffini, however, rose to his feet and argued that the words *vivere* and *crescere* were troubling insofar as they mutilated the judgment of Trent (Ruffini meant Vatican I; the Council of Trent never cited Vincent). Without giving a full explanation, Ruffini's implication was that if tradition is "living" and if understanding is "growing," then such development undermines the perduring stability and solidity of Roman Catholic doctrine.[100]

In certain quarters of Protestant Christianity, doctrinal development is regarded as a strategy by which new and alien ideas, beyond the witness of Scripture, are furtively smuggled into the church. *Sola scriptura* is intended to bear witness against precisely such illegitimate additions. Vincent would not be entirely unsympathetic to this point of view, and in order to forestall just such an occurrence, he offered significant safeguards against it. The Lérinian's adduction of a plurality of warrants is intended to assure that if some development is indeed to be accepted by the church as legitimate, then this understanding of Scripture is to have the agreement of significant sectors of ecclesial life. Vincent is not proposing the position that Vanhoozer—and traditional Protestantism generally—fears: a reading of Scripture that cavalierly presumes an identity or coincidence between the Bible and its ecclesial interpretation, thereby blunting the critical authority of the Word of God. For if the community is licensed to interpret Scripture, how can Scripture itself provide an enduring and trustworthy standard that judges the church, thereby acting as the one and only "norm that norms [but itself is] not normed [*norma normans non normata*]"? In this sense, the Reformers' plea echoes the age-old question of Juvenal: "Who will guard the guards themselves [*quis custodiet ipsos custodes*]?" But the Lérinian's thought is much too careful and theologically sophisticated to allow for an unqualified identity between Scripture and ecclesial authority. While Vincent does not endorse a starkly dialectical relationship between the Bible and the church, his complex hermeneutics eschews any naive presumption of coincidence.

At the same time, Vincent would certainly find affinity with what Vanhoozer calls the "meaning potential" in the biblical text, allowing the text to be further developed.[101] The Baptist theologian Timothy George speaks similarly: "The principle of *sola scriptura*, rightly understood, does not preclude, but rather calls for, a bona fide theory of doctrinal development."[102] I. Howard Marshall, another evangelical thinker, argues that postbiblical development is necessary. He says, Vincent-like, that any such development "must be based on continuity with the faith once given to God's people, and must be in accordance with what I have called 'the mind of Christ.'"[103] These evangelical theologians realize that development is possible when properly and homogeneously understood, thereby coming very close to Vincent's own point of view.

Roman Catholicism, well aware that there cannot be a naive presumption of identity between the Word of God and ecclesial teachings, has utilized several strategies to ensure that this point remains vibrantly alive in its contemporary theology. I cannot discuss these approaches at length here, but they must be mentioned in order to indicate that the relationship between Scripture and tradition is much suppler than is at times supposed.

Hierarchy of Truths

The decree on ecumenism at Vatican II (*Unitatis Redintegratio* §11) states, "When comparing doctrines, they [Roman Catholic theologians] should remember that in Catholic teaching there exists an order or 'hierarchy' of truths, since they vary in their relationship to the foundation of the Christian faith." Although the specific term "hierarchy of truths" was new, the idea itself was not, resonating with much of the earlier Christian tradition.

Vincent himself, avant la lettre, bears witness to an incipient hierarchy of truths, and so to the recognition that every church teaching does not possess the same weight. In two places in the *Commonitorium*, the theologian of Lérins gives indications of just this kind of analogical thinking. He says, for example, "We ought to research and investigate with great study the ancient consent of the holy fathers not in every small question of the divine law [Scripture], but only in those matters which pertain to the rule of faith [*in fidei regula*]." For Vincent, it is not essential to achieve unanimity "in every small question of the divine law [*in omnibus divinae legis quaestiunculis*]" (28.2). In the next chapter the Lérinian tells us that what is important is that "the interpretation of sacred Scripture should be guided by the one rule of the church's faith, especially in those questions on which the foundations of all Catholic doctrine rest [*totius catholici dogmatis fundamenta nituntur*]" (29.3). We cannot know for certain the kinds of limits that Vincent was imposing, but since his books (both the *Commonitorium* and the *Excerpta*) are concerned primarily with christological and trinitarian matters—questions that had been addressed by the prior ecumenical councils—we can surmise that these are the foundations on which unanimity is required.

It should not surprise us, then, that the young John Henry Newman, lamenting the divisions within Christianity, takes consolation in the fact that while Vincent insists on church unity, "in truth, he does not speak of *all* doctrine, but of the *'foundations'* . . . of Christian doctrine" (*Records of the Church* 25.5). The Anglican thinker concludes that these fundamentals "are contained in the Creed, and have been expanded at various times by the Catholic Church acting together; such are the doctrines of the Trinity, the Incarnation, the Atonement, and the like." In the 1837 *Via Media*, Newman, proving he was an astute reader of the *Commonitorium*, cites both passages referring to this Vincentian hierarchy and concludes, "That there are greater truths, then, and lesser truths, points which it is necessary, and points which it is pious to believe . . . seems undeniable."[104]

Yves Congar has observed that the idea of a hierarchy of Christian doctrine also exists in Lutheranism (where the fundamental elements are constituted by the teachings that speak clearly of Christ as Savior).[105] Contemporary Roman Catholic theologians have distinguished between a doctrine's content and the authority with which it has been taught—in other words, between its *centrality* to Christianity as opposed to the *certainty* with which the church teaches it. For example, the nineteenth- and twentieth-century Marian dogmas are taught with significant certainty, even though these teachings do not stand at the center of the Christian faith. The same is true of the definition of the papal magisterium's infallibility, which is not a foundational teaching of Christianity.[106]

In this question of the hierarchy of truths, we may discern an analogy with the "fundamental councils" discussed earlier. The primary and fundamental truths and councils are the commanding ones in whose authority secondary truths and councils participate. Just here multiple questions present themselves—questions that have prevented the notion of "hierarchy of truths" from achieving palpable ecumenical fruit. Does the lesser centrality of certain teachings, such as the Marian dogmas, mean that these will now be treated as adiaphora? Is there a danger that the very notion of hierarchy of truths detracts from the close interrelationship that necessarily exists among all the mysteries of divine revelation? Is it too easy to cite the well-known maxim "Unity in necessary things, liberty in doubtful things, charity in all things [*in necessariis, unitas; in dubiis, libertas; in omnibus, caritas*]" without determining the precise *necessarii* that are ultimately at stake?

Further complicating matters is the Roman Catholic church's insistence that all revealed truths must be believed "with the same divine faith." So, even though some truths are central and principal, all dogmas, no matter their "standing" in the hierarchy of truths, must be believed with the same act of faith that finds its origin in God's grace. Denial of any revealed truth, then, even one that is less "central," constitutes heresy. Karl Rahner thought that to insist on this theological point was to render the church's teaching on the hierarchy of truths illusory. He called for further distinctions if the notion of hierarchy were ever to bear ecumenical fruit.[107] The intriguing question is this: Roman Catholicism believes that certain doctrines are formally revealed by God; but may one make a distinction in the *type* of faith elicited by various revealed truths, using analogical reasoning as a hermeneutical key, depending on their relation to the foundational dogmas?

Further thought is necessary on this issue; yet the hierarchy of truths, which clearly finds a foreshadowing in Vincent's work, remains an important strategy with ecumenical potential. To return to the original point: the very notion of the "hierarchy of truths" shows that any "presumption of coincidence" between ecclesial teachings and the inspired Word of God must be undertaken in a highly nuanced manner.

Theological Notes

Theological notes or qualifications constitute another "strategy" by which Roman Catholicism displays that there is no naive identity between ecclesial teaching and the inspired Word of God. The traditional assignment of a "note" to a church teaching exists precisely to indicate that Roman Catholicism teaches Christian doctrine with different levels of authority and varying levels of certainty.[108] Of course, every Christian church presumes that its teachings are biblically founded; otherwise, why teach them at all? However, with the invocation of theological notes, the Roman Catholic church attests that there does not exist a simple presumption of coincidence between ecclesial teaching and the Bible. Thus theological qualifications are assigned precisely to militate against any such facile conjunction.

To cite a recent example, we may again invoke the 2007 statement of the International Theological Commission concerning the fate of infants dying without baptism. The Commission states:

> The affirmation that infants who die without Baptism suffer the privation of the beatific vision has long been the common doctrine of the Church, which must be distinguished from the faith of the Church. As for the theory that the privation of the beatific vision is their sole punishment, to the exclusion of any other pain, *this is a theological opinion*, despite its long acceptance in the West. (§40, emphasis added)

In other words, even theses held by theologians, bishops, and popes for a long period of time can be regarded as uncertain—as common and widely held theological opinions—never definitively established as irreversible "landmarks." Not every teaching of Roman Catholicism, then, is to be regarded as an irreformable doctrine. "Church teaching" should be understood as an analogical, not a univocal reality.

Precisely because theological notes witness to varying degrees of certitude, Roman Catholic theologians at times speak of reversals of church teaching.

Such reversals are not applicable to doctrines that have been irrevocably established and thus are "landmarks," to use Vincent's term again. But much "ordinary" teaching has never been definitively held.[109] As Karl Rahner has said, "It cannot be denied that . . . an authentic doctrinal pronouncement not only *can* in principle be erroneous, but in the course of history often *has been* actually erroneous."[110] At Vatican II, for example, one thinks of the reversals of ordinary teaching that occurred on such matters as ecumenism, the inclusive nature of church membership, and the *objective right* to worship God other than as revealed in Jesus Christ. In these and other matters, it became increasingly clear that the goal was not continued growth *in eodem sensu*.

If the possibility of reversals on the level of "ordinary" teaching did not exist, then it would necessarily be the case that every ecclesial teaching would be, ipso facto, infallible, a position that has never been held. While Roman Catholicism certainly regards even its ordinary teachings as biblical and truthful, definitive (Vincentian) landmarks are reserved only for those teachings that are advanced with solemn and formal authority. At Vatican II it was acknowledged that true continuity at times requires reform "insofar as the Church is an institution of men and women on earth" (*Unitatis Redintegratio* §6). Vincent, who was wedded to biological metaphors for growth, would understand that at times a healthy plant needs not only cultivation but also pruning to flourish properly.[111]

Authentic Pluralism

At Vatican II the Roman Catholic Church placed a decided accent on authentic pluralism within the unity of faith. One need only glance at the major passages on this question (*Unitatis Redintegratio* §§4, 6, 17; *Gaudium et Spes* §62) to see this position clearly enunciated. Much of the pluralism sanctioned by Vatican II was of the type that Vincent endorsed with his axiom "Speak newly, but never say new things [*dicas nove, non dicas nova*]," for the council was convinced that there could be complementary ways of expressing and understanding the Christian mysteries that did not jeopardize the deposit of faith.[112]

One example is that adduced by Joseph Ratzinger, who says that while Eastern Orthodoxy does not share with Roman Catholicism all elements concerning an intermediate state (purgatory), "What is primary is the praxis of being able to pray [for the dead], and being called upon to pray. The objective correlate of this praxis in the world to come need not, in some reunification of the churches, be determined of necessity in a strictly unitary fashion."[113] Ratzinger's statement approaches the position argued by Vincent that there need not be unanimity *in omnibus divinae legis quaestiunculis* (28.2). This may seem like a minor point, but just here it is a matter of identifying "smaller questions," which are not church-dividing issues. The *Commonitorium* allows

for a unity of faith and communion without agreement on "every little question," and it is just these points that Ratzinger is seeking to identify.

Unity within plurality is precisely the chief contemporary ecumenical issue.
How can there be a rich pluriformity, a diversity of theological, liturgical, and
spiritual expressions, but within a unity of faith and Christian doctrine?[114] How
can there be a theological pluralism that is nonetheless commensurable with
the deposit of faith once transmitted to the saints? At stake here is the well-
known axiom "Different but not contradictory [*diversi sed non adversi*]."[115]
This dictum (which Vincent would surely endorse on the basis of his *noviter,
non nova*) has a long history, often being invoked to show that the accounts
of the four evangelists, though different, are not incoherent. In the Middle
Ages, the axiom was adduced to demonstrate that the fathers of the church
yielded a *consensus patrum* despite apparent differences in their interpretation of the Scriptures. De Lubac, for example, points to the speech of John
Basil Bessarion at the Council of Florence, where Bessarion argues that there
exists a parallel between the consensus of the evangelists and the consensus of
church fathers, Greek and Latin. In both cases, variety in expression cannot
be understood as equivalent to opposition.

Diversi sed non adversi is again an important point at Vatican II, particularly
in the claim that different modes of expression "are often to be considered as
complementary rather than contradictory," thereby indicating that Eastern
and Western churches, although using different formulations, express the
same divine truth (*Unitatis Redintegratio* §17). Such a position has helped
clarify the diverse theological understandings of the eternal procession of
the Holy Spirit.[116] The possibility of complementary formulations may also
find some source in the well-known phrase of Thomas Aquinas, *Articulus
[fidei] est perceptio divinae veritatis tendens in ipsam* (*Summa theologiae,*
II–II q. 1 a. 6), which itself sums up the patristic legacy that no one expression of divine truth is ever entirely sufficient. Most important in the pursuit
of an authentic pluralism—in things *diversi sed non adversi*—have been the
ecumenical dialogues that have taken place since Vatican II. In these theological agreements, one sees the attempts by several churches to allow for an
expansive and commensurable pluralism that nonetheless protects the central
elements of the Christian faith.

These three "strategies"—the hierarchy of truths, theological notes, and
authentic pluralism—have been briefly mentioned for this reason: to show
that theological approaches exist in Roman Catholicism for avoiding a naive
identification between ecclesial teaching (tradition) and the Word of God. In
responding to Vanhoozer's concern—and that of the Reformation generally—
about the "presumption of identity" between the Bible and church doctrine,
these factors should be recognized as having the potential to advance the ecumenical discussion. In the *noviter, non nova* and the *quaestiunculae* (smaller
questions) of Vincent, we see these theological themes already adumbrated.

Rereception

The notion of "rereception" is often invoked as a way for churches to reexamine their own teachings as well as those of other Christian communities. Yves Congar, for example, calls for churches to practice a rereception of their own essential doctrines and creeds. As he says, the various churches now live fruitfully according to the doctrines of *Pastor Aeternus* (Dogmatic Constitution of Vatican I, 1870), the *Augsburg Confession* (Lutheran, 1530), and Palamism (Eastern Orthodox theology). How can these teachings be re-received in our day—not for the sake of abandoning them, to be sure—but for the purpose of thinking about them anew, taking account of their particular historical and cultural situations, the criticisms received from others, and the common cause of the gospel?[117] From a purifying rereception, disputed theological doctrines would likely emerge with new accents and emphases, perhaps leading to reformulations that are acceptable to a broader spectrum of Christians.[118] Rereception, then, has two aspects: internal and external. Churches must rereceive their own teachings, newly cognizant of the historical and cultural limitations that necessarily surround them.[119] And churches are simultaneously called upon to rereceive the creeds and teachings of other churches, integrating them, to the extent possible, into their own understanding of Christian doctrine. An example of this latter notion is provided by Louis Bouyer, in speaking of certain Roman Catholic councils: "All that the West can and must ask of the East is that the word of these [Western] councils should be accepted provisionally, with favorable prejudgment, as an essential, positive element for a broader and more profound common examination of the questions."[120]

It may be argued that it is difficult to justify the procedure of rereception on the basis of Vincent of Lérins's writings. His experience of the church was—despite heresies, schisms, and heated controversies—one of fundamental unity. One could argue on Vincentian grounds, then, that the universal church has never sought the opinion of those who do not belong to it, since the church necessarily proceeds without the approbation of others. Indeed, Vincent did not hesitate to cite the apostle Paul: "There must be heresies among you so that those who are approved are known" (1 Cor. 11:19; *Common.* 20.3). On the other hand, insofar as the Lérinian was, at every turn, deeply committed to the consentient unity of the *entire* church, it can surely be argued that he would see rereception as a salutary development, a way of restoring unity to the broken Christian communion. If Christians are able to rereceive the teachings of other churches as at least not fundamentally opposed to the gospel, or even as proper interpretations of it, then they are striving precisely for the consentient unity that Vincent argued was essential for any legitimate *profectus*.

Although good relationships generally exist among the various Christian churches and ecclesial communions, there remain significant doctrinal divisions. The rereception of church teaching—both internally and externally—would surely help to heal those doctrinal ruptures while still respecting the integrity of the rereceiving church. Many elements of complementarity may still be recovered and integrated into the living theology of the churches. Rereception would encourage a continuing and determined effort to implement Vincent's *noviter, non nova*.

Assuming that no church will simply change its fundamental position, then the question becomes this: How may we interpret various teachings in ways that do not sacrifice truth, to be certain, but that also consciously seek greater Christian unity? Given his own accent on consentient universality, Vincent serves as a reminder that particular churches should avoid establishing their own developments without seriously searching for the arguments of Christians beyond their own borders.

Continuing Development

The issue of proper development over time is a deeply contemporary one. Most churches are discussing a variety of doctrinal and ethical questions. Are the varying proposals that have been brought forward homogeneous with the prior tradition? Are they finding the support of Scripture, councils, theological doctors, and the *instinctus* of the faithful?

Let us take one example: In Roman Catholicism (and other churches), there has been considerable discussion about the possibility of women serving as ordained priests. Would this step constitute a complementary unfolding of the prior tradition? Or would it, rather, be an adulteration of the Christian faith? On the basis of Vincent's principles, I argue that this proposed *profectus* cannot be ruled out a priori. But for any such significant change to occur, the Lérinian would no doubt seek consentient warrants from the entire church: Holy Scripture as interpreted by the *corpus praepositorum*; the consensus of learned and esteemed theological doctors; the *phronēma* of the faithful generally; and the approbation of the bishop of Rome. Vincent well understood that developments necessarily occur over time. But organic growth must be measured by the criteria of *semper, ubique, et ab omnibus*—which, for Vincent, means the judgment of the entire church in the living transmittal and unfolding of the apostolic tradition.[121]

What of the insights of liberation theology, of process theology, and of feminist thought generally, to name only a few recent proposals? How does Christianity incorporate that which is legitimate in the teachings offered by these theologies while rejecting anything that may be inauthentic? Vincent's answer is clear. In formulating answers to emerging questions, we must distinguish between the proposals *in eodem sensu* with the prior tradition on the one hand, and on the other hand the developments that "transgress landmarks," that seek theological metamorphoses by transforming the essence of

Christianity into something else entirely. But how can we confidently make this distinction when one person's authentic *profectus* is another's pernicious *permutatio*? How can we be certain that some proposal or other is an organic and architectonic growth rather than a corrosive change *in alieno sensu*? How can we determine that our responses to contemporary questions are representative of the biblical and the apostolic tradition? Vincent would reply confidently: We have clear warrants for ensuring a proper response. Pride of place belongs to Scripture itself, which is capable of answering all questions. But to ensure that we have the proper interpretation of God's Word, we look to the bishops/overseers, particularly as gathered in ecumenical council; to the learned and holy theological doctors of the church; to the faith of the saints generally; and to the bishop of Rome (united with his colleagues). By examining the consensus of these *loci theologici*, we may determine whether some development is actually homogeneous with the prior tradition.[122] And we should realize that this accent on consensus is not simply a desire for political unity; it is rooted, rather, in the theological belief that the Holy Spirit is at work in all members of the church, guiding them to the fullness of truth. Vincent leaves largely implicit the pneumatological premises of his criteria, but they are always at work. The *Commonitorium* serves as an example that development is possible today, just as it occurred in the early church; yet organic and homogeneous growth finds its authentic sanction in the consensus of various centers of authority and apostolic tradition.

Conclusion

One may certainly agree with Harnack when he says of the Lérinian, "We really breathe freely when we study the attempt of this man to introduce light and certainty into the question [of tradition]."[123] Most Christians already share the Scriptures, the ancient councils, and the creeds of the early church—a significant common patrimony of faith. One challenge to the churches today is to move beyond the perennial stalemates that separate them from full communion. In the interests of achieving Christian unity, and of providing guidance on a significant array of contemporary questions, Vincent of Lérins can still offer compelling help. His work fosters a salubrious via media, interested neither in primitivism (despite some of his interpreters) nor a freewheeling and heterogeneous development. He regards the apostolic tradition, as recorded in Scripture, as a precious eternal standard and norm, even as he supports continuing development that is architectonically related to the earlier formulations of faith. He insists that the church's role is to guard ancient doctrine, "treating it faithfully and wisely [*vetera fideliter sapienterque tractando*]" (23.17), while at the same time "sanctioning the vigorous progress of this same doctrine [*crescat . . . et multum vehementerque proficiat*]" (23.3).

If Vincent of Lérins's reputation has suffered in recent times, this is intrinsically related to the foreshortening of his thought. One cannot cite Vincent's canon, dismiss it as a naively antiquarian and petrified fantasy, and then be done with the Lérinian. There is nothing in Vincent of the static dogmatism or flattening positivism of which he is sometimes accused. If this book accomplishes one purpose, I hope it will be to complicate the naive reception of the theologian of Lérins that one finds in various invocations of his work. Vincent's canon, stated at the outset of his *Commonitorium*, cannot be isolated from the thirty-one chapters that follow. Those chapters elucidate precisely how Vincent's famous rule is to be properly understood.

Vincent was clear that the central dogmas of Christianity have been taught *semper, ubique, et ab omnibus*. The entire *Commonitorium* witnesses that he is not proposing this maxim as some kind of empirically verifiable principle that could be easily disproved. As many authors have asked, which doctrine has been taught always and everywhere and by everyone? Vincent meant by his canon, rather, that in the decisions of ecumenical councils, preeminently, we have the Christian faith taught by the bishops/overseers of the entire world, and we therefore have the transmission of the apostolic tradition. Further, in the complex of theological *loci*—such as the consent of learned and holy doctors, the instinct of the Christian faithful at large, and the teaching of the bishop of Rome (with his colleagues)—one finds the apostolic faith preserved and its authentic development properly husbanded. The *catholica*, the *omnes*, both carefully conserves the deposit of faith even while allowing it to advance *in eodem sensu*.

Vincent is well aware that change occurs, that history surrounds us, and that time marches on. But while time devours all things, we can still seize from it that which profits to life eternal (*Common.* 1.3). Time is the canvas by which God allows us to preserve the faith once given in ancient Israel and in Jesus of Nazareth, as well as to identify its legitimate progression. The key to understanding Vincent is in keeping his two rules conjoined, with all their preservative and developmental senses. It is to recognize, further, that Vincent carefully outlines the criteria—one might say the grammar—by which the Christian faith is simultaneously conserved and developed.

I do not intend here to make overweening claims for Vincent's thought. Like all theologians, he has his weaknesses.[124] But the Lérinian does offer significant insights into a Christian notion of history and into the hermeneutics of doctrine. His work serves to remind us that the idea of doctrinal development is not a product of the Enlightenment, or of Romanticism, or of nineteenth-century evolutionary thought; instead, doctrinal development is truly rooted in the early Christian church and was strikingly brought to life by one of its most insightful theologians.

Vincent's thought can help the church both theologically and ecumenically, as it perennially faces new questions and needs to do so with a forcefully united

Christian witness. From his monastery on the shores of the Mediterranean Sea, Vincent was convinced that he had found in Jesus Christ the pearl of great price, which leads him again and again to insist with the apostle Paul, "Guard the deposit, Timothy!" But just as firmly he tells us that progress must occur in the church, indeed, *plane et maximus*.

Notes

Abbreviations

CCSL   Corpus Christianorum: Series latina. Turnhout: Brepols, 1953–.

Common.   Vincent of Lérins. *Commonitorium.* Edited by Roland Demeulenaere. In CCSL 64 (1985): 127–95.

DTC   *Dictionnaire de théologie catholique.* Edited by Alfred Vacant et al. 15 vols. Paris: Letouzey & Ané, 1903–50.

Moxon   Reginald Stewart Moxon, ed. *The Commonitorium of Vincent of Lérins.* Cambridge: Cambridge University Press, 1915.

PL   Patrologia latina [= Patrologiae cursus completus: Series latina]. Edited by Jacques-Paul Migne. 221 vols. Paris, 1844–65 (including indexes).

Preface

1. Ratzinger says, for example, that Vincent is now seen in a "dubious light" by historical research and "no longer appears as an authentic representative of the Catholic idea of tradition." See Joseph Ratzinger, "Dogmatic Constitution on Divine Revelation," in *Commentary on the Documents of Vatican II*, ed. Herbert Vorgrimler, 5 vols. (New York: Herder & Herder, 1969), 3:187.

2. José Madoz, *El concepto de la tradición en S. Vicente de Lérins* (Rome: Gregorian University Press, 1933), 189.

3. For reflections on how the study of early Christian writers might advance dialogue and unity, see "On Becoming a Christian: Insights from Scripture and the Patristic Writings" (Report on the International Dialogue between Classical Pentecostal Churches and the Catholic Church, 1998–2006), *Information Service* 129 (2008/III): 216–26, §§8–13, http://www.vatican.va/roman _curia/pontifical_councils/chrstuni/eccl-comm-docs/rc_pc_chrstuni_doc_20060101_becoming-a -christian_en.html.

Introduction

1. For more information on Vincent's life and work, one does well to consult the exhaustive and still useful introduction found in the critical edition of Moxon (see Abbreviations, above), xi–lxxxviii. See also "Vinzenz von Lérins," in *Theologische Realenzyklopädie* (Berlin: de Gruyter,

1993–), Band 35.1/2:109–11; G. Bardy, "Vincent de Lérins," in *DTC* 15/2: cols. 3045–55; and "Vinzenz von Lérins," in *Lexikon für Theologie und Kirche* (Freiburg: Herder, 2001), 10:798–99.

2. See Adolf von Harnack, *History of Dogma*, trans. Neil Buchanan, 7 vols. (New York: Dover, 1961), 3:229.

3. Moxon speculates that in referring to himself simply as *Peregrinus*, Vincent may have been thinking of passages such as Heb. 11:13, "They acknowledged themselves to be strangers and aliens on the earth" (2n3).

4. *Common.* 1.4. All subsequent references to the *Commonitorium* will list citations by chapter and sentence according to the critical edition and standard enumeration found in the *Commonitorium*, ed. R. Demeulenaere, in CCSL 64 (1985): 127–95. Demeulenaere notes (140), in fact, that he has rarely deviated from Moxon's earlier evaluation of the manuscript tradition. Demeulenaere's introduction also provides a solid bibliography of both older and more recent literature on Vincent's thought. The Migne edition of the *Commonitorium* may be found in PL 50:638–86. A widely available English translation is in *Nicene and Post-Nicene Fathers*, Series 2, ed. Philip Schaff and Henry Wace, trans. C. A. Heurtley (Grand Rapids: Eerdmans, 1978), 11:131–56.

5. See PL 58:1059–1120A, esp. 1097–98, §65. Demeulenaere's critical edition includes the relevant paragraph from Gennadius (CCSL 64:127), as does Moxon's work (xii). Gennadius's volume was likely written in the second half of the fifth century, probably around 490.

6. For an exhaustive treatment of the history of the Islands of Lérins, see A. C. Cooper-Marsdin, *The History of the Islands of the Lérins: The Monastery, Saints and Theologians of S. Honorat* (Cambridge: Cambridge University Press, 1913). For the nature of monastic life at Lérins, see Donato Ogliari, *Gratia et certamen* (Louvain: Leuven University Press, 2003), 111–18. Also useful is Friedrich Prinz, *Frühes Mönchtum im Frankenreich* (Munich-Vienna: R. Oldenbourg, 1965), 45–87.

7. Moxon, xiii. He adds that the theologians at the monastery, among whom are counted Vincent, Hilary (later of Arles), and Faustus (later of Riez), are "names alone sufficient to render the monastery of Lérins illustrious." See Moxon, 4n1.

8. Vincent tells us that the general Council of Ephesus (431) had been held three years prior to the writing of his *Commonitorium* (29.7). He also refers to a letter of Sixtus, bishop of Rome, which is dated September 15, 433 (32.2). These internal indications allow the date of the work to be fixed accurately.

9. Moxon, 6n3; with Demeulenaere agreeing, in CCSL 64:129. Demeulenaere observes that "Vincent uses this word [*Commonitorium*] in the sense of *aide-mémoire*" (128).

10. The critical edition of the *Excerpta Vincentii Lirinensis*, ed. R. Demeulenaere, may be found in CCSL 64 (1985): 197–231.

11. See José Madoz, *Excerpta Vincentii Lirinensis* (Madrid: Estudios Onienses, 1940). Idem, "Un tratado desconocido de San Vicente de Lérins," *Gregorianum* 21 (1940): 75–94.

12. Demeulenaere, ed., *Commonitorium*, in CCSL 64:133.

13. Basil Studer, "A Patristic Theology," in *History of Theology*, ed. A. Di Berardino and B. Studer, (Collegeville, MN: Liturgical Press, 1996), 1:465.

14. Prosper's work, in which the *Objectiones* are found, is titled *Pro Augustino responsiones ad capitula objectionum Vincentianarum*. See PL 51:177–86.

15. This thesis was first advanced by the Dutch humanist Gerardus Voss in the seventeenth century and was later endorsed by other historians and theologians such as G. Bardy in *DTC*, vol. 15/2: col. 3046. A French translator of the *Commonitorium* claims that "the parallels are striking between the *Commonitorium* and the *Capitula objectionum Vincentianarum*." See Michel Meslin, *Saint Vincent de Lérins: Le Commonitorium* (Namur: Les Éditions du Soleil Levant, 1959), 16–17. (The parallels noticed by Meslin and others have been called into question by O'Connor's detailed study. See n18 below.)

16. Moxon, 4n1.

17. Pierre de Labriolle, Introduction, in *Saint Vincent de Lérins*, ed. F. Brunetière and P. de Labriolle (Paris: Librarie Bloud, 1906), xciv. One should remember that de Labriolle's comments were made even prior to the discovery of the *Excerpta*, Vincent's tribute to Augustine.

18. William O'Connor, "Saint Vincent of Lérins and St. Augustine," *Doctor Communis* 16 (1963): 125–254.

19. Ibid., 164–65. Luis F. Mateo Seco makes similar points, arguing that only with difficulty may one reconcile the fact that the man who so faithfully followed Augustine in his christological and trinitarian doctrine—to the point of copying his phrases—is the same man who attacked so ardently his doctrine of grace. See Seco, *San Vicente de Lérins: Tratado en defensa de la antigüedad y universalidad de la fe católica* (Pamplona: Universidad de Navarra, 1977), 48–49.

20. O'Connor, "Saint Vincent of Lérins," 154–55.

21. S. Vincenzo di Lerino, *Il Commonitorio*, trans. D. Cesare Colafemmina (Alba: Paoline, 1967), 42–44. Colafemmina adds that while Vincent is not the author of the *Objectiones*, his writing is not without scattered semi-Pelagian and anti-Augustinian elements.

22. Demeulenaere, in CCSL 64:133. Rebecca Harden Weaver concurs that O'Connor's research has settled the question. See Weaver, *Divine Grace and Human Agency* (Macon, GA: Mercer University Press, 1996), 132. On the other hand, the controversy over the *Objectiones* is not entirely dead. When discussing this work, one author recently stated, "On the principle of not multiplying Vincents beyond necessity, this one [the author of the *Objectiones* mentioned by Prosper of Aquitaine] should be identified with a monk of Lérins who at the same period produced an antiheretical treatise known as the *Commonitorium*, and a set of excerpts from Augustine's trinitarian and christological writings." See Mark Vessey, "*Opus Imperfectum*: Augustine and His Readers, 426–435 AD," *Vigiliae christianae* 52 (August 1998): 264–85, esp. 278.

23. Although Vincent's *Excerpta* presents a strong argument against his authorship of the *Objectiones*, it does not conclusively settle the question. We cannot overlook the fact that Hilary, in his letter of complaint to Augustine about the monks of southern Gaul, says, "But I clearly ought not to pass over in silence the fact that they [the monks] claim to be admirers of Your Holiness [Augustine] in all your words and actions with this one exception [of predestination]." See "Letter 226," in *The Works of St. Augustine* (*Letters 211–70*), ed. Boniface Ramsey, trans. Roland Teske (Hyde Park, NY: New City Press), 4:95–104, esp. 101.

24. Moxon, 45n12.

25. See A. E. Burn, *The Athanasian Creed and Its Early Commentators* (Cambridge: Cambridge University Press, 1896). Moxon advances two cogent reasons against the thesis that Vincent borrowed from a preexisting Athanasian Creed: (1) Vincent never acknowledges any document as providing him with substantial material for his references; and (2) the material on the Trinity in the *Commonitorium* strongly reflects the impress of Vincent's own style, not having any whiff of quotations imported from elsewhere. See Moxon, lxx–lxxi.

26. See J. N. D. Kelly, *The Athanasian Creed* (London: Adam & Charles Black, 1964), 116.

27. Ibid., 117.

28. Ibid., 118. Moxon (lxix) had earlier reached a similar conclusion.

29. Kelly, *Athanasian Creed*, 123 and 118. Kelly concludes that the creed was likely written by some other resident of the monastery of Lérins, one who was strongly influenced by Vincent's thought.

30. Moxon, xvii.

31. Meslin (*Saint Vincent*, 10) characterizes Gennadius's claim about theft to be "pure invention."

32. Moxon, xix. Colafemmina (in *Il Commonitorio*, 18) also argues that Vincent published the second book in summary form in order not to exhaust his readers with a detailed examination of the Ephesine Council.

33. See José Madoz, *El concepto de la tradición en S. Vicente de Lérins* (Rome: Gregorian University Press, 1933), 184.

34. For a more comprehensive account of Pelagianism, with extensive bibliography, see Ogliari, *Gratia et certamen*, 2–5. Also see Jaroslav Pelikan, *The Emergence of the Catholic Tradition (100–600)* (Chicago: University of Chicago Press, 1971), 307–19.

35. M. Jacquin has argued that the term "semi-Pelagian" was probably coined only in the late sixteenth century, becoming a common usage from the early seventeenth century onward. Prior to this time, the more frequent terms invoked when referring to this position was "Massilian Pelagianism" (referring to the region around Marseilles) or *reliquiae Pelagianorum* (the remains of Pelagianism). See M. Jacquin, "À quelle date apparaît le terme *semipélagien?*" *Revue des sciences philosophiques et theologiques* 1 (1907): 506–8. Donato Ogliari thinks that the term "semi-Pelagianism" is incorrect, foreign as it is to ancient and medieval Christian literature and carrying ambiguous and even unjust connotations. Ogliari presents a cogent case for this position in *Gratia et certamen*, 6–9, with supportive bibliography. Added to this is the witness of the noted historian of the doctrine of grace, Henri Rondet, who spoke of the word "semi-Pelagianism" as "an equivocal term of sensitive usage." See Étienne Fouilloux, "Henri Bouillard et Saint Thomas d'Aquin (1941–1951)," *Recherches de science religieuse* 97 (April–June 2009): 177. While I am sympathetic with the position of Ogliari and Rondet, I maintain the traditional usage, given its familiarity in theological discussions about fifth-century Christianity.

36. See J. Reginald O'Donnell, "Introduction to Prosper of Aquitaine," in *The Fathers of the Church* (New York: Fathers of the Church, 1949), 7:339. For a discussion of John Cassian's position, as well as the entire controversy that existed in southern Gaul in the early fifth century, see Weaver, *Divine Grace and Human Agency*. For a review of the literature about Cassian, see Ogliari, *Gratia et certamen*, 10–12, 118–33. Owen Chadwick's study, *John Cassian* (Cambridge: Cambridge University Press, 1968), is singled out as particularly balanced.

37. Henri Rondet, *The Grace of Christ*, trans. Tad W. Guzie (Westminster, MD: Newman Press, 1966), 148.

38. Ogliari notes the alliance between the monastic communities of Marseilles and Lérins and writes of the "intimate relationship" that existed between Cassian and Honoratus (the founder of Lérins), particularly with regard to the "aim of monastic life and its underlying ascetical motivations, which they both drew from the traditions of the Eastern Church." See Ogliari, *Gratia et certamen*, 13; 116–18. Also on this point, see Hermann Josef Sieben, *Die Konzilsidee der Alten Kirche* (Paderborn: Schöningh, 1979), 164–70.

39. Moxon, 4n1. Madoz (*El concepto*, 65) is of the same mind, arguing that since the monastery of Lérins was in the region of Marseilles, it was certainly a focus of semi-Pelagianism. It should further be noted that one of the great champions of the semi-Pelagian position, Faustus of Riez (who wrote soon after Vincent's death), had also been a resident of the monastery at Lérins. For this reason, J. N. D. Kelly (*Athanasian Creed*, 119) concludes that although the monks of southern Gaul deeply admired Augustine's writings on the Trinity and the incarnation (relying here on Vincent's *Excerpta*), they "detested Augustine's teaching about grace and predestination."

40. So A. Solignac says, "Even if Vincent is not the author [of the *Objectiones*], he ought to be counted among the members of this [semi-Pelagian] movement." See Solignac, "Semipélagiens," in *Dictionnaire de spiritualité: Ascétique et mystique, doctrine et histoire* (Paris: G. Beauchesne & Sons, 1932–95), 14 (1990): 556–58, esp. 561. Cited by Ogliari, *Gratia et certamen*, 430n9. Pelikan (*Emergence of the Catholic Tradition*, 319) says the term "semi-Pelagian" is commonly used to describe the thought of the prominent theologians John Cassian, Vincent of Lérins, and Faustus of Riez.

41. Weaver, *Divine Grace and Human Agency*, 41.

42. Ogliari, *Gratia et certamen*, 4. John Henry Newman also found Augustine's doctrine of predestination to be idiosyncratic. In his translation of sections of the *Commonitorium*, the young Anglican thinker says that Augustine's "peculiar views of election were beyond, not to say, contrary, to those of the Church." See Newman, *Tracts for the Times*, vol. 2, *Records of the Church nos. 19–25* (1839; facsimile reprint, New York: AMS Press, 1969), Record 24.7.

43. Cooper-Marsdin, *Islands of the Lérins*, 74–75.

44. See PL 51:67B. An English translation of Prosper's letter is available in "Letter 225," in *The Works of Saint Augustine: A Translation for the 21st Century*, part 2, vol. 4, *Letters 211–70*, ed. Boniface Ramsey, trans. Roland Teske (New York: New City Press, 1990–), 4:87–94.

45. *Epistola XXI ad episcopos Galliarum*, in PL 50:528–30. See Ogliari, *Gratia et certamen*, 429. As Rondet (*Grace of Christ*, 151) says, "Celestine refused to get too involved and contented himself with general formulas." Cooper-Marsdin (*Islands of the Lérins*, 72) says that Celestine's letter is "vague and indefinite on the point at issue."

46. Without mentioning specific controversies, Vincent takes Celestine's letter as supporting his own reflections on the proper interpretation of doctrine. Vincent excitedly repeats the phrase "Let novelty not molest antiquity," just as Celestine counsels. But his crucial theological questions are these: How does one distinguish novelty from antiquity? And how might one properly identify illegitimate innovators? Precisely these questions animate the *Commonitorium*.

47. José Madoz, "El Canon de Vicente de Lérins," *Gregorianum* 13 (1932): 32–74, esp. 72. G. Bardy, writing several years after the discovery of the *Excerpta* in 1940, still argues that it is difficult to resist the conclusion that Vincent was writing against Augustine and predestination, even if the Lérinian does not dare to single out the great theologian by name. See Bardy, in *DTC*, vol. 15/2: col. 3049.

48. See Adolf von Harnack, *History of Dogma*, vol. 3, trans. Neil Buchanan (New York: Dover, 1961), 230n1; Pelikan, *Emergence of the Catholic Tradition*, 333.

49. See de Labriolle, Introduction, lxxxiv n. 4.

50. Moxon, 25n2.

51. See PL 50:530A.

52. See PL 45:1032. Quoted from Mary A. Lesousky, *The "De dono perseverantiae" of Saint Augustine* (Washington: Catholic University of America, 1956), 211, with translation slightly modified.

53. Moxon (109n10), for example, says that in this passage Vincent comes closest to an open reference to Augustine and his followers. According to the Augustinian view that Vincent is opposing, God predestines some to salvation and abandons others to hell, simply according to his sovereign divine will. For the Lérinian, this seems to be an extraordinary devaluation of human effort and human freedom, and it is on behalf of these gifts that Vincent is witnessing.

54. Ferdinand Brunetière, Preface to *Saint Vincent de Lérins* (Paris: Librairie Bloud, 1906), xiii.

55. Cooper-Marsdin, *Islands of the Lérins*, 75–78. Similarly, Luis Mateo Seco asks: Is it possible that the passage where Vincent speaks of the importance of seeking, asking, and knocking—and where he stigmatizes his opponents as belonging to a "conventicle," or little church (*Common.* 26.8)—has Augustine as its target? Could the small group that "conventicle" indicates be credibly attributed to Augustine, the great defender of the universal church against the Donatists? See Mateo Seco, *San Vicente de Lérins*, 186n174. Of course, is it not also possible that Vincent, fully aware of Pope Celestine's letter defending Augustine, used a smaller group in order to covertly attack certain Augustinian ideas?

56. Studer, "A Patristic Theology," 465. Studer (619n24) also observes that Vincent closes his *Excerpta* by saying that by opposing Augustine, one seems, "to be opposing the message of all the holy Fathers" (*Excerpta* 10.64–65).

57. Élie Griffe, "Pro Vincentio Lerinensi," *Bulletin de littérature ecclésiastique* 62 (1961): 26–31, esp. 26. In the following paragraph, I summarize Griffe's argument.

58. Griffe concludes that "one cannot truly say that [Vincent's] small book constitutes part of the 'semipelagian' dossier" (ibid., 30).

59. See R. Demeulenaere, "Préface," in CCSL 64:132. Demeulenaere cites several works in defense of Vincent, with an accent on O'Connor's exhaustive argument.

60. O'Connor, "Saint Vincent of Lérins," 142. We can, for the most part, agree with O'Connor's assessment, although the evidence from chapter 26—where Vincent speaks of

asking, knocking, seeking—does appear to betray some sympathy for the traditional position of the Massilian clergy.

61. Ogliari, *Gratia et certamen*, 5. Henri Rondet (*Grace of Christ*, 60) states that Orange took a very clear stand "against a predestinarian interpretation of Augustinism," anathematizing anyone who taught that "some souls are predestined for evil." Pelikan (*Emergence of the Catholic Tradition*, 329) judges that "Orange condemned some of Augustine's theology," but in comparison to the condemnations of the Pelagian and so-called semi-Pelagian positions, this was a "gentle rebuke."

62. See David Bentley Hart, "The Hidden and the Manifest: Metaphysics after Nicaea," in *Orthodox Readings of Augustine*, ed. George E. Demacopoulos and Aristotle Papanikolaou (Crestwood, NY: St. Vladimir's Seminary Press, 2008), 193–94.

63. Weaver, *Divine Grace and Human Agency*, 69.

64. Ogliari, *Gratia et certamen*, 8.

Chapter 1: Key Theological Themes in the *Commonitorium*

1. See *Saint Vincent de Lérins*, ed. F. Brunetière and P. de Labriolle (Paris: Librairie Bloud, 1906), v. José Madoz speculates that Vincent's work was probably unknown to the vast majority of medieval theologians, remaining buried in archives. See Madoz, *El concepto de la tradición en S. Vicente de Lérins* (Rome: Gregorian University Press, 1933), 183. This is the most likely explanation for the millennial silence. If the great theologians of the Middle Ages had been aware of the *Commonitorium*, they would likely have found Vincent's text, with its defense of Scripture and tradition against wanton innovations, deeply appealing.

2. See Adhémar d'Alès, "La fortune du *Commonitorium*," *Recherches de science religieuse* 26 (1936): 334–56.

3. Yves Congar states that, because Vincent refers to a universal criterion for Christian truth, apart from papal authority, "he was to be accepted by Protestants, Anglicans, Gallicans and, more recently, Old Catholics." See Congar, *Diversity and Communion*, trans. John Bowden (Mystic, CT: Twenty-Third Publications, 1985), 123. When the Old Catholics split from the Roman Catholic Church after the definition of papal infallibility in 1870 (under the leadership of the renowned church historian von Döllinger), they invoked Vincent's teaching as one significant motive for their action, making his canon into "the motto of their existence, the basis of their protestation." Ibid., 124.

4. John Henry Newman, *The Via Media of the Anglican Church* (London: Longmans, Green, 1901), 1:54–58.

5. Carl Braaten, *Principles of Lutheran Theology* (Philadelphia: Fortress, 1983), 55. The point made by Braaten—that since no teaching has been endorsed always, everywhere, and by everyone, Vincent's canon appears useless—is a judgment shared by many others. Aidan Nichols, for example, states, "The Vincentian canon . . . is notoriously hard to apply in its full rigor to any aspect of the faith whatsoever." See Nichols, *The Shape of Catholic Theology* (Collegeville, MN: Liturgical Press, 1991), 165. Recently, a well-known ecumenical group, while not unfavorable to Vincent, stated that "the rule articulated by Vincent of Lerins is not adequate, as it stands, to settle the question of doctrinal authority." See Le Groupe des Dombes, *One Teacher: Doctrinal Authority in the Church*, trans. Catherine E. Clifford (Grand Rapids: Eerdmans, 2010), 26.

6. See Joseph Ratzinger, "Dogmatic Constitution on Divine Revelation," in *Commentary on the Documents of Vatican II*, ed. Herbert Vorgrimler (New York: Herder & Herder, 1969), 3:187.

7. Yves Congar, *Diversity and Communion*, 124.

8. Yves Congar, *The Meaning of Tradition*, trans. A. N. Woodrow (1964; reprint, San Francisco: Ignatius, 2004), 71.

9. Barth is a highly astute interpreter of Vincent's work, even while disagreeing with it. He says of the Lérinian's accent on growth over time, "We cannot assess too highly the contribution

made by Vincent of Lérins in his theoretical elucidation of this matter, even when we remember that he was only formulating what had already been put into practical effect in the Church of his time." But Barth is convinced that, ultimately, Vincent defends an illegitimate marriage between Scripture and tradition. See Karl Barth, *Church Dogmatics*, trans. George Thomas Thomson and Harold Knight (New York: T&T Clark, (2004), I/2:548–51. I argue that Barth does not sufficiently acknowledge Vincent's marked accent on the Bible's uniquely foundational character.

10. Michel Meslin, *Saint Vincent de Lérins: Le Commonitorium* (Namur: Les Éditions du Soleil Levant, 1959), 21.

11. As an Italian translator (Colafemmina) of the *Commonitorium* says, while Vincent's formula "for its brevity and vigor has had great success, in practice [it] has been shown to be equivocal and insufficient." See Vincenzo di Lerino, *Il Commonitorio*, trans. D. Cesare Colafemmina (Alba: Paoline, 1967), 30–31.

12. So Meslin asks, what, precisely, is meant by everyone? Is Vincent speaking of a simple majority? And why does he tell us, in chap. 28, that his rule is not for older heresies but newer ones? Does this not render the rule entirely useless? See Meslin, *Saint Vincent*, 21.

13. The famous proverb "There are as many opinions as there are people [*tot homines, quot sententiae*]" finds its roots in both Terence and Cicero. See Moxon, 8.

14. Moxon (84) notes that while the Greek reads "empty talk" or "babbling," all of the Latin manuscripts, whether Vulgate or Old Latin, translated this as *novitates*.

15. See *Common.* 5.2. Vincent may find another source for this passage in Cyril's letter to John of Antioch (at the Council of Ephesus, 431): Cyril argues that the faith defined at Nicaea (325) cannot be changed. The bishop of Alexandria insists that not even a syllable of the creed may be altered since we must remember the words of Proverbs, "Transgress not the landmarks established by your fathers." See *Decrees of the Ecumenical Councils*, ed. Norman P. Tanner (Washington, DC: Georgetown University Press, 1990), 1:73.

16. For a brief history of the Synod of Ariminum (359) and its affirmation that the Son is "like [*homoios*]" the Father (thereby overturning the affirmation of Nicaea), see Leo Donald Davis, *The First Seven Ecumenical Councils (325–787)* (Wilmington, DE: Michael Glazier, 1987), 97–100.

17. Here and throughout the work, Vincent uses the word *sacerdotes* (priests) to refer to bishops. Moxon notes that this usage of *Catholici sacerdotes* to refer to bishops was common from the time of the third century. Madoz adds that *sacerdos* was a common word for bishops until the tenth century (*El concepto*, 168). When Vincent is specifically distinguishing priests from bishops, he uses the traditional language of *presbyter* for priest and *episcopus* for bishop (*Common.* 15.7).

18. Several authors suggest that, with regard to the *regula fidei*, Vincent is deeply influenced by Tertullian's *Prescription against Heresies* (esp. chap. 13). See Vincent's *Commonitorium*, ed. R. Demeulenaere, in CCSL 64 (1985): 131; de Labriolle, in *Saint Vincent de Lérins*, ed. F. Brunetière and P. de Labriolle, lxi; Moxon, 2; and Madoz, *El concepto*, 185–88. While such influence is likely true, it does not prevent Vincent from severely criticizing Tertullian for lapsing into heresy. Indeed, Tertullian serves as a sterling example of those brilliant but dangerous doctors who prefer their own opinions to the consentient authority of the entire church. Further, there is no significant reflection in the African theologian on the nature of proper development, the centerpiece of Vincent's theology of Christian doctrine.

19. For more on the term *regula fidei* in the early church, see Ronnie J. Rombs and Alexander Y. Hwang, eds., *Tradition and the Rule of Faith in the Early Church* (Washington, DC: Catholic University of America, 2010). Also see Yves Congar, *Tradition and Traditions*, trans. Michael Naseby and Thomas Rainborough (New York: Macmillan, 1967), 26–30; Heiko A. Oberman, *The Dawn of the Reformation* (Grand Rapids: Eerdmans, 1992), 272–73.

20. Notice that heretics say to Christians, *Discete furtim atque secretum* (*Common.* 21.8). Learning a matter of doctrine "furtively and secretly" is the very opposite of the Catholic faith, which is known everywhere and by everyone.

21. In Vincent's lament that even esteemed doctors can lead Christians astray, some have seen a
veiled reference to Augustine. But this is the unfortunate result of regarding the *Commonitorium*,
from beginning to end, as an anti-Augustinian tract. Vincent clearly goes on to discuss in detail
the teaching of Apollinaris and Nestorius. Of the latter, Vincent says, "Who would have supposed
that a man chosen for his position by the emperor, held in high esteem by the bishops and people,
who every day preached on the Scriptures and who refuted dangerous errors, could himself be
transformed from a sheep to a wolf?" (11.1–3). Of course, Vincent may indeed be concerned that
Augustine, too, is overstepping the boundaries of consentient theological agreement. But his polem-
ics are reserved for others. Élie Griffe, for example, is convinced that it is Nestorius, the archbishop
of Constantinople recently deposed by the Council of Ephesus (431), who is Vincent's primary
target. See Griffe, "Pro Vincentio Lerinensi," *Bulletin de littérature ecclésiastique* 62 (1961): 30.

22. *Ingemuit totus orbis, et arianum se esse miratus est.* See Jerome, *Dialogus contra Luciferia-
nos* (in PL 23:81). For more on the Synod of Ariminum, see R. P. C. Hanson, *The Search for the
Christian Doctrine of God* (Edinburgh: T&T Clark, 1988), 362–80; Lewis Ayres, *Nicaea and Its
Legacy* (Oxford: Oxford University Press, 2004), 160–66; and Davis, *Ecumenical Councils*, 97–100.

23. For Vincent, the church is aptly described as a good mother, continually nourishing her
children with the holy teaching of the Word of God (*Common.* 20.7; 27.1; 33.6).

24. Passages such as this one make it difficult to believe that the *Commonitorium* is, primarily, an anti-Augustinian polemic. Despite the theological differences between Augustine and
the monks of southern Gaul, did anyone regard Augustine as a man who had swallowed the
poisonous error of heresy? Let us remember that in Vincent's *Excerpta*, Augustine is presented
as the very exemplar of Christian belief.

25. As John Henry Newman would later say of Constantius and Ariminum: "He [Constantius]
fiercely persecuted the orthodox, assembled council after council to destroy the authority of the
Nicene [Creed], and at the end of his reign dragooned 400 bishops in the West and 150 in the
East into giving an indirect denial to the doctrine witnessed to and solemnly professed in 325.
Thus political influences told strongly against, not for, the triumph throughout Christendom of
the tradition of orthodoxy. The Creed of Nicaea was not the imposition of secular power." See
John Henry Newman, *Essays, Critical and Historical* (London: B. M. Pickering, 1871), 1:124.
Newman's point is that Nicaea represented the faith of the universal church while Ariminum
represented merely the triumph of political scheming.

26. The word *praeter* could also be translated as "beyond," and this would be an entirely
legitimate rendering of Vincent's meaning. I think, however, that "other than" is more precise
in this context since Vincent almost certainly takes the word *praeter* from the Latin translation
of Gal. 1:9 (*praeter id, quod acceptistis*), where the apostle Paul condemns those who preach a
gospel "other than" the one already received (*praeterquam quod accepistis*; in *Common.* 33.5).
Similar citations may be found at 8.1–4 and 24.12.

27. David Friedrich Strauss, *Die christliche Glaubenslehre* (Tübingen: C. F. Osiander, 1840),
1:71; cited in Peter C. Hodgson and Robert H. King, eds., *Christian Theology*, 3rd ed. (Philadelphia: Fortress, 1994), 72.

28. Ovid, *Metamorphoses* 15.234.

29. Various attempts have been made to identify the sources of Vincent's accent on development, but there is nothing that compares with his reflections on this matter. Tertullian had
spoken of the seed, stalk, and shrub in *De virginibus velandis* 1. But this is rudimentary in
comparison with the *Commonitorium*.

30. Vincent's chapter on development has most often caught the attention of careful authors. Meslin (*Saint Vincent*, 9), for example, calls this chapter "certainly the most important
of the treatise, whose later influence will be the greatest." Madoz (*El concepto*, 98) refers to this
chapter as "the other golden page of the *Commonitorium*" (along with the Vincentian canon).

31. Because of the undoubtedly strong preservative accent in Vincent's work, José Madoz is
very reticent in ascribing any notion of development to his thought. He says, for example, that

Vincent's law of development cannot countenance growth from a primitive and amorphous nucleus since the entire tone of the *Commonitorium* is against novelty (*El concepto*, 129n110). He also claims that Vincent's militant arguments against innovation disallow any notion of implicit faith gradually becoming explicit over the course of time (130). For Madoz, Vincent allows polishing and precision, but not actual doctrinal growth.

In my judgment, Madoz's reading is entirely too restrictive of the Lérinian's actual intentions, with Vincent's essential and unique chapter on development now extraordinarily narrowed in both meaning and scope. While often an astute interpreter of the monk of Lérins, Madoz copies the mistake of many by taking Vincent's first rule in a nakedly isolated fashion. Doing so forces Madoz to say that if we argue that Vincent's work sanctions a progression from implicit to explicit, we threaten the very integrity of the *Commonitorium*, given the restrictions imposed by the Vincentian canon itself (131, 133). But in holding this position, Madoz fails to take proper account of precisely *how* the dictates of the canon—ubiquity, antiquity, and universality—are known *in actu ecclesiae*. The canon only comes alive *in the living and concrete understanding of the church*. Madoz lapses, rather, to an understanding of antiquity as a remote, nebulous past—not antiquity as *still living and known, especially in the universal councils of the church*. On the Spaniard's reading, Vincent's law of development, his celebrated second rule, comes close to being an interpolation with little actual traction in the *Commonitorium* itself. Madoz's interpretation of Vincent's work is likely too heavily influenced by his firm belief (at least in 1933, when he published his major study) that the *Commonitorium* is written with "considerable preoccupation of opposing the argument from tradition to what he [Vincent] judged to be Augustinian novelties" (131). Consequently, even Vincent's sophisticated notion of development is entirely subordinated to his ardent polemic against innovations of any kind. Madoz's judgment, significantly flawed in my opinion, has been highly influential, particularly in Roman Catholic assessments of Vincent's work.

32. Vincent's comment—that the church neither subtracts nor adds to the dogmas entrusted to its care—perhaps finds its source in the Council of Ephesus's proscription, in its seventh canon, of adding anything to the Creed of Nicaea. A similar comment may be found in Cyril's letter to John of Antioch. See Tanner, *Decrees of the Ecumenical Councils*, 1:65, 73.

33. While Vincent does indeed stress the importance of ecumenical councils as witnessing to the ubiquity and universality of the church's judgments, these are not the only *loci* where such witnessing occurs, as we shall see.

34. Several authors have argued, rightly I think, that it is not Augustine's teaching on grace, but rather various christological errors (particularly those of Nestorius) that constitute Vincent's primary target. Meslin (*Saint Vincent*), for example, argues convincingly that Vincent was deeply influenced by the anti-Nestorian writings of John Cassian (13–14).

35. Vincent's use of the word *enucleare* is significant. He is "unfolding," or "laying open," the meaning embedded in Scripture with the help of councils. Madoz (*El concepto*, 129n110) argues that one may not speak of Vincent's work as defending development from a "nucleus," but the Lérinian's very word here seems to witness against this judgment.

36. Perhaps here we may usefully invoke the traditional distinction made between *traditio* and the *tradita*. The latter refer to the material contents of faith that are handed down and transmitted from generation to generation. These are the matters that Vincent is, indeed, trying to conserve (and properly develop). *Traditio*, on the other hand, refers to the active *practices* of the ecclesial community that maintain (and develop) the *tradita*. How are we to allow for legitimate advances without betraying fundamental identity? This is the question Vincent labors to answer.

37. Madoz, *El concepto*, 95, with original emphasis.

38. Colafemmina (trans., *Il Commonitorio*, 149) notes that the image of lining a cup with honey to conceal a bitter draught may be found in Lucretius, *De natura rerum* 4.11–17.

39. On the significance of councils for Vincent's thought, see Hermann J. Sieben, *Die Konzilsidee der Alten Kirche* (Paderborn: F. Schöningh, 1979), 156–64.

40. Modern scholarship continues to debate the precise teaching of Nestorius. That issue will not detain us here since our primary interest is not Nestorius's thought but the role of ecumenical councils in Vincent's hermeneutics of doctrine.

41. Earlier in the *Commonitorium* (22.2), Vincent says that the guardians and preservers of church doctrine, the "Timothy" of today, are "either the universal church generally or, in particular, the whole body of bishops/overseers [*vel generaliter universa ecclesia vel specialiter totum corpus praepositorum*]." Ecumenical councils clearly fulfill this Timothean role.

42. The citation of ten illustrious bishops/doctors by Ephesus should indicate that when Vincent speaks of *omnes* in his canon, this word should not be taken in a literal sense. Vincent cites only ten witnesses, though Ephesus itself lists twelve, leading Meslin to speculate that the smaller number is symbolic, with Vincent intending a parallel to the Decalogue (Meslin, *Saint Vincent*, 128n161). All of the witnesses listed, except for Cyprian and Felix (both from the third century), are relatively recent teachers, leading Moxon to say that in the list offered by Vincent, "antiquity . . . was not so well represented" (127n1). But Moxon misses Vincent's point. The Lérinian is convinced that an ecumenical council—composed of witnesses to Christianity from across the known globe—necessarily transmits the apostolic tradition. The *dates* of the "witnesses" are not important.

43. As earlier noted, the monks of southern Gaul recognized that their monastic way of life had Eastern roots. And in the controversy with Augustine over predestination, the Massilians appealed to the East as a sure warrant for the antiquity and universality of their own theology. Was anything like predestination, to the exclusion of one's merits and demerits, to be found in the approved masters of the church's *pars Orientis*?

44. While speaking frequently of the Councils of Nicaea and Ephesus, Vincent never mentions the Council of Constantinople held in 381. It is probable that this council was unknown to him. As Davis says, until the council of Chalcedon in 451, Constantinople was not regarded as ecumenical and thus "not of the stature of Nicaea." See Davis, *Ecumenical Councils*, 121–22. Karl-Josef Hefele remarks that while the Council of Ephesus speaks of Nicaea with great respect, it is "totally silent" as to Constantinople. See Hefele, *A History of the Councils of the Church*, trans. H. Nutcombe Oxenham (Edinburgh: T&T Clark, 1876), 2:370–72. Yves Congar notes that a decree attributed to Pope Gelasius (492–96) recognizes only Nicaea, Ephesus, and Chalcedon as ecumenical councils. See Yves Congar, "La primauté des quatre premiers conciles oecuméniques," in *Le Concile et les conciles*, by Bernard Botte et al. (Chevetogne: Éditions de Chevetogne; Paris: Éditions du Cerf, 1960), 76–109.

45. Vincent is one of the chief purveyors of a term that will become classical in later theology: *consensus patrum*, "the consent of the fathers." At the same time, the Lérinian would not disagree with a contemporary point made by Olivier Clément, who observes that sometimes only a single individual testifies to the truth, as Maximus the Confessor did in 658 during the Monothelite controversy. Eventually the episcopacy hears the voice of the prophet, giving "to this seemingly isolated opinion an ecclesial weight." See Clément, *You Are Peter: An Orthodox Theologian's Reflection on the Exercise of Papal Primacy*, trans. M. S. Laird (New York: New City, 2003), 14. In this case, the voice of a solitary theologian was eventually recognized by the entire church.

46. In other words, the objection is this: if the consent of theological doctors is not useful for every error, then what is the value of the *semper, ubique, et ab omnibus*? Harnack insisted that the Vincentian canon must be of limited use since, as Vincent here admits, it is not applicable to older heresies but only newer ones. Such alleged admission leads Harnack to state that the Lérinian's tradition principle is bankrupt. See Adolf von Harnack, *History of Dogma*, trans. Neil Buchanan (New York: Dover, 1961), 3:232n1. On this point, however, Harnack misunderstands Vincent's intentions, as we shall see below.

47. Vincent's theological strategy, invoking the authority of Scripture and councils to deal with older heresies, while applying the unified opinion of venerable doctors for newer heresies, is perfectly intelligible but, surprisingly, seems to have distracted even sensible commentators.

So Moxon (xlviii) says that, in this instance, Vincent admits that his rule is "valueless." A. C. Cooper-Marsdin (*The History of the Islands of the Lérins: The Monastery, Saints and Theologians of S. Honorat* [Cambridge: Cambridge University Press, 1913], 64) says that Vincent's tradition principle is partially lame. Madoz (*El concepto*, 96–97n22) argues that the Lérinian is not entirely clear on this point of newer and older heresies. The reason for this widespread misunderstanding may be identified. These commentators have not clearly seen that the Lérinian regards Scripture and universal councils (*semper, ubique, et ab omnibus*) as having *already* dealt with older heresies. Newer heresies—before a council can be called to denounce them—should be attacked by the consentient opinions of approved masters. Their unified witness will be able to fight the poison of heresy before it takes root in the body of Christ. But there is no sense whatsoever in collecting the theological opinions of approved masters when an older error has already been condemned by both Scripture and an ecumenical council. The very highest authorities have already been definitively invoked and have spoken with clarity. But clear condemnations, even by Scripture and the entire body of bishops/overseers, do not result in the immediate disappearance of egregious theological errors. Vincent is fully alive to the continuing strength of Arianism despite Nicaea's condemnation of this heresy over a century earlier.

48. Some have noted that this image is likely rooted in Cicero's similar statement about Plato. See Cicero, *Tusculanae disputationes* 1.17.

49. Vincent may be criticizing Origen's excessive allegorizing, which led the Alexandrian to misunderstand the teachings of the church. See Moxon, 73n1; and Meslin, *Saint Vincent*, 88n83.

50. At the end of his lament, Vincent changes course a bit and admits that Origen's books have been corrupted. But, he continues, even if he is not always the original author, many books published in his name have been a great trial for the church. Here it is not Origen but Origen's authority that is the chief problem (*Common.* 17.17–18). This last-minute correction shows that Vincent's entire disquisition about Origen is primarily meant as a lesson for the church rather than as a historically precise treatise: even the greatest theological doctors can lead the church astray when they innovate and fail to follow antiquity and consentient universality.

51. Vincent likely regarded Timothy as both a theological doctor and the bishop/overseer of Ephesus, something deduced from 1 Tim. 1:3 and from Eusebius's claim in his *Ecclesiastical History* 3.4.6. Vincent alludes to this when he exclaims, "O Timothy, O Bishop, O Interpreter, O Doctor [*O sacerdos, O tractator, O doctor*]" (*Common.* 22.6).

52. Some have argued that this sentence, with its drumbeat of titles—*sanctus, doctus, episcopus, confessor, martyr*—is aimed directly at Augustine. See Moxon, 115. The young John Henry Newman, in his 1834 partial translation of the *Commonitorium*, also cites Augustine's views on election as illustrative of this sentence. See *Tracts for the Times*, vol. 2, *Records of the Church nos. 19–25* (1839; facsimile reprint, New York: AMS Press, 1969), Record 24.7. But is it truly the case that Augustine is Vincent's antagonist here? Augustine, of course, was not a martyr. Why, then, could this description not refer to Nestorius, bishop of the prominent see of Constantinople, who is the *Commonitorium*'s chief target? Or the Pelagian bishop Julian, also strongly condemned by Vincent? Or could the theologian of Lérins have been thinking of the fact that the Donatists continually appealed to Cyprian, the bishop universally known for his sanctity, learning, and martyrdom (and whose opinion on the rebaptism of heretics was dismissed by the church at large)? In fact, Vincent is concerned to show that *any* lone thinker, despite his genius, talent, holiness—remember his comments on Origen—can be a great trial for the church if he adulterates the faith with idiosyncratic teaching. It is surely possible and perhaps even likely that Vincent is also thinking of Augustine's comments on predestination, but if so, he is placing these reservations within a much more comprehensive reflection on theological epistemology. For Vincent, agreement about a proper *profectus* and an improper *permutatio fidei* always requires a consentient opinion of the church, not the interpretation of one maverick individual, no matter how talented or personally dedicated to Christ.

53. Vincent never uses the word *laici* in the *Commonitorium*, although the idea is implied by his use of the word *clerici* (4.6; 24.5). Vincent generally retains the New Testament usage of "saints" (e.g., *contra omnes sanctos*, in 22.2) and at times "faithful" (as in *omnes fideles*, in 24.5).

54. It has long been noted that the word "pope [*papa*]" was used commonly of bishops in the ancient world. In the *Commonitorium*, however, Vincent reserves this title to the bishop of Rome.

55. The term "apostolic see" was also in wide usage in the early church, designating all sees claiming an apostle as their founder. As with the term *papa*, so also *sedes apostolica* is limited by the Lérinian to refer to Rome. Of course, Rome is the only apostolic see in the West, where Vincent is writing.

56. Stephen's phrase has come down to us only in its citation in *Letter 74* of Cyprian of Carthage as *nihil innovetur, nisi quod traditum est* (in PL 3:1174–78).

57. Madoz, *El concepto*, 177–78. See also Moxon, 24n10.

58. *Sancio* is used by Vincent when referring to the injunction laid down by the apostle Paul to the Galatians, "Walk in the spirit and not in the desires of the flesh" (Gal. 5:16), a commandment established for all ages (*sancta sunt*, in *Common.* 9.4). The same verb is used when referring to the Council of Ephesus authoritatively determining the rules of faith (*de sanciendis fidei regulis*, 29.8).

59. The argument is that Vincent, with his excited repetition of Celestine's phrase *si ita res est* [if the case be so], is covertly asking the pope: "Who, in fact, is introducing novelty into Christianity—the monks of southern Gaul or Augustine?" This speculation may be correct, but we can hardly be certain that Vincent's comments are slyly directed against Augustine. After all, Vincent has just finished a long disquisition on the errors of Nestorius. For Celestine's letter to the bishops of Gaul (no. 21), see PL 50:528.

60. Rome's unique witness is also implicitly adduced by Vincent when he notes that Julian of Eclanum failed to unite himself (*incorporare*) to the interpretation (*sensus*) held by his colleagues and so presumed to separate himself (*excorporare*) from them (*Common.* 28.15). It was Julian's failure to adhere to the condemnation of Pelagius's teachings circulated by Pope Zosimus that led to his deposition. See Moxon, 118.

61. John Henry Newman, perhaps unsurprisingly, takes Vincent's reference to *caput orbis* as indicating the primacy of the Roman see. See Newman, *An Essay on the Development of Christian Doctrine* (London: Longmans, Green, 1894), 161.

62. Madoz, for example, argues that the Vincentian canon of *id teneamus* can be reformulated as *id tantum teneamus*. In other words, we should hold *only* that which has been believed everywhere, always, and by everyone. Madoz adds that Vincent rejects not only that which is *contra* (against) his canon, but that which is *praeter* (beyond) his first rule as well. See Madoz, *El concepto*, 111, 133. As we have seen, Madoz's thesis is hamstrung by his tendency to read the Vincentian canon in isolation. In response, I argue that (1) Vincent is not insisting on some gossamer ghost of antiquity. The church possesses the means to know the teaching of antiquity and thus the ability to distinguish a true from a false development *today*, particularly through its universal councils; and (2) what is "beyond [*praeter*]" Vincent's first rule, if it is to have any concrete meaning at all, is that which has not been sanctioned as a legitimate development by means of the specific *loci theologici* that Vincent has presented. If one attempts to understand the Vincentian canon apart from the specific and living warrants that Vincent identifies—councils, doctors, and so on—then the first rule is so indeterminate that it would be impossible to identify that which is actually *contra* and that which is actually *praeter*. Indeed, *virtually the entire body of Christian doctrine would supersede the Vincentian canon if it were read as a bare rule without further specification.* For which doctrine has been held universally and always and by everyone? Reading Vincent's canon in isolation is, unfortunately, the trap that too often ensnares Madoz's reading of the Lérinian's work.

Chapter 2: The Theological Reception of Vincent of Lérins

1. It is arguable, in fact, that the traditionally Anglican appropriation of the monk of Lérins went a long way, through Newman, toward correcting certain ecclesiological excesses of Roman Catholicism.

2. Yves Congar, *Diversity and Communion*, trans. John Bowden (Mystic, CT: Twenty-Third Publications, 1984), 123. Perhaps representative of this position is A. C. Cooper-Marsdin, writing at the beginning of the twentieth century: "Vincent represents a principle which is not that of the modern Roman or Greek Church, and far more nearly represents the attitude of the Anglican Communion." See Cooper-Marsdin, *The History of the Islands of the Lérins: The Monastery, Saints and Theologians of S. Honorat* (Cambridge: Cambridge University Press, 1913), 63. He modifies this evaluation slightly by adding that Anglicans usually appeal to a closed canon of tradition while Vincent also admits a *progressus fidei*.

3. John Henry Newman, *Apologia pro vita sua* (London: Longmans, Green, 1895), 197. Originally published in 1864 (London: Longman, Green, Longman, Roberts & Green), a new edition appeared the following year.

4. John Noonan, for example, is representative of this opinion when he baldly states, "The inventor of the idea that Christian doctrine develops is John Henry Newman." See Noonan, *A Church That Can and Cannot Change* (Notre Dame: University of Notre Dame Press, 2005), 3.

5. Thomas O'Loughlin is one of the few writers who have explored the link between Newman and Vincent. As O'Loughlin says, "Newman had an immense regard for him [Vincent] and knew his work intimately." And he rightly observes that the Lérinian was "a crucial source for Newman." See O'Loughlin, "Newman, Vincent of Lérins and Development," *Irish Theological Quarterly* 58 (1991): 147–66, esp. 149, 163. While O'Loughlin properly accents Newman's reliance on Vincent, he limits his study to a few areas of agreement between the *Commonitorium* and Newman's *Essay on Development*, centering particularly on Newman's seven notes or tests (cf. John Henry Newman, *An Essay on the Development of Christian Doctrine*, edition of 1845, ed. J. M. Cameron [Harmondsworth: Penguin, 1974]). We intend a much broader analysis here.

6. Newman's selections from Vincent's *Commonitorium* may be found in *Tracts for the Times*, vol. 2, *Records of the Church nos. 19–25* (1839; facsimile reprint, New York: AMS Press, 1969), Records 24–25. They are identified in the text as *Records* and cited by record number, period, page number.

7. Worth noting is that a decade later, in the 1845 edition of his *Essay on Development*, Newman identifies the seven characteristics he adduces to distinguish a proper from an improper development and calls them "tests"—just as he had in this translation of Vincent—only later changing the term to "notes." The reasons for this terminological alteration are unclear. Gerard McCarren argues that the criteria are better called "notes" since "one should not expect to construct upon them a proof which would be convincing to anyone . . . who approached them with an open mind." See McCarren, "Are Newman's 'Tests' or 'Notes' of Genuine Doctrinal Development Useful Today?" *Newman Studies Journal* 1, no. 2 (2004): 57.

8. These papers, written in 1833–36, were collected and published in a one-volume edition in 1840. The pagination that follows is from John Henry Newman, *The Church of the Fathers*, ed. Francis McGrath (Notre Dame: University of Notre Dame Press, 2002), 375–90.

9. Newman mentions no specific example, but it is likely that he is insisting here, as he had earlier, on the necessity of infant baptism and the importance of episcopal succession.

10. This 1836 essay later appeared in *Essays Critical and Historical* (London: Longmans, Green, 1907), 1:102–37. Page numbers in the text refer to this edition.

11. Forty years after their original release, Newman republished the *Lectures* as the first volume of *The Via Media of the Anglican Church* in 1877. See John Henry Newman, *The Via Media of the Anglican Church*, vol. 1 (London: Longmans, Green, 1901). Page numbers in this section refer to this volume.

12. For a convenient list of corruptions consistently opposed by the young Newman, see Avery Dulles, *John Henry Newman* (London: Continuum, 2002), 73.

13. In a footnote to the *Lectures on the Prophetical Office of the Church*, added for the 1877 republication of the work (and so in his Roman Catholic period), Newman says, "Surely this unmanageableness [of Vincent's canon] is a reason against Vincent's rule being the divinely appointed instrument by which Revelation is to be brought home to individuals. . . . If this rule is all that is given us for the interpretation of Scripture or of Antiquity, it is a *lucus a non lucendo*," i.e., an explanation that fails to help (57n7). Newman's insistence on the "troublesome" and "unmanageable" nature of Vincent's canon—characterizations found in both his early and later work—indicate that he did not fully understand how Vincent's first rule was integrated into the entire *Commonitorium*. This flaw will be discussed more fully in the conclusion to the chapter.

14. O'Loughlin rightly says of the *Essay on Development* that "the whole piece is written with Vincent hovering in the background." See O'Loughlin, "Newman, Vincent of Lérins and Development," 157. Indeed, one may legitimately argue that from 1834 to 1845 Newman had the *Commonitorium* constantly in mind, continually reflecting on the hermeneutical criteria by which one could separate truth from heresy.

15. John Henry Newman, *An Essay on the Development of Christian Doctrine* (London: Longmans, Green, 1894), 29–30, 36. The 1894 text is a reprint of the 1878 edition of the work. Page numbers in this section refer to this volume.

16. In fact, Newman's demolition of the Vincentian canon, I will argue, applies to the rule as understood by the theologians of his day (and often down to our own time), but not the rule as Vincent intended it to function in the life of the church. The first rule cannot be taken in isolation from Vincent's extended chapter on development.

17. The "rule" to which Newman refers is found in canon seven of the Council of Ephesus as well as in Cyril's letter to John of Antioch. The latter document insists that no one has the freedom "to alter any expression or to change a single syllable" of the creed. See *Decrees of the Ecumenical Councils*, ed. Norman P. Tanner (Washington, DC: Georgetown University Press, 1990), 1:73.

18. Newman, *Essay on Development*, 303n8. Newman is likely referring to Gregory's *Epistle 102*, the second letter to Cledonius. At the Council of Florence (1439), the Eastern theologians argued that the second ecumenical council (Constantinople, 381) legitimately added to the Creed of Nicaea since there was yet no prohibition against so doing. Out of respect for Ephesus's prohibition against creedal modifications, the word *Theotokos* was not added, even though it would have been apt to do so. See Joseph Gill, *The Council of Florence* (Cambridge: Cambridge University Press, 1959), 149–50.

19. See McCarren, "Newman's 'Tests' or 'Notes'?" 56.

20. Speaking of the notes, Owen Chadwick has said, "No one ever believed in the operation of these seven tests. No one believed in them when the book [*Essay on Development*] first came out and no one has believed in them since." See Chadwick, *Newman* (Oxford: Oxford University Press, 1983), 47.

21. George Lindbeck has said, "We are often unable . . . to specify the criteria we implicitly employ when we say that some changes are faithful to a doctrinal tradition and others unfaithful." But both Vincent and Newman do indeed seek to specify those particular criteria. See Lindbeck, *The Nature of Doctrine* (Philadelphia: Westminster, 1984), 7. Cited by McCarren, "Newman's 'Tests' or 'Notes'?" 49.

22. Since he makes no significant comment on these passages in the 1877 republication of *Lectures*, we may safely conclude that his mind remained unchanged.

23. Newman, *Via Media*, 1:309. Page numbers in this section refer to this volume.

24. In an 1877 footnote just prior to this passage, Newman offers a Roman Catholic addendum that does not change his fundamental position: "That the informations of Scripture were of the first importance with the early Church is indisputable, and I do not wish so far to modify what

is said in the text." He adds, however, that while Scripture possesses a unique "sacredness and power," other documents became important and authoritative as time passed (*Lectures*, 320n6).

25. Dulles, *Newman*, 78.

26. Newman, *Essays, Critical and Historical*, 1:123. Historians generally regard the number 318 as symbolic rather than literal.

27. Ibid., 1:127–28.

28. Newman, *Via Media*, 1:207. Citations in this paragraph are from this work.

29. In the early twentieth century, the Anglican theologian Darwell Stone noted that some Anglican historians dismissed the Second Council of Nicaea (787) because its decisions were rejected in the West by the provincial council of Frankfurt in 794. Stone argues, however, that Nicaea II should be accepted since what Frankfurt rejected is not the careful distinction between honor (due to images) and worship (due only to God) that Nicaea II taught. See Darwell Stone, *Outlines of Christian Dogma* (London: Longmans, Green, 1900), 313–14.

30. Newman, *Via Media*, 1:203.

31. Ibid., 1:212–13.

32. Dulles, *Newman*, 93.

33. Newman, *Apologia pro vita sua* (1864), 256.

34. Dulles, *Newman*, 93.

35. Ibid., 93–94. Dulles notes that the exact number of departing bishops remains a subject of some dispute (98n56).

36. Ibid., 94. In a similar vein, see Louis Bouyer, *Dictionary of Theology*, trans. Charles Underwood Quinn (Tournai: Declée, 1965), 103.

37. Vincent himself would likely deplore the absence of the *pars Orientis* of the church at an ecumenical council and would perhaps question the validity of the consensus reached without this significant segment of Christendom. I am not aware of Newman's indicating this same concern for Eastern Christianity, surprisingly so given his wide knowledge of the Eastern fathers.

38. See John Henry Newman, "The Strength and Weakness of Universities: Abelard," in *Historical Sketches* (reprint, London: Longmans, Green, 1906), 3:192–202, esp. 200.

39. Newman, *Essay on Development*, 338, 343.

40. Dulles, *Newman*, 142; citing John Henry Newman, *The Idea of a University Defined and Illustrated* (London: Longmans, Green, 1896), 384. Rationalism is always Newman's opponent, whether found in philosophy, theology, or biblical criticism. This is why he was at pains to show that human knowing is much more complex than mere Lockean evidentialism, leading him to accent the illative sense and the intuitive appraisal of evidence. For Newman's comments on Locke, see *Essay on Development*, 327.

41. Newman, *Essay on Development*, 337.

42. Newman, *Via Media*, 1:xlvii.

43. Ibid.

44. Newman, *Apologia*, 267.

45. Ibid., 267–68.

46. John Henry Newman, "Letter to the Duke of Norfolk," in *Certain Difficulties Felt by Anglicans in Catholic Teaching Considered* (London: Longmans, Green, 1910), 2:176.

47. Ibid., 2:321.

48. Newman, *Via Media*, 1:xlvii–xlviii.

49. Letter of February 5, 1875; cited by Dulles, *Newman*, 101.

50. See John Henry Newman, *On Consulting the Faithful in Matters of Doctrine*, ed. John Coulson (New York: Sheed & Ward, 1961), 71. For how Vincent's work is invoked in *Ineffabilis Deus* (Pope Pius IX's 1854 bull declaring the Immaculate Conception), see Thomas G. Guarino, "Vincent of Lérins and the Hermeneutical Question," *Gregorianum* 75 (1994): 491–523.

51. Newman, *On Consulting the Faithful*, 63, 73. A parallel may be noted in Eastern Orthodox thought. The 1848 encyclical of the Eastern patriarchs refers to the bishops as the "judges"

and the faithful as the "shields" of truth, "thus extending the fundamental theme of 'reception' to the entire people of God." See Olivier Clément, *You Are Peter: An Orthodox Theologian's Reflection on the Exercise of Papal Primacy*, trans. M. S. Laird (New York: New City, 2003), 13.

52. For the criticisms lodged against Newman's thesis, see Dulles, *Newman*, 114nn33–34.

53. Newman, *Via Media*, 1:54.

54. Ibid., 1:54–55. In an 1877 footnote (and so during Newman's Roman Catholic period), he says that highest authority must speak last; i.e., Vincent's canon is intended for the discussion *preceding* the exercise of papal authority (54n6).

55. Ibid., 1:321.

56. In his 1834 annotated edition of the *Commonitorium*, Newman never translates the sections where Vincent describes Pope Stephen as in the forefront because of the "authority of his see," nor does he translate those sections at the end of the treatise where Vincent explicitly appeals to the authority of the bishop of Rome.

57. See Newman, *Essay on Development*, 302. Page numbers in parentheses refer to this volume. For more extended accounts of the "Robber Synod/Council" of Ephesus (449) and the trial of Eutyches (Council of Chalcedon, 451), see Aloys Grillmeier, *Christ in the Christian Tradition*, trans. J. S. Bowdon (London: Mowbray, 1965), 456–65. Also Leo Donald Davis, *The First Seven Ecumenical Councils (325–787)* (Wilmington, DE: Michael Glazier, 1987), 176–80.

58. Newman adds, "At Ephesus it had been declared that the Creed should not be touched; the Chalcedonian Fathers had, not literally but virtually, added to it; by subscribing to Leo's Tome, and promulgating their definition of faith, they had added what might be called 'The Creed of Pope Leo'" (313).

59. Another example that Newman adduces is the controversy surrounding the document known as the *Henoticon* of the emperor Zeno, issued in 482 and attempting to reconcile Chalcedonians and Monophysites. Newman observes that large segments of the East fell under the spell of this document, which abandoned the definition of Chalcedon (*Essay on Development*, 319). Rome consistently opposed the *Henoticon* as fundamentally anti-Chalcedonian, again leading Newman to praise the role of the bishop of Rome in ensuring that any later developments are consistent with the prior tradition.

60. Newman, *Apologia*, 256.

61. Dulles, *Newman*, 93.

62. Newman, *Via Media*, 1:55.

63. Another similarity between Vincent and Newman is in Vincent's claim that we should "speak newly, but never say new things [*dicas nove, non dicas nova*]" (*Common.* 22.7). Newman, too, was a proponent of using the vocabulary and ideas of his time to express the Christian faith. As Dulles (*Newman*, 79) says, Newman "argued vigorously for the irreversibility of dogmas, not necessarily in their wording, but in their meaning."

64. Dulles, *Newman*, 151.

Chapter 3: The Enduring Ecumenical Importance of Vincent of Lérins

1. Yves Congar, *Diversity and Communion*, trans. John Bowden (Mystic, CT: Twenty-Third Publications, 1984), 124. The young Joseph Ratzinger makes a similar comment, explaining that Vatican II did not cite Vincent because the council "has another conception of the nature of historical identity and continuity. Vincent de Lérins's static *semper* no longer seems the right way of expressing [this] problem." See Joseph Ratzinger, "Dogmatic Constitution on Divine Revelation," in *Commentary on the Documents of Vatican II*, ed. Herbert Vorgrimler (New York: Herder & Herder, 1969), 3:187.

2. José Madoz, *El concepto de la tradición en S. Vicente de Lérins* (Rome: Gregorian University Press, 1933), 189, 191.

3. Ibid., 189.

4. Ibid., 190.

5. Ibid., 191.

6. Lord Halifax, ed., *The Conversations at Malines, 1921–1925* (London: Philip Allan, 1930). At the discussions between Roman Catholics and Anglicans at Malines, there was frequent reference to Vincent (and frequent misunderstanding of his canon). So the Roman Catholic Van Roey says that Vincent's rule cannot be taken "in an absolute or exclusive sense, as if the antiquity of a dogma of faith was the essential condition of its authenticity." Of course, Vincent *does* insist on the note of antiquity. But he sees ecumenical councils as necessarily drawing on the apostolic tradition (and so protecting antiquity) even if some teaching has not been fully articulated in the past. This is why the Lérinian can say in reference to ecumenical councils, "What antiquity venerated without comprehension, let posterity now understand" (*Common.* 22.7). See Lord Halifax, *Conversations at Malines*, 171–72.

7. See Georges Florovsky, *Bible, Church, Tradition: An Eastern Orthodox View* (Belmont, MA: Nordland, 1972), 52. Another Eastern theologian, Vladimir Lossky, betrays a similar misunderstanding of the Vincentian canon. Reflecting the traditional misconstrual of Vincent's work, Lossky argues that if the first rule were strictly invoked, certain essential church teachings would be unacceptable, such as the establishment of the canon of Scripture and the term *homoousios* itself. See Lossky's work *In the Image and Likeness of God*, ed. John H. Erickson and Thomas E. Bird (Crestwood, NY: St. Vladimir's Seminary Press, 1974), 159. But Lossky overlooks the fact that Vincent invokes his rule precisely to *defend* the teaching of Nicaea—which for him is the quintessential instantiation of *semper, ubique, et ab omnibus*. This is why Vincent, far from neglecting the *homoousios*, mounts a spirited defense of the term *consubstantialis Patri* (*Common.* 13.9). (I am grateful to Daniel J. Lattier for bringing to my attention the comments on Vincent's canon by both Florovsky and Lossky. Lattier has treated aspects of the Eastern Orthodox reception of the Lérinian in an unpublished paper titled "Orthodox Readings of Vincent of Lérins.")

8. Florovsky, *Bible, Church, Tradition*, 53. After condemning Vincent's criterion, Florovsky (like Newman) comes closer to the Lérinian's actual point of view. For example, he says that the whole body of the church has not only the right but also the duty of certifying church teaching. He continues, "The conviction of the Orthodox Church that the 'guardian' of tradition and piety is *the whole people*, i.e., the Body of Christ [referring here to the Encyclical Letter of 1848 of the Eastern Patriarchs], in no wise lessens or limits the power of teaching given to the hierarchy." Is Florovsky's claim different from Vincent's statement that the guardians of the deposit of faith, the Timothy of today, are *vel generaliter universa ecclesia vel specialiter totum corpus praepositorum* (*Common.* 22.2)?

9. C. S. Lewis, speaking of moral principles, endorses just this kind of development, arguing for growth that is "development from within." He explains, "There is a difference between a real moral advance and a mere innovation." Of the former, he says, "Anyone who accepted the old would at once recognize the new as an extension of the same principle." Lewis's formulation is cognate with Vincent's notion of doctrinal development. C. S. Lewis, *The Abolition of Man* (New York: Collier Books, 1947), 58.

10. Of course, essential philosophical issues attend the question of continuity, discontinuity, and the nature of temporality. And the questions pertaining to historicity and hermeneutics loom large in contemporary theology. For my treatment of these issues at length, see Thomas G. Guarino, *Foundations of Systematic Theology* (London: T&T Clark, 2005).

11. Pope John XXIII, in *Acta apostolicae sedis* 54 (1962): 792, For Vatican II formulations similar to that found in the opening speech, see *Gaudium et Spes* §62; and *Unitatis Redintegratio* §§4, 6, 17.

12. Yves Congar, *A History of Theology*, trans. Hunter Guthrie (Garden City, NY: Doubleday, 1968), 18–19. More recently, Giuseppe Alberigo has called this distinction one of the decisive motifs of the council. See Alberigo, "Facteurs de 'Laïcité au Concile Vatican II," *Revue des sciences religieuses* 74 (2000): 211–25.

13. Several theologians have insisted that a change in form is always and necessarily a change in content. I argue that while there is an element of truth in this statement, it does not require the conclusion that the essential meaning embodied in one formulation cannot be transferred to a new one. For the context/content distinction, as well as the philosophical issues connected with this question, see Thomas G. Guarino, *Foundations of Systematic Theology* (New York: T&T Clark, 2005), 149–52, 169–208.

14. John of Damascus, *On the Divine Images*, trans. David Anderson (Crestwood, NY: St. Vladimir's Seminary Press, 1980), 71. Gregory Nazianzen expresses the very same thought in the fourth century: there exists "a great deal of diversity inherent in names" for it is a matter of "meanings rather than words." See his *Oration* 31.24.

15. Karl Barth, *Church Dogmatics*, ed. G. W. Bromiley and T. F. Torrance (Edinburgh: T&T Clark, 1956), I/2:627.

16. See Hans Boersma, *Nouvelle Théologie and Sacramental Ontology: A Return to Mystery* (New York: Oxford, 2009). Luther himself experienced a "crisis of form" in the Christianity of the sixteenth century, thinking that only an abandonment of Scholasticism, in favor of the original power of the gospel, could recover Christian vitality.

17. Henri Bouillard, *Conversion et grace chez s. Thomas d'Aquin: Étude historique* (Paris: Aubier, 1944), 219.

18. For Johannes von Kuhn's thought on Vincent, see his *Einleitung in die katholische Dogmatik* (Tübingen: Laupp, 1846), 1:105–10.

19. The Romanian Orthodox theologian Dumitru Stăniloae is surely right when he endorses the employment of new words, metaphors, and formulas in order to express the mystery of salvation. But this process cannot be understood as simply encasing a disembodied content within a new form, for "it is impossible to separate language and content so clearly as that." See Stăniloae, "The Orthodox Concept of Tradition and the Development of Doctrine," *Sobornost* 5 (1969): 652–62. Cited by Daniel J. Lattier in "The Orthodox Rejection of Doctrinal Development," *Pro Ecclesia* 20, no. 4 (2011): 389–410, esp. 400. For a similar concern about the context/content distinction, as lodged by the Roman Catholic International Theological Commission in 1989, see Thomas G. Guarino, *Revelation and Truth* (Scranton, PA: University of Scranton Press, 1993), 159–60.

20. In his *Letter to Maximos* (*Epistle 9*) of 361, Basil discusses a possible reformulation of the word "consubstantial." See Georges A. Barrois, ed., *The Fathers Speak* (Crestwood, NY: St. Vladimir's Seminary Press, 1986), 122–23.

21. This is a crucial point in understanding Vincent. When he says *dicas nove, non dicas nova*, he is talking about the landmarks established by ecumenical councils—and, in particular, the illegitimate attempt to overturn Nicaea by Ariminum in 359, an assembly that haunts him. The Lérinian is certainly not saying that there cannot be a further development in the sense of *res amplificetur*.

22. Henri de Lubac, *The Motherhood of the Church*, trans. Sr. Sergia Englund, OCD (San Francisco: Ignatius, 1982), 91.

23. Yves Congar, *The Meaning of Tradition*, trans. A. N. Woodrow (1964; reprint, San Francisco: Ignatius, 2004), 117. Surprisingly, an incisive theologian like Congar does not recognize that these wise words are entirely reflective of Vincent's own thought. There is no doubt that the deposit is to be guarded, as Scripture counsels, but in such a way that authentic progress and growth are equally sanctioned. As earlier noted, Congar was likely under the influence of Madoz's 1933 study of Vincent (*El concepto*). It is also possible that Congar was still somewhat resentful of the dragooning of the Lérinian (in truncated form) by the antimodernist papal statements of the early twentieth century.

24. In a recent statement, Benedict XVI traces the notion of continuing progress in the church to Bonaventure's work in the thirteenth century. He argues that the Franciscan's understanding of history is an innovation in comparison with the church fathers: "*Opera Christi non deficiunt, sed proficiunt*: Christ's works do not go backward, they do not fail but progress. . . . Thus

St. Bonaventure explicitly formulates the idea of progress and *this is an innovation in comparison with the Fathers of the Church* and the majority of his contemporaries." (Benedict XVI, Audience of March 10, 2010, emphasis added; see http://www.vatican.va/holy_father/benedict_xvi/audiences/2010/documents/hf_ben-xvi_aud_20100310_en.html). In this statement, Benedict misses the marked accent on development in Vincent, a lacuna that may go back to his reservations, as a young theologian, about the Vincentian canon.

25. I discuss Protestant thinkers who defend some form of *prima scriptura* in "Catholic Reflections on Discerning the Truth of Sacred Scripture," in *Your Word Is Truth*, ed. Charles Colson and Richard J. Neuhaus (Grand Rapids: Eerdmans, 2002), 96–97.

26. Kevin J. Vanhoozer, "Scripture and Tradition," in *The Cambridge Companion to Postmodern Theology* (New York: Cambridge University Press, 2003), 149–69, esp. 167. See also Vanhoozer's work *The Drama of Doctrine* (Louisville: Westminster John Knox, 2005), 151–65.

27. For a discussion of Basil on this point, see Guarino, "Catholic Reflections on Discerning," 79–101, esp. 84–85.

28. For a summary of these revised positions, see Avery Dulles, *Revelation and the Quest for Unity* (Washington: Corpus Books, 1968), 65–81.

29. Martin Luther, *Assertio omnium articulorum M. Lutheri*; cited by Yves Congar, *Tradition and Traditions*, trans. Michael Naseby and Thomas Rainborough (New York: Macmillan, 1967), 141n1.

30. Congar, *Tradition and Traditions*, 487.

31. As Congar notes, many Roman Catholic theologians hold "that all the truths necessary for salvation are contained, in one way or another, in the canonical Scriptures." See Congar, *Meaning of Tradition*, 106.

32. Thomas Aquinas, *Commentary on the Gospel of John*, chap. 21, lectio 6.

33. For recent research on this issue, see Guarino, "Catholic Reflections on Discerning," 82–86.

34. Congar, *Tradition and Traditions*, 422.

35. Congar, *Meaning of Tradition*, 100. (This passage was kindly brought to my attention by Eduardo Echeverria). Congar was fond of quoting Thomas Aquinas: "We believe the successors of the apostles and prophets only in so far as they tell us those things which the apostles and prophets have left in their writings" (*De veritate*, q. 14 a. 10 ad 11).

36. Congar liked to cite a phrase of Luther as indicating that Luther himself might not be against a certain notion of development: "What is not against Scripture is for Scripture and Scripture is for it [*quod non est contra Scripturam pro Scriptura est et Scriptura pro eo*]." See *Briefwechsel* 2:426–27; cited by Congar, *Tradition and Traditions*, 143n3.

37. As a recent Lutheran–Roman Catholic dialogue rightly says, "It is clear that for him [Vincent] the tradition expressed in the Fathers and Councils is not another source besides Scripture, but is instead the very truth of Scripture as this is articulated in the church." See Lutheran–Roman Catholic Commission on Unity [of] The Lutheran World Federation [and] Pontifical Council for Promoting Christian Unity, *The Apostolicity of the Church: Study Document* (Minneapolis: Lutheran University Press, 2006), 152n349.

38. See Congar, *Diversity and Communion*, 93. Louis Bouyer notes, "There is no official list in existence of the councils which have in fact been ecumenical." See Bouyer, *Dictionary of Theology*, trans. Charles Underhill Quinn (Tournai: Desclée, 1965), 104. Similarly, Vittorio Peri states, "There does not exist, on the part of the ecclesiastical magisterium, the explicit recognition of a list which establishes as ecumenical the twenty or twenty-one councils normally cited when counting them." See Peri, *I concili e le Chiese* (Rome: Studium, 1965), 12. At the same time, as Peri reports, theologically and canonically, Roman Catholics normally speak (including Vatican II) of twenty-one councils (48).

39. Peri, *I concili e le Chiese*, 12–13.

40. Louis Bouyer, *The Church of God*, trans. Charles Underhill Quinn (Chicago: Franciscan Herald Press, 1982), 552.

41. *Acta apostolicae sedis* 66 (1974): 620. Paul VI also stated, in a 1971 letter to Patriarch Athenagoras, that between the Roman Catholic Church and the Orthodox churches "there already exists a communion which is almost complete—though still short of perfection." See E. J. Stormon, ed., *Towards the Healing of Schism* (New York: Paulist Press, 1987), 232.

42. In a suggestive article, Bertrand de Margerie argues that the medieval councils may be recognized as possessing true ecumenicity, although in an imperfect manner. See his "L'Analogie dans l'oecuménicité des conciles, notion clef pour l'avenir de l'oecuménisme," *Revue thomiste* 84 (1984): 425–45, esp. 432–33.

43. Congar argues that one may speak of a hierarchy of councils and even of sacraments (just as Vatican II spoke of a hierarchy of truths); see Congar, "The Notion of 'Major' or 'Principal' Sacraments," in *The Sacraments in General: A New Perspective*, ed. Edward Schillebeeckx and Boniface Willems, Concilium 31 (New York: Paulist Press, 1968), 21–32.

44. John Henry Newman, *The Via Media of the Anglican Church* (London: Longmans, Green, 1901), 1:206.

45. See Yves Congar, "La primauté des quatre premiers conciles oecuméniques," in *Le Concile et les Conciles*, by Bernard Botte et al. (Chevetogne: Éditions de Chevetogne; Paris: Éditions du Cerf, 1960), 76–109.

46. Newman, *Via Media*, 1:252.

47. See Martin Luther, "On the Councils and the Church," in *Luther's Works*, ed. J. Pelikan and H. Lehmann (Philadelphia: Fortress, 1966), 41:9–178. Luther accepts the first four councils of the church as warranted by Scripture. But, he adds, if one had to acknowledge ecclesial teaching on the basis of conciliar authority alone, "then I myself would not believe the council" (58).

48. Samuel M. Powell, *The Trinity in German Thought* (Cambridge: Cambridge University Press, 2001), 22.

49. Karl Rahner's 1954 essay "Chalkedon—Ende oder Anfang?" was redacted as "Current Problems in Christology," in *God, Christ, Mary, and Grace*, vol. 1 of *Theological Investigations*, trans. Cornelius Ernst (Baltimore: Helicon, 1969), 149–200, esp. 149.

50. Nicaea II (787) insists that one "characteristic of an ecumenical council is the homogeneity of the doctrine taught . . . with that of prior ecclesiastical councils recognized and acknowledged as ecumenical." See Peri, *I concili e le Chiese*, 27. Here one sees confirmed the Vincentian principle of homogeneous development.

51. The mutual "re-reception" of the teachings of various churches will be discussed more fully below.

52. Avery Dulles, *A Church to Believe In* (New York: Crossroad, 1982), 103–32, esp. 109.

53. Luther, too, does not hesitate to invoke Vincent's favorite passage (1 Tim. 6:20–21), although often to condemn philosophy as a profane novelty infecting the gospel. See, e.g., *Luther's Works*, 2:124–25.

54. See Nelson H. Minnich, "The Role of Schools of Theology in the Councils of the Late Medieval and Renaissance Periods: Konstanz to Lateran V," in *I Padri e le scuole teologiche nei concili*, ed. J. Grohe, J. Leal, and V. Reale (Vatican City: Libreria Editrice Vaticana, 2006), 59–95. Also idem, "The Voice of Theologians in General Councils from Pisa to Trent," *Theological Studies* 59 (1998): 420–41.

55. Newman, *Via Media*, 1:xlvii.

56. Joseph Ratzinger, *Theological Highlights of Vatican II* (1966; reprint, New York: Paulist Press, 2009), 144.

57. J. M. A. Vacant, *Études théologiques sur les Constitutions du Concile du Vatican d'après les actes du Concile* (Paris: Delhomme & Briguet, 1895), 2:302. Like Newman, Vacant insists that before any development is sanctioned by the church's pastors, there must be an extended period of theological discussion and testing, of years or even centuries. In this regard he notes Vincent's statement that growth occurs *aetatum ac saeculorum gradibus* (*Common.* 23.3). See Vacant, *Études*, 2:302–3, 307.

58. In our own day, Karl Rahner has spoken of the difficulty of determining if a new theological proposal has properly performed its preservative as well as developmental task. He argues that theology will necessarily generate a certain amount of friction precisely because of its dual goal. See Rahner, "Yesterday's History of Dogma and Theology for Tomorrow," in *God and Revelation*, vol. 18 of *Theological Investigations*, trans. Edward Quinn (New York: Crossroad, 1983), 3–34.

59. See Olivier Clément, *You Are Peter: An Orthodox Theologian's Reflection on the Exercise of Papal Primacy*, trans. M. S. Laird (New York: New City, 2003), 13. Also Florovsky, *Bible, Church, Tradition*, 53.

60. John Henry Newman, *On Consulting the Faithful in Matters of Doctrine*, ed. John Coulson (1859; reprint, New York: Sheed & Ward, 1961), 71.

61. For Newman's position on post-Nicene controversies, as well as the challenges to his historical recounting of them, see Dulles, *Newman*, 105–6.

62. See Newman, *On Consulting the Faithful*, 63.

63. Vatican II sought to counteract a Roman Catholic tendency, particularly after Vatican I in 1870, to place too great an accent on papal centralism. So Gustave Thils has commented, "Theology after 1870 generally left it [the theme of the infallibility of the faithful] in the shadows." See Thils, *L'Infaillibilité du peuple chrétien "in credendo"* (Paris: Desclée, 1963), 6.

64. Congar, *Tradition and Traditions*, 397. At the same time, Congar lodges reservations against any naive understanding of the sense of the faithful: "Too much must not be attributed to the *sensus fidelium*, not only in view of the hierarchy's prerogatives . . . but [also] in itself. . . . The body of the faithful is infallible in the living possession of its faith, not in a particular act or judgment." See Yves Congar, *Lay People in the Church*, trans. D. Attwater (Westminster, MD: Newman Press, 1965), 288. And as Olivier Clément (*You Are Peter*, 14) rightly observes, sometimes only a single individual testifies to the truth, as Maximus the Confessor did in 658 during the Monothelite controversy. Eventually the episcopacy hears the voice of the prophet, giving "to this seemingly isolated opinion an ecclesial weight." The prophetic voice of a single theologian or doctor is also accented by Florovsky, in *Bible, Church, Tradition*, 52.

65. International Theological Commission, "The Hope of Salvation for Infants Who Die without Being Baptized," January 19, 2007, http://www.vatican.va/roman_curia/congregations /cfaith/cti_documents/rc_con_cfaith_doc_20070419_un-baptised-infants_en.html.

66. For a contemporary analysis of the *sensus fidelium* (primarily from a Roman Catholic point of view), see Ormond Rush, *The Eyes of Faith* (Washington, DC: Catholic University of America Press, 2009). See also Aidan Nichols, *The Shape of Catholic Theology* (Collegeville, MN: Liturgical Press, 1991), 221–31.

67. Edward Giles, ed., *Documents Illustrating Papal Authority, A.D. 96 to 454* (London: SPCK, 1952), 252.

68. As Giles points out, Celestine's own letter to the Council of Ephesus, translated into Greek and read to the gathered bishops, states: The Holy Spirit wills that "all of us should perform that office which he thus entrusted in common to all." Celestine's own accent, then, is on the *common* action of the bishops/overseers in council. See ibid., 249.

69. See *Luther's Works*, 36:108. I say "formal" because there is no indication in Vincent's study that the bishop of Rome could teach something different than that taught by the church universal.

70. Michel Meslin, *Saint Vincent de Lérins: Le Commonitorium* (Namur: Les Éditions du Soleil Levant, 1959), 12.

71. See Augustine, *Contra epistulam Parmeniani*, in PL 43:101.

72. As earlier mentioned (in the introduction), when Prosper of Aquitaine and Hilary appealed to Pope Celestine (ca. 430) on behalf of Augustine's theory of grace—directly against the view of the monks of southern Gaul—Celestine issued a letter warmly praising Augustine's work (although without taking a stand on the disputed questions of grace and predestination).

73. As Tillard says, while Vatican II did not change the "letter" of *Pastor Aeternus* (the Vatican I decree on the papal teaching office), its vision is that of the "more balanced and lucid elements in the minority of Vatican I. In other words, the minority of Vatican I has become the majority of Vatican II." This is simply to say that those at Vatican I who opposed a too-great papal centralism were ultimately victorious at Vatican II. See J. M. R. Tillard, *The Bishop of Rome*, trans. John de Satgé (Wilmington, DE: Michael Glazier, 1982), 35.

74. Dulles, *Newman*, 96.

75. It was just this concern about centralism that led Charles Gore, an Anglican theologian at Malines, to state that many developments in the Roman church were providential. But there existed elements in the Anglican, Orthodox, and Protestant churches that belonged to the Christianity of the New Testament and were more in accord with modern democratic sentiments. Gore is clearly referring to a more consensual, less centralized understanding of the church. See Lord Halifax, *Conversations at Malines*, 55.

76. Walter Kasper, *Harvesting the Fruits* (London: Continuum, 2009), 133. On the Petrine ministry specifically, see 133–37.

77. The North American document of October 2, 2010, "Steps Towards a Reunited Church: A Sketch of an Orthodox-Catholic Vision for the Future" (http://www.usccb.org/beliefs-and -teachings/dialogue-with-others/ecumenical/orthodox/steps-towards-reunited-church.cfm), offers important suggestions. The statement calls upon the churches to "recognize each other as authentic embodiments of the one Church of Christ, founded on the apostles." In a reunited church, the role of the bishop of Rome would be "by ancient custom, the 'first' of the world's bishops," and his primacy would mean "not simply honorific precedence, but [also] the authority to make real decisions, appropriate to the contexts in which he is acting" (no. 6a). At the same time, the pope's leadership would be realized by way of a "serious and practical commitment to synodality and collegiality" (no. 6a).

78. Tillard, *Bishop of Rome*, xii.

79. Although I am moving immediately to the disputed issue of the Roman Catholic Marian dogmas, I do not intend to overlook the significant ecumenical convergences on the person and role of Mary in salvation history. Many evangelical Christians, for example, while rejecting the material content of the Immaculate Conception as unbiblical (since Rom. 3:23 teaches that all have sinned), nonetheless recognize the uniquely gracious election accorded to Mary, who remains "an extraordinary model of the call to discipleship and the life of holiness." See "'Do Whatever He Tells You': The Blessed Virgin Mary in Christian Faith and Life; A Statement of Evangelicals and Catholics Together," *First Things*, no. 197 (November 2009): 49–59, http://www.firstthings.com/article/2009/10/do-whatever -he-tells-you-the-blessed-virgin-mary-in-christian-faith-and-life.

80. Congar, *Meaning of Tradition*, 118–20. Congar understands Vincent in a highly restrictive sense, with an accent almost entirely on strict preservation. As noted earlier, in my judgment, Congar, with other Roman Catholics of his generation, read Vincent through the lenses of Madoz's influential 1933 study (*El concepto*) and in reaction against the use of Vincent's thought by Roman antimodernist documents (at the beginning of the twentieth century) that cited the Lérinian in a cramped fashion (e.g., the 1910 Oath against Modernism, http://www .papalencyclicals.net/Pius10/p10moath.htm). As a counterpoint, it is worth recalling that earlier theologians—such as John Henry Newman, Johann Adam Möhler, Johann E. Kuhn, and Antonio Rosmini—never saw Vincent's thought as only preservative; indeed, the exact opposite is the case. Surely Vincent's analogies—seeds' maturing over time and the body's gradually coming to full stature—indicate that he was well aware of evolution according to type, and so his undoubtedly preservative instincts are balanced by his recognition of propulsive, genetic growth. Would Vincent, then, who wrote soon after the Council of Ephesus and who stoutly defended that council's bestowal of the title *Theotokos* on Mary, have necessarily found the Marian dogmas of later centuries to be "transforming one thing into something else [*aliquid ex alio in aliud*

transvertatur]" (*Common.* 23.2), or would he instead have seen them—materially speaking—as constituting an organic development of the seeds originally sown in the apostolic tradition?

81. In one of the ironies of theological history, Congar—taking Vincent as a strict antiquarian—argues that the Immaculate Conception violates the first rule because it does not preserve antiquity. On the other hand, Karl Barth, a highly perceptive interpreter of Vincent, unhesitatingly recognizes the Lérinian's accent on growth according to type, yet rebukes him because of it. Barth finds Vincent's *noviter, non nova* (as well as Vincent's call to arrange the gems of divine doctrine with wisdom and grace; *Common.* 22.6) to be insidious, because hidden in that *noviter* is an accent on development. Barth concludes his evaluation of Vincent with his usual vigor: "The Reformation was needed for the lie [that apostolic tradition could develop beyond the letter of Scripture] to come to fruition even in the measure in which it did so at Trent." See *Church Dogmatics*, I/2:550–51. While Barth sees Vincent's accent on development more perceptively than either Congar or Ratzinger, he fails to acknowledge that the Lérinian's notion of development is deeply rooted in Scripture and in a polycentric, weblike understanding of ecclesial interpretation.

82. See Anglican–Roman Catholic International Commission, *Mary: Grace and Hope in Christ* (London: Continuum, 2006), 61–68, esp. 64n60.

83. Surely the *subsistit in* of *Lumen Gentium* §8, insofar as it is an attempt to recognize and acknowledge the significant elements of Christian faith and practice found outside Roman Catholicism, intensifies the importance of authoritative theological *loci* as they exist within all Christian churches.

84. Karl Barth, *Karl Barth's Letters, 1961–1968*, ed. J. Fangmeier and H. Stoevesandt, trans. Geoffrey W. Bromiley (Grand Rapids: Eerdmans, 1981), 135. For recent ecumenical evaluations of Mary, see Carl E. Braaten and Robert W. Jenson, eds., *Mary, Mother of God* (Grand Rapids: Eerdmans, 2004). For a specifically Lutheran evaluation, see Anja Ghiselli, "The Virgin Mary," in *Engaging Luther*, ed. Olli-Pekka Vainio (Eugene, OR: Wipf & Stock, 2010), 173–85.

85. This is not to say, however, that Vincent did not make his opinion known. When he cites Celestine's strong letter to the bishops of Gaul against recent innovative tendencies, Vincent excitedly repeats Celestine's words *si ita res est* (if the case be so). To the pope's claim that novelty in the church cannot be tolerated, Vincent is perhaps responding: "Who is truly introducing novelty into the church? Are the monks of Gaul guilty? Or is it Augustine, with his teaching on predestination?"

86. I do not here enter into the disputed interpretations of these phrases, noting only that Vincent stood in a tradition in which Rome's authority, however understood, was already acknowledged.

87. Newman, *Via Media*, 1:54–55.

88. Even at Vatican I, Vinzenz Gasser, the chairman of the Doctrinal Commission, in responding to the question, "In what sense is the infallibility of the Roman pontiff absolute?" stated: "In no sense is pontifical infallibility absolute. For absolute infallibility belongs only to God, the first and essential truth. All other infallibility . . . has its limits and conditions, and this is true as well of the infallibility of the Roman pontiff." See G. D. Mansi et al., *Sacrorum conciliorum, nova et amplissima collectio* (Graz: Akademische Druck- u. Verlagsanstalt, 1960–61), vol. 52, cols. 1214A–B. Cited in Gustave Thils, *L'Infaillibilité*, 50–51. Also important in interpreting Vatican I is the work of Joseph Fessler, secretary of that council, whose moderate book, *The True and False Infallibility of the Popes* (New York: Catholic Pub. Society, 1875), Newman praised for its "wise and gentle minimalism." See Dulles, *Newman*, 94.

89. Of course, accenting the pope's role within the college of bishops/overseers necessarily calls to mind the statement of Vatican I that the solemn teachings of the pope are irreformable "of themselves and not from the consent of the church [*ex sese, non ex consensu ecclesiae*]." We cannot enter this complex issue here, but the phrase in question was elaborated in a determinate historical context, entailing unique circumstances. As one author has noted, the phrase *ex sese*

was "not intended to eliminate the broader patristic and theological notion of consent by the Church." See Walter H. Principe, *Faith, History, and Cultures: Stability and Change in Church Teachings* (Milwaukee: Marquette University Press, 1991), 20. Avery Dulles adds that the phrase was not intended to separate the bishop of Rome from the college of bishops or the entirety of the church. See Dulles, *A Church to Believe In*, 144–45.

90. Indeed, all Christians may be analogically denominated "vicars and legates of Christ." Vincent would probably affirm that the "saints" properly "guard the deposit" precisely because they are legates of Christ.

91. Tillard, *Bishop of Rome*, 39. In *Ut unum sint* of 1995, John Paul II came very close to this position: "When the Catholic Church affirms that the office of the Bishop of Rome corresponds to the will of Christ, [the church] does not separate this office from the mission entrusted to the whole body of Bishops, who are also 'vicars and ambassadors of Christ'" (§95).

92. Summing up much recent scholarship on the issue is James F. Puglisi, ed., *How Can the Petrine Ministry Be a Service to the Unity of the Universal Church?* (Grand Rapids: Eerdmans, 2010). See also Carl E. Braaten and Robert W. Jenson, eds., *Church Unity and the Papal Office* (Grand Rapids: Eerdmans, 2001).

93. If, from a Roman Catholic perspective, the church of Christ is found truly, if not fully, in other Christian churches, then surely logic demands that any proposed *profectus* requires the careful weighing of the insights of these churches.

94. Mansi, *Sacrorum conciliorum . . . collectio*, vol. 13, cols. 207–10. See Peri, *I concili e le Chiese*, 21–34.

95. Mansi, *Sacrorum conciliorum . . . collectio*, vol. 13, col. 210.

96. Peri, *I concili e le Chiese*, 27.

97. Andrew Louth, "Is Development of Doctrine a Valid Category for Orthodox Theology?" in *Orthodoxy and Western Culture*, ed. Valerie Hotchkiss and Patrick Henry (Crestwood, NY: St. Vladimir's Seminary Press, 2005), 45–63, esp. 46–47. Page numbers in this paragraph refer to this article.

98. At the same time, Louth (ibid., 60) approvingly cites a Romanian Orthodox theologian who says that development of doctrine represents "the spontaneous process of unfolding of what is already given in the apostolic and unsurpassable confession of Christ as 'God and Lord.'" If this position means that revelation is given fully and once and for all in Christ Jesus, and that any development must be a harmonious unfolding of the revelation once delivered to the saints, then it is not clear to me how this position differs from Vincent of Lérins or even modern Roman Catholic theories of development. Of course, differences exist on whether particular *matters* are truly developments or corruptions; it is the *idea* of development expressed here that seems quite Vincentian.

99. Daniel Lattier has recently provided an important counterargument to the claim that Eastern Christian writers have formed a solid consensus against the idea of development of doctrine. See Lattier, "Orthodox Rejection of Doctrinal Development," 389–410.

100. I explain Vincent's role at Vatican II more fully in "Tradition and Doctrinal Development: Can Vincent of Lérins Still Teach the Church?" *Theological Studies* 67 (2006): 34–72.

101. Vanhoozer, *Drama of Doctrine*, 352–53. Hans Boersma observes that Vanhoozer even introduces the notion of doctrinal development into his work, commenting that "its acceptance is surely significant for an evangelical theologian." See Hans Boersma, "On Baking Pumpkin Pie," in *Calvin Theological Journal* 42 (2007): 237–55, esp. 251.

102. Timothy George, "An Evangelical Reflection on Scripture and Tradition," in *Your Word Is Truth*, ed. Colson and Neuhaus, 9–34, esp. 31.

103. I. Howard Marshall, *Beyond the Bible* (Grand Rapids: Baker Academic, 2004), 79.

104. Newman, *Via Media*, 1:253–54.

105. Congar, *Diversity and Communion*, 128. Charles Gore offers an illustration of this distinction in Anglican thought when he says at Malines, "The essential point is the distinction between

fundamental dogmas and dogmas that are not fundamental." See Lord Halifax, *Conversations at Malines*, 59. Offering a concrete example, Lord Halifax (*Conversations at Malines*, 77) observes that Rome, *in articulo mortis* (at the point of death), allows Orthodox priests to absolve Roman Catholics. Does this not mean that the sacraments and infallibility are not on precisely the same footing?

106. The infallibililty of the papal magisterium rests on the more foundational teachings of Christ's continual presence to the church and the infallibility of the church as a whole. For this distinction between centrality and certainty and a fuller discussion of the hierarchy of truths, see Guarino, *Revelation and Truth*, 142–46.

107. For an extended discussion of Rahner's position, see ibid., 146–50.

108. A comprehensive treatment of theological notes is provided by Francis A. Sullivan, *Creative Fidelity: Weighing and Interpreting Documents of the Magisterium* (New York: Paulist Press, 1996).

109. For further details, see Guarino, *Revelation and Truth*, 158–61.

110. See Karl Rahner, "Magisterium and Theology," in *God and Revelation*, 54–73, esp. 57.

111. In this book there is no need to attend to the contemporary intra–Roman Catholic debates on continuity, discontinuity, and reform as found in the documents of Vatican II. The hermeneutical arguments are complex, but the crux of the issue is this: Did this council reverse, distort, or contravene definitively established landmarks? If so, then Vincent himself would condemn it. Or did it, at times, reverse "ordinary" teaching (e.g., prior prohibitions of Roman Catholics engaging in ecumenical discussions and prior papal condemnations of religious freedom, understood as the *objective right* of men and women to worship God other than in Jesus Christ)? I think the latter is clearly the case. No definitive or solemn Roman Catholic teaching was reversed by Vatican II. However, the ecclesial reversal of even ordinary teachings, especially those teachings that had been held for a long time and promulgated with papal authority (such as various statements against religious freedom), seems to some to be a pernicious fulfillment of what Vincent described as the song of heretics: "Condemn what you used to hold, and hold what you used to condemn. Reject the ancient faith and the dictates of your fathers and the deposits of the ancients" (*Common.* 9.8). This issue is at the root of the continuing debates and even schism within contemporary Roman Catholicism. It is important to remember, however, that when Vincent speaks of "transgressing landmarks" in the *Commonitorium*, he is always referring to definitive and solemn conciliar teaching.

112. I discuss the notion of legitimate plurality at Vatican II and afterward in *Foundations of Systematic Theology*, 143–53, 188–98.

113. See Joseph Ratzinger, *Eschatology* (Washington, DC: Catholic University of America Press, 2007), 233.

114. As Cardinal Mercier repeatedly said, in the context of the Anglican–Roman Catholic dialogue at Malines, the goal is an Anglican Church united to Rome but not absorbed by it. See Lord Halifax, *Conversations at Malines*, 57–58.

115. I highlight two important articles about this axiom: Hubert Silvestre, "*Diversi sed non adversi,*" *Recherches de théologie ancienne et médiévale* 31 (1964): 124–32; and Henri de Lubac, "A propos de la formule: *diversi sed non adversi,*" *Recherches de science religieuse* 40 (1952): 27–40. (I am grateful to Marcus Plested for bringing the latter essay to my attention.)

116. So the Orthodox theologian Olivier Clément says, "In the end, it is not a question of denying the Latin tradition, but of showing that there are two differing approaches, of which both are legitimate and neither in any way contradicts the other." See Clément, *You Are Peter*, 81. See also the excellent statement "The Greek and Latin Traditions regarding the Procession of the Holy Spirit," *Information Service* 89 (1995/II–III): 88–92; published under the heading "The Vatican Clarification on the Filioque with Commentary," in *L'Osservatore Romano*, September 20, 1995, 3, 6, http://home.comcast.net/~t.r.valentine/orthodoxy/filioque/vatican_clarification.html.

117. Congar, *Diversity and Communion*, 171. Congar's small book, although now thirty years old, remains important because of a wealth of proposals of how re-reception can serve the unity of the churches.

118. George Hunsinger's *The Eucharist and Ecumenism* (Cambridge: Cambridge University Press, 2008) is a good contemporary example of this, showing how the Reformed theology of the Eucharist may be creatively retrieved and broadened by taking account of the teachings of other churches.

119. In Roman Catholicism, for example, the declaration *Mysterium Ecclesiae* of 1973 accented the fact that doctrinal teachings, while true, are limited by certain linguistic and conceptual forms. See *Acta apostolicae sedis* 65 (1973): 403. I discuss how this document is important for the hermeneutics of doctrinal statements in Guarino, *Foundations of Systematic Theology*, 150–51, 215–16.

120. Bouyer, *Church of God*, 552. Yves Congar also discusses this kind of "exogenous" rereception in "Reception as an Ecclesiological Reality," in *Election and Consensus in the Church*, ed. G. Alberigo and A. Weiler, Concilium 77 (New York: Herder & Herder, 1972), 43–68.

121. Risto Saarinen has recently stated that by approving women's ordination, certain Protestant traditions show that one can maintain "a high regard for tradition with a dynamic and flexible view of gender roles." See Saarinen, "Fire, Iron, and the Eucharist: Some Questions for George Hunsinger," *Pro Ecclesia* 19 (2010): 267–72, esp. 271. In my judgment, Vincent *could* approve of the ordination of women as constituting a legitimate *profectus fidei* (since such a practice would not transgress definitively established landmarks). At the same time, he would likely insist that, in order to avoid the danger of an idiosyncratic adulteration of the faith, such an advance would require the consentient agreement of the various warrants he adduces. (Of course, various bishops of Rome have spoken to this issue. I leave aside the question, debated by Roman Catholic theologians, of the precise theological weight of John Paul II's Apostolic Letter of 1994, *Ordinatio sacerdotalis*.)

122. Karl Rahner, specifically invoking Vincent, says that the church is bound to "abide by the faith of preceding generations *in eodem dogmate eodem sensu eademque sententia*." But he notes that any development provokes some anxiety as to whether we have indeed properly maintained the faith. I add to Rahner's comment that precisely because of this legitimate concern, Vincent insists on multiple centers of ecclesial consensus to underwrite and warrant any proposed *profectus*. See Karl Rahner, "Basic Observations," in *Ecclesiology, Questions in the Church, the Church in the World*, vol. 14 of *Theological Investigations*, trans. David Bourke (London: Darton, Longman & Todd, 1976), 3–23, esp. 13–14.

123. Adolf von Harnack, *History of Dogma*, trans. Neil Buchanan (New York: Dover, 1961), 3:229.

124. For example, while the work of the Holy Spirit envelops the *Commonitorium*, there is very little explicit reflection on pneumatology. And reform in the church has almost no role in Vincent's thought, although his incipient reflection on the hierarchy of truths allows for a modicum of it.

Index